ANTISEMITISM IN THE UNITED STATES

Edited by **LEONARD DINNERSTEIN**
The University of Arizona

WITHDRAWN

HOLT, RINEHART AND WINSTON

New York • Chicago • San Francisco • Atlanta
Dallas • Montreal • Toronto • London • Sydney

Cover illustration: Desecrated tombstones, Stein Joelson
Lodge Cemetery, Totowa, New Jersey, November 12,
1961. *(UPI)*

Figures for the map on page iv are taken from *American
Jewish Yearbook, 1970*, pp. 345–346.

CONTENTS

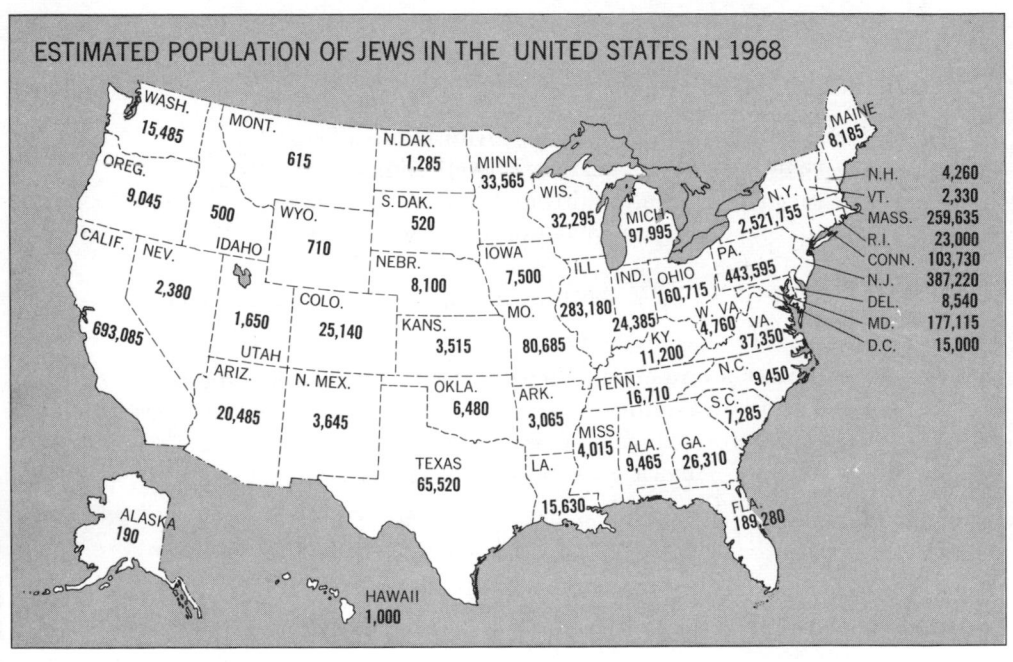

ESTIMATED POPULATION OF JEWS IN THE UNITED STATES IN 1968

WASH. 15,485
MONT. 615
N.DAK. 1,285
MINN. 33,565
WIS. 32,295
MICH. 97,995
MAINE 8,185

OREG. 9,045
S.DAK. 520
IDAHO
WYO. 710

CALIF. 693,085
NEV. 2,380
UTAH 1,650
COLO. 25,140
NEBR. 8,100
IOWA 7,500
ILL. 283,180
IND. 24,385
OHIO 160,715
PA. 443,595
N.Y. 2,521,755
W. VA. 4,760
VA. 37,350

500

KANS. 3,515
MO. 80,685
KY. 11,200

ARIZ. 20,485
N. MEX. 3,645
OKLA. 6,480
ARK. 3,065
TENN. 16,710
N.C. 9,450
S.C. 7,285

TEXAS 65,520
LA. 15,630
MISS. 4,015
ALA. 9,465
GA. 26,310
FLA. 189,280

ALASKA 190

HAWAII 1,000

N.H.   4,260
VT.   2,330
MASS.   259,635
R.I.   23,000
CONN.   103,730
N.J.   387,220
DEL.   8,540
MD.   177,115
D.C.   15,000

INTRODUCTION

Antisemitism is a complex phenomenon. It is an expression of antipathy toward Jews ranging from a mild form of disparagement to complete hatred. In the United States it has manifested itself frequently in social and economic discrimination but there have been political curbs as well.

From one point of view Jews had greater freedom and opportunity in the United States than anywhere else before in the Christian world. Hundreds of Jews arrived from Spain, Portugal, and the German states (some via Brazil, others via England) during the colonial period, and save for some voting restrictions and bans upon becoming lawyers or doctors in some colonies, they could engage in any economic or social endeavors that suited them.

During the eighteenth, nineteenth, and early part of the twentieth century a growing nation needed people, and the United States welcomed newcomers. Protestants of northern Europe were the most favored groups but others came as well. Jews constituted less than 1 percent of the immigrant influx before the 1890s. The thousands who came from the German states and eastern Europe did not set up any major enclaves but scattered throughout the land. Most of them prospered and tried to adapt themselves as quickly as possible to American customs. As a result of their small numbers and unobtrusiveness, there were few incidents of antisemitism in this country before the end of the nineteenth century. One major exception, however, was the period of the Civil War. The tensions generated during the conflagration created such intense anxieties that Judaeophobia (the nineteenth-century expression for hostility toward Jews) erupted in both the North and the South. Jews were condemned in both sections for alleged profiteering and treasonous activities,

Stagnating wages and farm prices in the United States in the late nineteenth century intensified antisemitism. Farm prices began falling in the early 1880s, and the nationwide depression in the 1890s affected factory workers as well as farmers. A number of disgruntled Populists, socially displaced Brahmins, and urban dwellers, looking for an explanation for the causes of their miseries, focused upon bankers and immigrants. Jews were visible among both groups. The House of Rothschild was one of the best-known banking concerns in the world. In the United States August Belmont, who was born Jewish, and Jacob

Schiff, head of Kuhn Loeb, stood out prominently among the nation's bankers. Since many of the economically unsophisticated blamed the depression upon the manipulation of wily financiers, grievances against mythical Shylocks soon surfaced.

The increasing number of immigrants from southern and eastern Europe and the dominant racist thoughts of the era also contributed to the emerging hostility toward Jews. Italians, Jews, and Slavs constituted the bulk of the newer immigrants in contrast with the British, Irish, Germans, and Scandinavians who made up the majority of older settlers. The East European Jews, as well as many of the other newcomers, dressed oddly and worshiped according to traditions foreign to large numbers of American Protestants. These Americans held to views of Anglo-Saxon superiority and considered the new arrivals as inferior beings who would mongrelize the race and neutralize established virtues. Moreover, the newer ethnic groups, most of whom were antagonistic to all other elements in the population except their own compatriots, eyed one another warily. As a result of these varying tensions and prejudices more and more antisemitic incidents occurred. Fights broke out in the crowded urban ghettos, organizations blackballed Jewish members, job discrimination appeared, residential areas erected religious barriers, and resorts invited "Christian guests only."

The increasing evidence of antisemitism alarmed thoughtful Jews who had come to the United States before the 1890s. They too had reservations about the influx of East European Jews but in time recognized their responsibility to help these adjust. They set up organizations to help Russian, Polish, Hungarian, Rumanian, Austrian, and other Jews make the transition between the old and the new worlds. In addition, defensive groups to combat prejudice and discrimination appeared. In 1906 some older American Jews, primarily of German ancestry, established the American Jewish Committee, and seven years later B'nai B'rith, a Jewish fraternal order, founded its Anti-Defamation League.

Despite growing interest in the subject, the roots of American antisemitism have not been examined carefully by historians. Isolated antisemitic incidents and remarks are found in numerous works on other topics in American history, but the lack of in-depth studies makes it difficult to ascertain whether they were indeed isolated or part of a systematic pattern. Many American historians assume that prejudice toward Jews in this country has been largely an aspect of hostility toward aliens and that as Jews have become assimilated this antagonism has waned. This is partly true. During nativistic outbursts in the 1890s and 1920s Jews were only one of the targets. It is also true that as Jews have, in varying degrees, absorbed the dominant values in American society antisemitism has diminished. However, one must consider in addition the image of the Jew in Christian teaching and the common assumption that Jews are particularly clever and avaricious in business dealings. These beliefs have existed for centuries and are not related to America's experience with nativism or immigration.

In Europe and the United States outbursts of antisemitism have occurred in times of social crisis. The causes of these outbreaks of religious bigotry have been subject to comprehensive analyses by psychologists, psychiatrists, political scientists, sociologists, ministers, priests, and rabbis. Although the analysts find some common ingredients, almost all of them emphasize a particular aspect as being crucial. Certainly, different factors predominate under different circumstances but religious teaching, psychological frustrations, and economic insecurity commonly provide a fertile breeding ground for the development of antisemitism. These causes are discussed in the following sections.

In the volume's first essay, an overview, Melvin Tumin asks, "What is antisemitism?" Then, very briefly, he proceeds to answer his own question. Tumin identifies the four major aspects of antisemitism as (1) a belief that Jews are distinguishable from non-Jews, (2) a fear of Jews, (3) a desire to keep them at a distance, and (4) a willingness to discriminate against them. In the rest of the essay he attempts to identify Jews, to indicate how they fit into the American scene, and to pinpoint the ways in which Jews are different from non-Jews. He also touches upon the roots of antisemitism, the types of people likely to be prejudiced, and the different ways antisemitism is expressed. These last points are developed at somewhat greater length in the other sections.

The next four selections focus on the roots of antisemitism. Horace Kallen, a Jewish philosopher, writes that "the roots of the special Jewish difficulty is [*sic*] the position of the Jews in the Christian religion. If you can end this teaching that the Jews are the enemies of God and of mankind you will strike anti-Semitism at its foundations." Kallen acknowledges, though, that social crises engender fears which in turn lead to anger (later psychologists paraphrased this idea and explained it as frustration which leads to aggression). Nevertheless, Kallen devotes a good deal of his argument to the thesis that because the Jews are the villains in the Christian schema—having once been the Chosen People but then rejecting the Savior—they are the enemies of both God and mankind. Consequently, "Jew" has been a word to curse with in Christian societies even for those who have never seen a Jew. If Kallen's views are correct, how can one explain pre-Christian hostility toward Jews? Is it possible that religious teaching must be combined with other factors before hostility blooms?

In the next selection Otto Fenichel, a psychoanalyst and follower of Sigmund Freud, takes a broader view. He insists that rather than coming from a specific cause, prejudicial behavior emerges under certain complex conditions. Writing in 1940, in the context of a European world dominated by Nazi racism, Fenichel explains the phenomenon of antisemitism as a combination of sociological, historical, political, and psychological factors. He emphasizes as well that gentiles use the Jew as a displacement substitute. People are antisemitic, he notes, because they cannot stand some of their own emotions, because they cannot express their antagonisms toward those in authority, or, finally, because they are miserable and need a scapegoat whom they can blame for their oppressions. For antisemitism to operate, of course, more than psychological phenomena must be present. "The full utilization of the psychological facts," Fenichel concludes, "is only possible under certain economic and political circumstances."

While Fenichel emphasizes psychological maladjustment combined with political and economic developments, Gorham Munson, witnessing the growth of antisemitism in the United States in the 1930s, subordinates all other considerations to the importance of economics. "Whatever else it is," Munson observes, "anti-Semitism is a poverty problem." Poor people, humiliated and insecure because of their own hunger and deprivation, gain psychological succor by seeing others worse off than themselves. This, Munson believes, makes life easier to bear for those at the bottom of the economic ladder. Obviously influenced by the problems Germany had faced in the 1920s and early 1930s before turning to Adolph Hitler for solution, Munson concludes that the promise of a new economic order is necessary to capture the popular imagination and turn people away from totalitarianism and one of its by-products—antisemitism.

Munson's argument sounds good, but certain incidents of American hostility toward Jews in the twentieth century suggest that economics is less than crucial. Societal causes may generate mass hostility, but individual prejudice is frequently nurtured by other factors. The antisemitism of Henry Ford and Lawrence Lowell, President of Harvard University in the 1920s (to be discussed by Morton Rosenstock), did not result from economic deprivation, and there are examples of antisemitic demagogues like Tom Watson of Georgia in 1914–1915 and Gerald L. K. Smith of Arkansas in the 1930s and after, for whom political opportunism seems to be the key element. But because antisemitism occurs also among those who are not economically deprived, can we ignore economic factors completely?

Another variation on the roots of antisemitism which warrants attention is the point that Arnold Rose, a sociologist, emphasizes. In the United States, Rose writes, people have associated Jews with economic success, political radicalism, and quick adaptiveness to a changing world. "Historically such traits are connected with life in cities and so are Jews. The Jews are the urban people *par excellence.*" Jews are hated also, Rose continues, because they are associated with both capitalism and communism, essentially urban phenomena. Such forces are too impersonal to *hate;* consequently "the Jews are hated . . . as a symbol of city life." Many urban dwellers have a nostalgia for country life and the rural virtues because they cannot adjust to city life. The "symbolic projection of hatred of the city onto the Jews allows the prejudiced person to destroy the city and to escape the city, and at the same time to keep it and live in it." When reading the selection by Rose see if you can find any similarities between his views and those of Otto Fenichel. Another question worth pondering is whether Rose has been so selective in his presentation that he describes only one, albeit an important, aspect of antisemitism rather than *the* root cause.

The first historians to examine the origins of twentieth-century antisemitism in the United States, the subject of the next group of selections, published their findings in the 1950s. To some extent, interestingly enough, their conclusions support Arnold Rose's contentions that antisemitism is tied in with hostility to the city. Oscar Handlin, in his seminal essay, "American Views of the Jew at the Opening of the Twentieth Century," writes that before the 1890s Americans generally had a favorable image of the Jew. Although they saw him as a peddler, pawnbroker, or old-clothes dealer concerned with money, this stereotype "involved no hostility, no negative judgment." Evidence of changes in American attitudes, Handlin believes, occurred during the last decade of the nineteenth century when one of the severest depressions in American history displaced numerous farmers and laborers. The pace of industrialization and the growth of cities wrought profound changes in society which those adversely affected could not explain. Unable to rationalize their experiences, some blamed the Jew as the arch-villain. They saw him as the omnipotent financier and international conspirator. "If all trade was treachery and Babylon the city," Handlin writes, "then the Jew—stereotyped, involved in finance, and mysterious—stood ready to be assigned the role of arch-conspirator." It was this suspicion, Handlin concludes, that finally changed the American image of the Jew after 1900. Unfortunately, Handlin does not deal with the blatant incidents of antisemitism which had occurred before the 1890s, such as the restrictions on voting, the courtrooms which barred Jewish testimony, the stores destroyed by mobs bent on "getting the Jew," and the preachers who railed against those who would not accept the true faith. Moreover, modern psychologists would question whether stereotypes poking fun at designated groups could, as Handlin claims, involve no hostility or negative judgment.

Richard Hofstadter, in *The Age of Reform,* seems to begin where Handlin stops. Hofstadter, however, probes more deeply into the agrarian psyche and arrives at the conclusion that "the Greenback-Populist tradition activated most of what we have of modern popular anti-Semitism in the United States." Neither Greenbackers nor Populists engaged in antisemitic riots or pogroms, Hofstadter writes, and their hostility expressed itself primarily in verbal attacks; nevertheless, the fact that they could accept the view that an "international gold ring" controlled by Jews kept them in economic bondage suggests their receptiveness to bigotry under trying circumstances. As Hofstadter points out, they needed a human scapegoat to excoriate for the unexpected and bizarre changes occurring to them, and the Shylock image, personified by the House of Rothschild, suited their purposes.

John Higham has done much more extensive research in antisemitism than either Handlin or Hofstadter, and has reached relatively similar conclusions. Although he also finds antisemitism to be primarily a Gilded Age phenomenon, he points out, as well, that both positive and negative stereotypes of the Jew had existed in this country as early as the Jacksonian era, and that antisemitism at the end of the nineteenth century flourished primarily in those areas which combined social discontent with aggressive nationalism. Higham acknowledges the antisemitism of the Populists, but he believes that their prejudices came more from nationalistic than from economic impulses. By concluding, though, that "the typical native American formulation of anti-Semitism may be described as pseudoagrarian," Higham aligns himself with those who find antisemitism a salient characteristic of the Populist movement.

The view of Populism as a source of American antisemitism has been challenged by defenders of the nineteenth-century agrarian reformers. Frederic Cople Jaher, who scrutinizes Populist ideology in his study *Doubters and Dissenters,* takes exception to the views of historians who see the origins of twentieth-century antisemitism in Populist beliefs. Jaher does not deny that hostility existed, but he finds that Populists "were no more antagonistic toward Jews than toward other groups; and that, even though individual Populists may have disliked Jews, the movement as a whole was not anti-Semitic." Other historians, including Norman Pollack, Walter Nugent, and C. Vann Woodward, have argued in a similar vein. They have written about the democratic and reformist aspects of the Populist movement and have emphasized the struggles of an agrarian group trying to restructure and improve American society. But even where a group is struggling to obtain legitimate goals, can the use of the Shylock image be wholly innocent or merely a stray aspect of relatively little significance? Is it possible, moreover, that the Populists were not more antisemitic than others in the United States but that the American heritage contains the seeds with which antisemitism is nurtured?

Analyses of particular antisemitic episodes in the United States, presented in the next group of selections, may help readers understand what factors generate the noxious sentiment. Aside from the Civil War and the Populist eras, detailed studies are available only for the twentieth century. Three examples have been chosen for illustration. The ingredients in each case vary widely, and a search for a common denominator is difficult. If antisemitism can erupt in a southern city during the Progressive era, in a prestigious university in the 1920s, and all over the nation during the 1930s, can one isolate any single factor as the dominant cause? Since tensions generated by changes in society and economic grievances have been present throughout the twentieth century, one must ask: how powerful is the religious motive? At what point, if any, does Christian teaching that the Jews killed Christ sway people's views? How much antisemitic feeling is disguised and rationalized not as hostility to Jews but as responses to specific events? Also, while prejudice is the harboring of hostile attitudes toward any one group or individual, discrimination is the acting upon these feelings. A key question to keep in mind is what specific incident or action, if any, triggers discriminatory behavior. The three case studies which follow afford sufficient opportunity to note the divergent circumstances which lead to intense hostility toward Jews.

In the first study Leonard Dinnerstein discusses what happened in a southern city in 1913. The murder of a thirteen-year-old girl gave rise to the single most violent episode of antisemitism ever witnessed in the United States. Atlanta had grown quickly during the previous two decades, but the promise of a bountiful life had not been fulfilled for the rural workers who had flocked to the city. Low wages, long hours, and squalid tenements produced high crime rates and racial conflicts. Finally, in 1913, a gruesome murder horrified the populace, while accusing a Jewish factory superintendent of the crime provided a focus for their accumulated frustrations. Added to this was the Baptist and Methodist religious heritage which stressed that the Jews had killed the Savior and that they could not be forgiven until they acknowledged Jesus Christ as the Messiah. Social disorder in Atlanta no doubt stimulated the attack upon Frank. But would that have been enough of a reason without the religious heritage?

Large-scale discrimination against Jews had begun early in the twentieth century as evidenced by newspaper advertisements for resorts, housing accomodations, and employment specifying "Christians only." After World War I Harvard University shocked Jews all over the nation by inaugurating a restrictive admissions policy, the subject of the selection by Morton Rosenstock. It is "the most disturbing manifestation of anti-Semitism" in American history, one rabbi exclaimed, while another Jew dubbed Harvard "an intellectual Ku Klux Klan." Despite the anger of the Jewish community, the new Harvard quotas remained. Many gentile students and alumni supported the limitations because they felt that the presence of too many Jewish students "threatened the Anglo-Saxon character of the college." Legally, of course, a private university can determine its own qualifications for admissions. But do private institutions have moral obligations to society which transcend legal rights? Should students be excluded—or admitted— on the basis of religion?

David J. O'Brien in the last essay of this section deals with Father Coughlin, who won wide support from Catholics and other Americans during the New Deal era. Although Coughlin did not begin his crusade for "Christian Justice" with open attacks upon Jews, his analyses were strikingly reminiscent of some Populist orators of the 1890s. He identified the monetization of silver and the destruction of the Federal Reserve System with the dictates of Christianity. Coughlin then "discovered" that the financial oligarchy of the United States was Jewish and, what is more, that Jews supposedly controlled the press and propagandized against Christians. Because of the dire economic plight of most Americans during the great depression of the 1930s, many poorly educated and unsophisticated individuals responded favorably to the priest who could identify the causes of their hardships so easily. Coughlin's strength grew during the decade. He added an attack upon atheistic communism to his repertoire and explained in 1938 that antisemitism in this country was growing "because the people sense a closely interwoven relationship between communism and Jewry. . . ." The 1930s also witnessed the rise of persecution of Jews by Hitler in Germany and the indiscriminate brutalities of Joseph Stalin in Russia. In the United States many Americans, including large numbers of Catholics, tended to agree with Coughlin that communism was a greater menace than fascism. They deplored what they considered relative American indifference to Russian policies while treatment of the Jews in Germany received greater and greater condemnation. At one point Father Coughlin, whose radio audience was estimated to be between 30 and 45 million listeners every week in 1932, admitted that the *real* need was for Jews to "openly profess the divinity of Christ" and that the "Jewish problem" would continue so long as Jews refused to accept the "spiritual brotherhood of Christ." Does a statement of this kind support Kallen's views and suggest that religious heresy rather than economic or political differences shaped Coughlin's opinions? Also, how much can you rely on what people like Coughlin profess to be the *real* problem?

The final selections in this book assess black antisemitism. Within the past decade much has been written on the subject. Are blacks generally antisemitic or are they not? Answers to this question have abounded in treatises, pamphlets, surveys, analyses, and journalistic diatribes. The argument has focused on three points: whether blacks are as antisemitic as non-Jewish whites, whether they are antisemitic because they are antiwhite, or whether they are antisemitic because they want a scapegoat.

The issue of black antisemitism reached nationwide audiences during the strike of public school teachers in New York City during the autumn of 1968. The trouble began the previous spring when the administrator of an experimental local school district (predominantly black) dismissed a number of union teachers (predominantly Jewish) on the grounds that their presence was inimical to the successful operation of the schools. The teachers protested, the union supported them, and an independent commission established to ascertain the validity of the complaint concluded that the local school board did not prove that the teachers' performances were unsatisfactory. The local administrator then agreed that the teachers might return, but when they did so, they claimed that they were being harassed, and the union called a strike. At this point labor issues, racial antagonisms, and public hysteria became so enmeshed that it is difficult, even in retrospect, to separate fact from fantasy and rhetoric from reality. By the time the teachers returned to their classes, the dispute had opened a veritable Pandora's box of prejudices. Scores of commentators, laymen and scholars alike, investigated the situation and turned out an avalanche of studies detailing the new wave of alleged antisemitism.

Aside from the excesses of a few militants, however, the views of the blacks toward the Jews do not seem to be significantly different from those discussed by Kenneth Clark, the social psychologist, in 1946. At that time he pointed out that mutual negative stereotyping existed among both Jews and Negroes, and he pinpointed the reasons in a cogent manner. Both groups are insecure in

American society. Hostility toward one out-group allows another to feel closer to the in-group. Furthermore, minorities imbibe the dominant cultural attitudes, and although they deplore prejudice against themselves, they are less concerned with the treatment of others. Clark also mentioned the perennial Negro stereotypes of the biased Jewish merchant, the exploitive Jewish housewife, and the greedy and avaricious Jewish landlord who allegedly charges high rents and provides less than minimal services. He acknowledged, however, that much of the prejudice might be no more than displaced aggression, a means of expressing antiwhite feeling, and a way of maintaining and solidifying group identity.

Clark's analysis, and many other articles published in the last few years, including one by James Baldwin, acknowledge that black antisemitism exists. But where Clark is scientific and dispassionate in his treatment of the subject, Baldwin seethes with rage. After first cataloging the black man's grievances against society in general and the Jew in particular, he states that white Protestants in the United States are primarily responsible for black prejudice. Nevertheless, Baldwin continues, the Jew "is singled out by Negroes not because he acts differently from other white men, but because he doesn't. . . ."

Rabbi Robert Gordis finds Baldwin's essay nothing but "a passionate justification of Negro anti-Semitism today." In a direct response to Baldwin, Rabbi Gordis admits that some Jews may have been guilty of sins of omission and commission but he notes, as well, that the contributions of Jews to civil rights causes have been greater than those of other whites. Rabbi Gordis interprets black antisemitism as a result of socioeconomic deprivation and Christian teaching. It is also, he points out, a way for the black man to identify "with the dominant white majority, give vent to his pent-up hostilities and indulge a sense of imaginary superiority." Rabbi Gordis advises the Negro to engage in greater self-help and urges him to stop scapegoating Jews. Hatred, he concludes, is not the way to uplift oneself.

The problems raised in these essays do not exhaust the ramifications of antisemitism in American life. Much more research in depth is needed for a fuller understanding of its development in the United States. No doubt many of the conclusions reached within this collection will require serious modification as fresh material is unearthed and fuller analyses emerge. The field for historical inquiry is wide open. The task should prove beneficial for a greater understanding of minority group life in the United States.

In the reprinted selections footnotes appearing in the original sources have in general been omitted unless they contribute to the argument or better understanding of the selection.

MELVIN M. TUMIN (b. 1919) is professor of sociology and anthropology at Princeton University. Among his many published works are *Desegregation* (1958) and *An Inventory and Evaluation of Research and Theory in Anti-Semitism* (1960). In the following essay Tumin asserts that "in all important cultural regards, the average American Jew is indistinguishable from the average American non-Jew, except in place and form of worship." Is such a statement a denial of a rich cultural heritage? Are there any tangible or intangible characteristics which distinguish different ethnic groups from one another? Or is Tumin, in attempting to point out the fallacies of stereotypical impressions, also denying that there are differences among groups of people other than religion? Moreover, are all stereotypes fallacious, or are they merely exaggerations —hence, distortions—of some frequently observed characteristics?*

Melvin M. Tumin

What Is Antisemitism?

If someone were to show you photographs of four well-known personalities and instruct you to point out which were Jewish, you would probably react in the following way. Like most people who have taken such tests, you would begin to look for some identifying clues and would manage to find some, no matter how subtle and vague. Why?

The instruction to distinguish Jewish from non-Jewish sets in motion a particular way of looking at things, and the mere search for differences brings to mind the numerous things most people seem to have heard about "Jewish-ness." When tests like this are scored, it turns out that most of the guesses are wrong; non-Jews are identified as Jews as often as the reverse. Yet almost no one who has been a subject for this kind of test has refused to take it or has protested about it on grounds that such identifications could not be made. The implication seems clear: many people believe Jews are different and can be sorted out from non-Jews, no matter how similar they may at first appear.

What Is Anti-Semitism?

By itself, this belief in the identifiability of Jews need not concern us. But, if and when this belief is accompanied by some kind of fear of Jews—a feeling that they

*Melvin M. Tumin, "What is Anti-Semitism?" 15 pp. Published by the Anti-Defamation League of B'nai B'rith, New York, 1966. Originally entitled "Anti-Semitism in America."

ought to be kept at a distance, and a desire to deny them certain rights enjoyed by others—then we have the phenomenon called anti-Semitism. These then are the major ingredients:

1. A belief that Jews are different, that they can be identified and distinguished from non-Jews;

2. Some kind of fear of them;

3. A desire to keep them at a distance;

4. A willingness to discriminate against them—in schools, jobs, residence, social clubs, resorts, and other such places.

As you can see, full-fledged anti-Semitism involves not only beliefs and feelings, but actions. The beliefs and feelings we call prejudice; the actions we call discrimination. It is very important to make this distinction, for they do not necessarily go together. We have found prejudiced people who do not discriminate; and, curiously enough, people who discriminate even though they are not prejudiced. At the extremes, of course, we find people who do both, or neither. An understanding of the difference between prejudice and discrimination, of the ways in which they may work with or against each other, is essential to a discussion of anti-Semitism.

Let us begin with prejudice. What are some of these anti-Semitic beliefs? A tally of the most frequent stereotypes shows the following:

Jews are too clannish—but they are always trying to mix in;

Jews are international financiers—and also international communists;

Jews are too materialistic—and also too spiritual and moral;

Jews are too concerned with business—and at the same time too bookish and intellectual;

Jews are aggressive and pushy—but they are also too withdrawn, too ascetic, too introverted.

We can see that these beliefs cover a whole range of characteristics—and their opposites. The fact that people can hold such mutually contradictory beliefs shows us that rational logic is absent from prejudice. The more extreme stereotypes show us something even more important. For when the anti-Semite insists, as the more fanatic ones do, that the Jew is an agent of the Devil; that he dotes on ritual murder of non-Jewish children; that he is plotting to seize control of the world—then we know we are dealing with sick and distorted minds. We might wish to laugh at these wild and ludicrous notions, but they cannot really be safely ignored. But for the moment, let us concentrate on the ordinary, non-fanatic anti-Semites and their beliefs. Are any of their ideas true? What are the facts about the Jews? Are they indeed so different? So strange? So fearsome?

Who Are "the Jews"?

When we try to answer these questions, the first difficulty we encounter is finding the group called Jews. Who are they? Whose characteristics shall we collectively examine? The most obvious thing that strikes us in America today is that a great many different kinds of persons are called Jewish or call themselves Jewish. They range over the entire gamut of physical type: they are short and stocky, tall and thin, dark and swarthy, fair and light. So, too, they range over many cultural characteristics. Southern Jews speak English with Southern accents; Boston Jews have Boston accents. Nearly all of them speak only English. A small handful of the older Jewish population still can speak Yiddish, but most often do not; and an even smaller per cent know any Hebrew. Jews differ greatly in their religious beliefs and practices as well; although most would, of course, if forced to choose, prefer the Old Testament to the New, and a monotheistic view of the universe to a polytheistic. There are Jews in virtually every occupation available in America—farmers, unskilled laborers, clerks, salespeople, managers, proprietors of small and large businesses, semiprofessionals, professionals.

While America, as one nation, presents a picture of a diverse Jewish group, the international picture is even more complex. English Jews resemble other Englishmen in their speech, their dress, their patterns of manners, their loyalties, their national identification. In the same way, French Jews resemble other Frenchmen. And so it goes. In every country, the persons called Jews are more like their non-Jewish countrymen than they are like Jews of other countries.

Yet, persons called Jews identify themselves as such even if they share with other Jews virtually no distinctive characteristics that they do not also share with non-Jews. And it is equally true that much of the non-Jewish community continues to be especially aware of persons called Jewish and seems to be ready at all times to identify and respond to Jews in special ways. Why? Why this persistence of a common identity, both by the Jews themselves and by others, even though there are no accurate identifying criteria?

An Old Way of Life in a New World?

To answer this question, we have to go back to the history of the Jews. In Europe, the Jews were isolated and restricted. They were frequently forced to live in ghettos or special sections of the country. They were often restricted to certain occupations and often denied the right to own and farm the land. They

were denied admission to schools. They were often harassed, denied the opportunities of citizenship and normal community life, and at times threatened with violence, destruction of property, and even physical extinction. As a result of this persecution, they often doubly intensified their group solidarity, their consciousness of kind. They developed their own schools, their own language, common attitudes toward the world.

Persecution also made them champions of democracy and morality and fair play. Denied normal opportunities for pursuit of social and economic improvement, they developed the quite correct idea that if a Jew was to be given a chance, he had to do twice as much, show twice the capability of the non-Jew. Hampered in the free exercise of trade and business by the laws of medieval society, it was quite natural that Jews should develop the need to be doubly active and energetic in the pursuit of their livelihoods. These attitudes toward themselves, the non-Jewish world, and the requirements for survival in a hostile society are the attitudes that Jewish immigrants brought over with them to America. But within a relatively short time, many of them found that their former distrusts and suspicions and the needs for special group solidarity were not nearly as relevant and applicable to America as they had been in the old country.

As they probed and tested the American environment, they developed an increased confidence in the openness and fairness of American society. Presented with the opportunity for free public education, with virtually no quota system until the college level was reached, they worked hard and often made great sacrifices to see that their children got an education. Having for thousands of years been devoted to the idea of the importance of reason and intellect and learning, it was natural for them to have grasped the American opportunity as avidly as they did. Following the example of their non-Jewish neighbors, many Jews devoted themselves assiduously and with considerable skill to social, educational and economic betterment.

While this was going on, another thing of great importance was happening to the Jews. They were quickly and surely losing whatever distinctive culture they had brought over with them from Europe. Within a short span of approximately two generations, virtually every "old country" cultural characteristic by which the Jewish group could conceivably be identified has disappeared from the American scene—and in all important cultural regards, the average American Jew is indistinguishable from the average American non-Jew, except in place and form of worship.

How is it, then, that there are still many people who emphasize the strangeness of Jews? Many of these so-called Jewish traits are no more characteristic of Jews than non-Jews, and all of them are acquired traits which disappear rapidly when the social milieu no longer requires them. Why is it, then, that people continue to believe that these learned traits are inborn and true of all Jews everywhere?

How Do People Become Prejudiced?

To start with the obvious, one reason such prejudices exist is that they are learned. We acquire our biased definitions of group characteristics in the learning situations we experience as children. In the Jewish case, the dominant images are ancient images, European-formed, products of systems of total discrimina-

tion. They took root and were confirmed at the time of the immigrations of past generations. The problem here is that these images, once formed, are very hard to change or eradicate.

Stereotypes and prejudices have real tenacity in the minds of individuals and, when transmitted, in the mind of a whole society. This fact dare not be forgotten by those who have any power over the formation of young minds: teachers and parents and those connected with the mass media —TV, radio, magazines, books. For the images transmitted to our children today are the images they will have in their minds when they are adults. In short, the ordinary everyday learning during childhood is the first and major source of prejudice against Jews as well as others. Unfavorable and biased ideas are transmitted to children by an adult who has learned them from adults before him and has not felt the necessity or the obligation to re-examine his mental images in the light of the concrete evidence around him.

Once infected with prejudice, it is very hard for most people, unless they make a conscious effort, to learn from what they see around them. This is because of a process called *selective perception*. By that we mean simply that people tend to see what they want to see and what they have been taught to see. They tend more often to see the kind of things that confirm their ideas and simply do not notice or respond to contrary evidence. If a child has been taught that Jews are special, he will tend to notice when they behave differently from the way he does. He will not be very impressed with the vast majority of times when they are the same as he. This is why it is so crucial not to transmit prejudices to children.

Another crucial factor that accounts for the persistence of stereotypes and prejudices is that they are explanations which, though false, have the advantage of simplicity. Ascribing an inherent trait to a whole group is very convenient; one can then either dismiss the group, or, at the very least, one can behave on the basis of a blanket reaction without having to stop and consider each individual case. One can see the dangerous attractiveness of this mechanism in a society which is daily increasing in pace and complexity of life.

Why Some People and Not Others?

But we have still not answered the deeper question—why? Why do some people respond to the teaching of prejudice and others not? Why are some people more violent and others more passive in their prejudices? And why do most people resist attempts to rid them of their prejudices? Obviously because prejudice fulfills a need, or perhaps several needs.

To discover these needs that prejudice satisfies, we have to ask a more general question: namely, why are so many of us receptive to unfavorable and hostile ideas about *any* group of people? We are dealing, in almost all cases, with some kind of fear: fear of competition, fear of loss of standing, fear of the strange. Most adults seem deeply concerned with how well they rate with others around them, with their social standing and prestige. This uneasiness, this fear of possible loss of status makes us tend to keep distance from people whom others consider inferior; we do not want their low rank to rub off on us. Because we do not feel secure about ourselves, we tend to be fearful about people whom we have already learned to regard as different.

A second factor to be taken into account is that in America and in other countries, the cultural pattern demands that one

take personal credit for any success one has achieved. As a corollary, that same pattern demands that we ourselves shoulder the blame for any of our failures. Unfortunately, most of us are ill equipped—we are not inwardly strong enough—to shoulder the blame for our own failures, or our own lack of distinction. We, therefore, need someone or some group, some scapegoat, on whom to dump the blame we cannot ourselves accept. Most of us are ordinary people, yet we are driven to command as much prestige as possible and to make ourselves appear as successful as possible. And, if we fail in any important way, we find it psychologically convenient to blame others for our lack of distinction or for our failures. Thus, the relatively unsuccessful businessman may find it very convenient to blame his lack of success on his Jewish competitors.

Some studies of anti-Semitic behavior suggest that many young men and women experience considerable difficulty in their relationships with parents who are overbearing, overdemanding, reticent about giving approval, or incapable of expressing real affection. These relationships make the child feel that he is unworthy and undeserving of love. As young people grow up, many find this sense of their unworthiness intolerable. They cannot bear the psychological pain this causes. They are therefore eminently susceptible to ideas which say that one's troubles are due not to any lack in oneself, but to strange, conniving, immoral people who make trouble, and who cause societies to function badly. Thus, out of a deep sense of personal insecurity, children frequently become adults who are all too sensitively attuned and receptive to the idea that certain "types" and groups are responsible for all that is bad and destructive.

This need to blame others for one's own inadequacies is not limited to the behavior of individuals. Certain other scientific studies suggest the following: when groups one belongs to and identifies with are themselves shaky in social standing, then these groups will collectively seek out a group scapegoat on whom to project their own worries and anxieties. Even nations, when under the stress of social and economic upheaval, may behave much as the individual does in seeking a place to lay and displace the blame. Often, too, this scapegoating is engineered by unscrupulous leaders who wish to grasp or maintain power by giving people an outlet for their dissatisfactions, thus, diverting their attention from the real sources of their difficulties. The mass phenomenon of vicious anti-Semitism in Germany under Hitler is a horrible case in point.

These are some of the reasons why people are responsive to prejudice and some of the conditions under which this prejudice gives rise to discrimination. It remains for us to analyze the reasons why some prejudiced people do *not* act out their prejudice in the form of discrimination.

Most of the people who have some unfavorable ideas about Jews also have other values that are important to them: fairness, a belief in democracy, a commitment to decent behavior — the ingredients of what Gunnar Myrdal has called "The American Creed." As a result they prefer to keep their communities peaceful and democratic rather than indulge in the costly luxury of discrimination. In recent years, such people have been considerably helped by the existence of laws which prohibit discrimination, though these laws do not, of course, attempt to prohibit the private feelings of prejudice. The positive value of being law-abiding thus enters into the balance against prejudice and restrains it from taking the form of overt discrimination.

In short, it is possible, we now know, to interpose restraints and balances, consisting of customs, community themes, law, and democratic ideals, in between the private feelings of prejudice and the public actions which comprise discrimination.

The "Polite" Bigot

The bulk of persisting anti-Semitism in the United States is practiced not by loud-mouthed agitators and crackpots, not by neo-Nazis, but by the so-called "gentle people of prejudice," the polite bigots — those who would hardly, if ever, insult a Jew to his face or discriminate against him openly and candidly. Rather the so-called gentleman anti-Semite simply sees to it that wherever possible he keeps Jews out of jobs, out of his neighborhood, out of his schools, out of his clubs. He does not do this openly in terms of anti-Semitism, for if one were to ask him frankly, he would insist he is not anti-Semitic but only that he feels he has a right to choose his neighbors, his business associates, his fellow club members. He cannot usually face up to his own anti-Semitism. Yet he practices it. In explaining it away as simply a matter of personal preference, he attaches an apparent certification of unimportance to his undemocratic and socially dangerous activity. To be sure, no single act of antisemitic discrimination can be said to be dangerous to our society. But when we add up all the single acts, we find that somewhere between 15 and 30 per cent of employment agencies in major cities systematically discriminate against Jewish job applicants; probably an equal number of undergraduate colleges and professional schools and universities do so. Perhaps an even larger number of real estate operators and neighborhood associations try to bar Jews from their residential areas; and an even larger per cent of social clubs and associations manage to exclude Jewish applicants by one device or another. In these fields, in these problems, we have examples where law or community pressure could do a great deal towards elimination.

When one thinks of the possible ways in which to eliminate or reduce both the prejudicial beliefs and the discriminatory actions, there comes to mind the role of the schools and of teachers in the shaping of attitudes of young people. Where the school curriculum manages to convey both the facts about the contributions of all people to the development of civilization and the idea of the crucial importance of fair play for the strengthening of our country, then both prejudice and discrimination are reduced to a minimum. Fortunately, for some years now, a number of excellent persons have worked very hard and very productively at the task of creating materials that can be effectively used in classrooms to teach these important facts and to convey forcefully the important idea of fair play.

Because the teacher is such an impor-

tant model of behavior for the children and young men and women in her classroom, her own behavior must be absolutely above reproach. Under any and all circumstances her words and her deeds must show that she stands firmly committed to the idea that all human beings, regardless of religion or ethnic origin, deserve equal respect and equal treatment. Any deficiency in these regards on the part of a teacher—no matter how subtle—is quickly seized upon by students—the teacher's attitudes and preferences quickly become the attitudes and preferences of the students.

To sum up then: prejudice is learned. It is learned by young people from those who stand in positions of authority and respect: their parents, their teachers, the local community leaders, their national leaders. At every level of influence, then, every person can and does make his contribution to the determination of the attitudes and practices of the oncoming generation. The more models of prejudice there are in the community, the more is prejudice spread to the next generation; but, similarly, the more models of fair play and equal respect there are in the community, the more is the younger generation likely to believe in and practice democracy during its own adult life.

The philosopher HORACE KALLEN (b. 1882) has had a long and distinguished career, and is author of more than a dozen books, including *College Prolongs Infancy* (1932), *Cultural Pluralism and the American Idea* (1956), and *Liberty, Laughter and Tears* (1968). There is hardly a subject of philosophical inquiry which he has not examined. In the following selection he argues that Christian teaching is at the core of antisemitism. If this is so, however, how can hostility toward Jews in the non-Christian world be explained? Is it possible that, using the same material as Kallen, one can develop an even more powerful argument for xenophobia or social disorganization as being the root cause of antisemitism?*

Horace Kallen

Christianity and Antisemitism

There is today not a Christian country in the world without its modicum of anti-Semitism. This communal passion obtains, indeed, wherever Christianity has reached. Christian sectaries in China or Japan, in India or Arabia participate in it no less than Christian sectaries in Germany or Hungary, in Russia or in the United States. It is present regardless of contrary attitudes, contradictory interests, opposed ideals. It appears in the most unexpected quarters and in the most varied and complicating forms. It justifies itself by the most antagonistic reasons, and it passes from one to another, from any to all, from all to any with the somnambulistic heedlessness of a sleepwalker. Its basis is an emotion. Its origin is a gospel. Its biography is a sequence of rationalizations in which the emotion seeks a publicly acceptable symbol. Its origin, nature, and present behavior present one of the most ironic and revealing chapters in the picaresque tale which makes up the history of the European mind.

The immediate background of present-day anti-Semitism is, of course, the Great War. The soil and matrix of its current forms are the passions which were the life of the war and which did not die when the war ended.

War and battle are acute crises in the life of man. The body is regimented, the spirit is crowded and cornered. Action loses its civilized delicacies, feeling its finenesses. Against surrounding, imminent, ever-nearing death a great anger

*Horace Kallen, "The Roots of Anti-Semitism," *The Nation,* 116 (February 28, 1923), 240–242.

develops, and a greater fear. The nice balances of peace-time habits break down. Inhibitions break down. Action and feeling become the simple elemental drives and sensibilities of the beast; behavior falls into primary and primitive patterns of defense and offense; thought becomes simplified and infantile.

A condition ensues which has its varieties but the living urge of which is always a dynamic fear, the same in all cases of it. As manifested in individuals this condition has gone by the generic name *shell-shock*. But social groups also are capable of undergoing fundamental disturbances whose animating source is fear and whose compensating emotion is anger. The collective fear projects itself upon the enemy. The enemy becomes really a symbol of the fear he evokes. The deeper the fear, the more evil the enemy. This view of the enemy becomes altogether independent of the facts in the case; the emotion generates its "facts" for itself. Hence the removal or disappearance of the outward cause or occasion for the emotion does not mean the immediate or even quick subsidence of the emotion itself. It grows by what it feeds on, even when it feeds on itself. So the removal, by the peace, of Germany as the evoking occasion of the emotion did not destroy the emotion. It survived and incarnated itself in a new symbol. This new symbol was bolshevism. The bolshevists, the world over, replaced the Germans as the incarnation of ultimacies in evil, and a *Walpurgisnacht* of the cruelties of fear ensued from Viborg to Naples, from Moscow to Washington.

In the course of time bolshevism lost its power as a channel for expression of the war emotion. But new sources of nourishment discovered themselves. Europe had begun to disintegrate. The institutional life of states, their industry,

their commerce, their agriculture, their education, and very obviously their governments, were cracked at their foundations and crumbling in their superstructures. If the war emotion was a basic fear focalized by the enemy, the emotion of the peace was the same fear nourished by the disintegration of the customary institutional supports of private life. The peace was a more radical case of community "shell-shock." The community began to fight illusions. One such battle with illusion is anti-Semitism.

Anti-Semitism is a chronic aspect of Christian history. It becomes acute during social crises and subsides in prosperity. The course it runs begins usually at some point of social disturbance where the cause is hidden and the distressful emotion is strong. The Jews are then declared to be the hidden cause, and the emotion is enchanneled by and projected upon this symbol. Although there have been times when the common people, led usually by a Christian priest or monk, have been the initiators of anti-Semitic manifestations, the more customary source has been some disturbed or dislocated beneficiary of social privilege. Anti-Semitism has served very largely as an instrument of the upper classes. Its history in Central Europe during the last four years—from Poland to Rumania —its history in the United States, from Henry Ford to Lawrence Lowell and the Ku Klux Klan, are not exceptions. The obscene tale of the making, the dissemination, the emotional elaboration of the burlesqueries called the Protocol of the Elders of Zion reveal the frightened snarl and melodramatic strut of professional anti-Semites, scattered by political upheaval from all the scrapheaps of privilege of Europe. The matter of interest is not, however, that this nonsense was invented, but that being nonsense it should so readily, so almost inevitably, serve to integrate social fear and malaise. Why are the Jews the perennial devil of the piece?

The answer lies in the Christian religion itself, in the status which Christianity assigns to the Jews and the burden it sets and binds upon them. The answer lies in the role which Christian teaching plays in the make-up of the Western mind.

In broad outline, this teaching has for all sects an identical content, which may be called the Drama or Epic of Salvation. It tells of a first man created perfect and sinless to dwell forever in the bucolic bliss of Eden. This first man was endowed with free will, and through the solicitation of the first woman exercised it, bringing "death into the world and all our woe." For God is just, and man's first disobedience merited no less than eternal death. But God is also merciful, and His mercy tempered His justice. The latter should be satisfied and yet man be saved. To this end it was preordained that a certain group of the human family should be chosen under covenant, for especial communion with God, that among the descendants of this family God should send His only-begotten son to be born, to live poorly, and to die ignominiously upon the cross, a vicarious atonement for Adam's original sin, to be buried and on the third day to rise again and take His place in heaven upon the right hand of God. Then all those who believed this tale and accepted this atonement would be saved from the consequences of Adam's sin. All those who did not believe and refused the atonement would be damned. By the incarnation, crucifixion, and resurrection the world became divided into a congregation of the saved and a congregation of the damned.

The fortunate vessels of God's mercy which was to temper His justice were the Jews. They were the original chosen people. To them God revealed Himself, His law, His purposes. Their history is signalized by manifestations of divine favor. As one of them, finally, the Savior dwelt on earth in the flesh, as man. But the Jews, instead of believing the tale of the Savior, repudiated it. Instead of accepting the atonement, they rejected it. They were made the instruments of His passion and death. Thereupon God's justice manifested itself anew. The old covenant was superseded by a new one, the old testament by a new. Divine favor was withdrawn from the Jews. The Chosen People became the Rejected People. From the crucifixion to the time of the Second Coming, they were doomed to live outside the fellowship of the saved, outcasts and outlaws, the brand of a sort of cosmic Cain upon their brows, their hands against every man's, every man's against them.

In the Christian system, then, the Jews are assigned a central and dramatic status. They are the villains of the Drama of Salvation. The gospel in which they so figure was carried to the farthermost corner of the European world. It became a part of the cultural inheritance of all the races of Europe, imparted equally to peer and to peasant. Nowhere in Europe could there be a village to whose inhabitants the word "Jew" did not denote the Rejected People who had once been chosen, who had denied the Savior and crucified Him, who were thus the enemies of God and of mankind. Whatever else the masses and classes of Europe might not know, the nature and destiny of the Jew they knew. Most of them lived and died without ever exchanging a word with one of the race, but to all of them the word "Jew" was full of evil meaning. This meaning derived from no concrete experience with Jews. It was simply an emotional reaction to their name in the tale —a reaction that might vary from discomfort, repulsion, or malaise to flaming hatred. It was a reaction established in early childhood through the teaching of the most solemn and impressive personalities in the child's small world. The word "Jew" became a stimulus which touched off this emotion. It was aroused by every object and person to which the word was applied. It was a word to curse with.

I have written as if this were all in the past. But it is not. The pattern of the generic Christian response to the word "Jew" is in its essentials the same that it ever was. The teaching is in its essentials the same that it ever was. Anti-Semitism is an organic part of it. How much so, may be observed in those instances of young people who come from communities where there are no Jews but who have an extraordinarily passionate anti-Jewish complex. I have had numbers of such in my classes. I have seen them associate on terms of warmest intimacy with fellow-students until the students were labeled for them, or labeled themselves, as Jews; and I have had occasion to observe the alteration of attitude which the application of that term to a personality evoked. I have discussed Anti-Semitism with Christianized Chinese and Japanese who had never been exposed to the secondary, non-religious anti-Jewish prepossessions. The reaction seemed in all cases the unconscious response of a habit whose base was the religious preconception—the definition of the central role and status of the Jew in the Christian system.

Wherever this system is taught the preconception is transmitted. People are not conscious of it; it lies in the unconscious subsoil of the mind and gives tone and pattern to their contacts with Jews. Neither experience nor the liberalizing influences of the humaner disciplines, neither science nor higher criticism nor free society seem much to modify its influences. Even the liberal movements in the church itself are without much effect upon it. Rather do all these acquirements become grist for the mill and afford the original feeling new and more modern symbols of expression. In principle and practice the pseudo-science of the brilliant economist Sombart has no different drive from the mythologies of Henry Ford; the vaticinations of Renan and Gobineau have the same dynamics as the phobias of Daudet and Lothrop Stoddard; the hysterical anthropology of Houston Stewart Chamberlain is a rationalization of the same nature as the anthropological mythology of Madison Grant. In even so detached and contemplative a spirit as George Santayana the Sunday-school bogy rose, when Europe was shaken, as a body for the new fear, to explain and assuage it. How many thousands of essentially free minds succumbed to it when inundated at the expense of Henry Ford with floods of anti-Semitic literature— forgeries so clumsy, inventions and lies so palpable that, with any other people as their theme, they would have been thrown into the waste-basket with a laugh! But because the Jews were their theme scores of friends and acquaintances of high intelligence, liberal spirit, radical interests and association have asked me, troubled, whether there could really not be anything in it. Those to whose attention I called the underlying preconception which mothered the question, recognized it upon consideration, acknowledged it, and to that degree were freed of it. For most, it is not so easy. The thing lies too deep and too forgotten.

Mr. Heywood Broun, therefore, seems too optimistic for the future of his son. The occasion which evoked his optimism is worth quoting at length, for it is an apt illustration of the point:

H. 3rd informed me that he couldn't play with Margaret any more. We didn't know who Margaret was, and yet the break seemed unfortunate. We asked him why he couldn't play with Margaret any more, and he said "because she is a Jew." Naturally that suggested another inquiry. "Because the Jews killed Christ," said H. 3rd. No, at the present moment H. 3rd is no more intelligent in his attitude toward race questions than the president of Harvard University, and he will be five on his next birthday. . . . Of course H. 3rd is going to grow out of all that rubbish. He may pick up catchwords from Ku Kluxers, but after all he is a reasonable human being and we can argue with him and even spank him.

Attitudes that Sunday-schools the world over impart automatically to children at five may be deep buried and forgotten at five and fifty, but they are not extirpated, nor translated. They make a subsoil of preconceptions upon which other interests are nourished and from which they gather strength.

The insurgence of anti-Semitism at Harvard, as everywhere, draws its energy from this subsoil. The case of Harvard is very richly in point, for in most of its features it is a reduplication — Harvardized — of the sordid class-conflict that prevails in the undergraduate society of most American institutions of learning and that goes on in the State institutions as the war of "Greek" and "barbarian." Its very interesting precipitation as a "Jewish question" gives it unique evidential point. Consider. The life of that academy, like the life of all other endowed institutions of learning in the United States, goes on in two dimensions. One is ostensibly intellectual; the other is social. The first is organized about the classroom; the second is organized about the undergraduate club or fraternity. The classroom form is in the main a disagreeable price which those seeking the social cachet of being "college men" must pay for the privilege of participating in the clubroom form. Undergraduate feelings, interests, and ambitions are integrated by the latter; it sets the standards and establishes the patterns of undergraduate life. This is an antique arrangement maintaining itself victoriously against perennial challenge. The challenge is called democracy, but the necessary basis of democracy, particularly in the academic world, is social heterogeneity and intellectual diversification. Harvard, in the heyday of Eliot's presidency, had plausible claim to being such a democracy. It troubled his successor from the beginning, and the latter's whole policy has been aimed at the restoration of social homogeneity, of something akin to intellectual uniformity.

Harvard College was created to be a sectarian academy whose primary purpose was to breed Puritan preachers, and from the outset, through many generations, Harvard kept up a sectarian homogeneity of students and faculty. The inevitable processes of secularization, the demands of the new learning in science and in industry, diversified the faculty and dispersed it socially. With the student body, however, the new influences worked otherwise. The homogeneity of "Harvard families" was in no relevant sense broken up. The masses of newcomers became simply a heterogeneous aggregate of individuals among whom the aborigines maintained their associations in superior and unbreached detachment. Membership in the clubs was conditioned upon family relations, mitigated by wealth, school connection, and by athletic distinction. In this way the class conflict of the world outside reproduced itself in the college yard.

In recent years there have been added to the categories of this conflict—rich and poor, well-born and plebeian, gentlemen and grind—another pair: native and foreign born. There has been a conspicuous increase in the number of foreign-born students, children of recent immigrants, in American colleges. Of these foreign-born students by far the larger number were Jews. The fact of their being Jews gave the conventional social issue its distinctive twist. Qualities characteristic of an economic grade could be referred to racial origins and sanctioned by the always active, if mostly unconscious, religious prejudice.

And so it was. While the Jews were few in number the discrimination against them was lost in the mass of class exclusions. As their numbers grew the discrimination grew, and grew in the degree that they developed to the full the traits of the most traditional and approved undergraduate social life—minus, of course, the Back Bay. They automatically submitted themselves to the completest assimilation possible, but they found that it takes two to effect an assimilation. Willing as they might be to fuse with the Christians, the Christians would not fuse with them. No clubs, no fraternities, few athletic teams, could find any place for them—with rare exceptions. Willy nilly, whether as amateur Gentiles or natural Jews, they were thrown back upon each other for the fellowship of college life. They created in their own circles what was refused them when they sought a wider one—the clubs, the fraternities, and such, which are the acme of undergraduate society, and they created them

and lived and moved in them in the closest possible imitation of the prevailing approved and emulated traditional type.

Of course, the proper sort of undergraduate and professor—those who, in the language of the Hairy Ape, "belonged"—grew scared and disturbed. But for a long time nothing could be done—save by snobbery and innuendo—that would not lead to the public shame of an exposure of the effective overt motives in the anti-Jewish sentiment. After the armistice, action became easier and more plausible. The propaganda of Czarist émigrés, the disseminations of Henry Ford, the association of Jews with "Reds," the resurgence of the Ku Klux Klan, the veiled though known and publicly discussed limitations upon Jews at Columbia, New York University, and other universities, provided a sympathetic social atmosphere and an encouraging academic precedent. Accusations of moral inferiority sprang automatically to the lips of their opponents and have not been withdrawn though proved to be false. Then the attack was shifted to the proposition that beyond a certain proportion—15 per cent, precisely—Jews are not assimilable. And so on. Anti-Semitic Europe—Hungary, Rumania, Germany, *et al.,* greeted these declarations with glee, and declared their own practices completely justified by them.

Of course the various rationalizations of his policy offered by Mr. Lowell and his defenders are excuses, not causes, in the case. For the fact is that it is not the failure of Jews to be assimilated into undergraduate society which troubles them. They do not want the Jews to be assimilated into undergraduate society. What really troubles them is the completeness with which the Jews want to be and have been assimilated. As every boy may yet be President, so, though perhaps with less certainty, every poor man's son might yet be a gentleman, and after a certain probation admitted to the society of gentlemen born. But if he is the son, not only of a poor man but of a poor man (or even of a rich) of the people who rejected the Savior and were rejected by God, then his apparition—on his own—in gentleman's guise becomes a mockery, a vexation, and an irritant. Unaware of the unconscious roots in the emotions of ancestral religion men seek to justify this irritation and vexation by varied and contradictory rationalizations. But the root of the special Jewish difficulty is not racial, nor economic, nor caste. It does not arise in connection with any Christian stock involved—whether in America or in Europe—in similar racial or economic or caste differences. The root of the special Jewish difficulty is the position of the Jews in the Christian religion. If you can end this teaching that the Jews are enemies of God and of mankind you will strike anti-Semitism at its foundations.

A prominent psychoanalyst of the twentieth century, OTTO FENICHEL (1897–1946), author of *Problems of Psychoanalytic Technique* (1941) and *The Psychoanalytic Theory of Neurosis* (1945), had an international reputation in theoretical as well as clinical psychoanalysis. Forced to flee Berlin after Adolph Hitler assumed power, in 1938 he arrived in California, where he spent the remainder of his life. As a victim of Nazi aggression and as a man well versed in sociology, philosophy, and psychiatry, Fenichel was in a particularly apt position to analyze the roots of antisemitism. As can be expected from a person so widely trained, he sees that hostility toward Jews results from a combination of factors, but emphasizes in particular its psychological derivation. In reading this selection, see if you can find any evidence of personal experience. Would this necessarily distort the evaluation?*

Otto Fenichel

Psychoanalysis of Antisemitism

Please do not expect too much from me. Antisemitism is a very complicated phenomenon. If one wishes to understand it, sociological, historical and political points of view must be employed as well as the psychological one, and opinions vary very much with regard to the relative significance which psychology has in the understanding of social phenomena. I do not like to estimate it too highly and am of the opinion that we can only throw light on one side of the problem, it is true, a side which would remain quite dark without our help. And so that you may not expect me to explain everything, I will begin by telling you of a discussion which I had with a colleague, who, it appeared to me, over-estimated the value of psychology in such connections which lead us straight to the point.

At that time I had a controversy with certain analysts with regard to their attempts to transfer the knowledge which they had gained by examining the mental conflicts of individual neurotics to socially and historically important mass-psychological phenomena, in too simple a manner. I was of the opinion that one must keep the following differences in mind. The actions of a person are determined from two sides, first by the current influences to which the person is

*Otto Fenichel, "Psychoanalysis of Antisemitism," *The American Imago,* I (March 1940), 24–39. Footnotes omitted.

subjected and to which he reacts, and secondly by the instinctual structure which he brings with him and which determines what these reactions will be. This structure for its part consists of biological factors on one side and all the early influences on the other side. A psychological description must therefore describe current experience and structure. But there is one category of phenomena in which one can relatively slight the current experiences, and place all the importance on the structure, — these are the neurotic phenomena. A neurotic is characterised by the fact that he does not react to current experiences in an appropriate way but with a definite pattern of reaction which he developed in his childhood. Therefore analysts who are occupied the whole day with neurotics, tend to underestimate the current experiences and overestimate the structure even when they examine social phenomena. But in the case of the historically important mass-psychological phenomena it is just the other way around. The instinctual structure of human beings has remained relatively unchanged in the course of historical times. It cannot be the chief factor needed to understand the changes within these times. Of importance here is the current and external stimulant which works very differently in different times and communities on the relatively constant structure, and just those current facts which affect whose groups in the same, or in a similar way. The colleague with whom I had this argument considered this point of view to be a betrayal of psychoanalysis. "For example," he said, "let us examine a phenomenon such as antisemitism. Whole masses of people are filled with senseless and contradictory feelings of hatred against a certain race. Logical thinking has lost all power against these emotions, the irrational, the original blind destructive instinct suddenly breaks out against an innocent object. Where in this case is the current factor which can explain this? Is this not an outstanding example to show that only the scientific investigation of the irrational forces in man, the psychoanalysis of the instincts, can explain it?" I retorted with a question: "Is the instinctual structure of the average man in Germany different in 1935 from what it was in 1925?" Surely not. The psychological mass basis for antisemitism, whatever that may be, existed in 1925 too, but antisemitism was not a political force then. If one wishes to understand its rise during these ten years in Germany, one must ask what happened there during these ten years, not about the comparatively unaltered unconscious. It is true, when one knows what happened one can only understand the reaction of the masses if one also understands *what* is reacting, that which is aroused or inhibited or displaced in the structure, and for this one needs psychoanalysis. In order to gain this understanding let us therefore begin at the surface and descend gradually to the depths. The principle thing which changed during those ten years was above all that an antisemitic mass propaganda was started. The effectiveness of this propaganda has been the chief thing which has altered the attitude of the masses in this respect. But why did the propaganda work? What was present in the masses which made them believe what they were told? The answer that it was mass-suggestion will not suffice, as the problem is: how and why did this suggestion work? It is certain that the first thought is that people are most ready to accept suggestions which bring them some advantage. What advantage does antisemitism bring to the average man?

Well, for instance the prospect of obtaining a job which has been taken away from a Jew. We certainly do not want to underestimate this, but one sees at the first glance that such an explanation is not sufficient, that it is too superficial because it is too unspecific. Let us ask in order to get further, what purpose does the spreading of antisemitic propaganda serve? And there we can perhaps learn more from Czarist Russia than from Germany. The protocols of the Wise Men of Zion were forged by the Czarist police, and they know for what purpose they forged them. As a result of the general misery there was a rebellious tendency directed against the ruling powers. If the propaganda succeeds the Jews will be thought to be the cause of the poverty and not the authorities, and the revolutionary tendency will have been redirected against them. The terrible pogroms showed that this intention succeeded. The advantage which antisemitism gave to the average person was different from that of a prospect of a job. They were in a conflict between the rebellious tendency and the respect for authority, in which they had been trained. Antisemitism gave them the means of satisfying both these contradictory tendencies at the same time; the rebellious tendency by destructive actions against defenseless people, and the respectful one by the clear conscience which they had, as these actions had been carried out at the command of the ruling powers. They could believe that their own enemies were also the enemies of the ruling powers.

This, undoubtedly correct but not yet sufficiently deep and specific, theory of antisemitism we will call the "scapegoat theory." As you know, the Jews used to load all their sins on to a goat and then drive it out into the desert in order, themselves, to become pure in this way. In this way the ruling classes load their sins on to the Jews. Before I go on I would like to mention in this connection a good article by Arnold Zweig, which shows how deep this conception of the Jews as scapegoats is anchored in the soul of the German people. Zweig analyses a folk-tale by Grimm, the story of "The Jew in the Thorn." In it is told of a man-servant who having been swindled out of his wages, manages to get the money from a Jew, instead of from his master, and the chief point is, he feels himself absolutely in the right in cheating the Jew, because he had served his seven years honestly. Zweig rightly points out that all the features of modern antisemitism are strongly marked in this folk-tale which is centuries old, dating at least from the time of the Bauernkrieg, 1500. At that time, too, there was a ruling class which needed to deflect mass-displeasure directed against themselves and then, too, apart from this mass-displeasure there was a mass-preparedness to submission, a change in the structure of the masses caused by education. Their conscience worried them when they dared to think of going against the authorities, and they were therefore grateful if they could let out their rage without anything happening to their master, without his being angry, and against an opponent who dared not defend himself.

But we must go on. This explanation is still not specific enough. The next problem, which presents itself, a problem which Zweig also did not neglect, is: Why are the Jews so suitable as displacement-substitutes? Is it just chance that in such a situation an antisemitic propaganda is instituted and not, say, a propaganda against redheads? Surely not. There must be something in the mass-mind which meets antisemitism half way, the Jew must be the "born scapegoat" for their hosts. That he is preferred to the redheads he owes to his history, which shows how often he has proved his worth as a scapegoat.

Why is this role so fatally suitable to him?

The first attempt at answering this question is a rational one. First, the Jew has always been more defenseless than the redhead. Secondly, when the social order, or rather, disorder, produces much misery then he whom this misery affects is seldom in a position to discover its origin, partly because the connections are too complicated and partly because the existing ruling class does everything it can to make the true connections unrecognizable. The point is then to find someone in his surroundings who appears to him to be the cause of his misery. For centuries it has been the Jew, on the one hand as money-lender, on the other hand as dealer, who has appeared to those who were confronted with financial need as the representative of the power of money; quite apart from the circumstance how much Jewish poverty there was at the same time. And then it is a problem in itself what drove the Jews away from the productive trades into commerce. We do not want to underestimate this point either. We must remember that the Armenians, too, who were persecuted by the Turks just as the Jews have been persecuted by the Russians and Germans, were the commercial people among their Turkish hosts. But we cannot free ourselves from the impression that we should not place too much importance on this condition, that it only serves to strengthen other things which come from more unconscious depths, and which we do not yet know. We must also mention that this point of their being the commercial people is not admissible in some cases

of social phenomena analagous to antisemitism, for instance the persecution of negroes in America. The American negroes were slaves, and their ostracism is a result of the historical and social troubles which arose around the problems of slavery. But these negroes have another characteristic which makes them suitable as scapegoats: they are black. The Jews have also been viled by the antisemites because of their cultural or physical "racial" peculiarities. They, too, were black, not their skins, but their hair, and are foreign in their customs and habits, in their language, their divine service, and their everyday life which is so interwoven into their divine service. The foreignness they share with the Armenians, negroes and the gipsies, and this must be the secret which made the people believe them to be the wicked evildoers. People who are of the same kind as oneself, and as the ruling powers are, one does not suspect of evil, but people who look different and speak differently and behave so differently, they may be capable of anything.

Here the question of antisemitism begins to leave the field of the psychology of the antisemitic people and to go over to the psychology of the Jews. The obstinacy with which the Jews have resisted assimilation through the ages, although the ghetto system should have been encouragement enough, although other people in a similar position have, during the course of history, repeatedly been absorbed by their hosts—this is a problem the examination of which would lead too far. Let us accept this as a fact. The Jews retained their peculiarities, and their hosts did not understand them. These peculiarities, however, were remarkable. They came partly from the time when they were an independent state, and partly from later times. Cult and holy literature were from that old past and had an oriental stamp, in their clothes and everyday language they were fixated at quite a different period, they had retained peculiarities of their hosts, which these hosts had themselves long since given up. Their strangeness worked at the same time as something archaic, as something left over from ancient times, which one had oneself overcome, like the gipsies have retained their nomadism among the settled nations.

What does all this mean psychologically? For primitive thinking that which is foreign is always something peculiar. Even today we meet every foreigner in a contradictory, as we say, ambivalent, manner. The essential quality of foreigners is that one does not know them yet, therefore does not know what one can expect from them. Perhaps, it would be as well to be on good terms with them, or perhaps it would be better to make them harmless as quickly as possible. How different it must have been in olden times, when the nations came less frequently into touch with each other, when the cultural peculiarities of each were much more strongly marked. The foreigners might bring advantages through inventions they had made, or be a danger if they were more advanced in the technique of arms. In the ancient world foreigners were "sacer," a peculiar word, which meant both holy and cursed at the same time. The strangeness of the Jews was of a special kind, because of its archaic character which was combined with an indisputable mental superiority in certain spheres, which perhaps was made use of quite often by the commercial Jews to take advantage of the other people. The Jews were clever, and at the same time connected with old primeval powers with which one had, oneself, lost touch. Who knows what one could expect from

them, and if the authorities said they were bad, then it was surely so, for one's own poverty was obvious.

Therefore, what could one expect from them? What phantastic evils were they capable of? We can begin here with ritual murder and the poisoning of wells, but must also relate other things. Let us look at any antisemitic literature. We read again and again, the Jews are murderers, are filthy and debauched.

The first question must again be to find the rational part in these accusations. But this cannot be found. The Jew is a merchant and as such may often be a swindler, but the criminal statistics show that Jewish murderers are rarer than those of any other race. The religious laws of the Jews prescribe particular cleanliness, and although the impoverished Jewish towns are undoubtedly very dirty, they are not more and probably less so than the Polish, White Russian and Russian peasant villages; and with regard to sexuality the Jews do not tend to excesses any more than any other nation. The accusations made against the Jews are creations of the peoples' fancy and these we will now investigate in connection with the archaic foreignness which the Jews really possess for other races.

In psychoanalysis we are in the habit of saying: "The patient is always right." What do we mean by this? That even the most senseless neurotic phenomenon has a hidden meaning for those who understand how to read it, that even the maddest obsession of a lunatic contains a bit of truth if it is not taken literally but in its latent meaning, and that in order to find this latent meaning one must take seriously everything that is said. In reality the Jews are not to a greater extent murderous, dirty or debauched. What can be understood by a latent meaning of the assertion that they are? That murderous, dirty and voluptuous tendencies are really concealed somewhere; the question is, where? That the Jew is in this case, too, a scapegoat, a displacement substitute, and we must search for the real sinner.

As you know *Freud* has taught us that everybody struggles all his life with repressed instincts, which continue to exist in the unconscious, and that among these original instincts, murderous tendencies and sexual impulses play the chief part, and just those sexual impulses which are considered objectionable, low and dirty. The lust to kill, love of dirt and low voluptuousness, these are the things which people try carefully to keep hidden in their unconscious. One measure of this striving is to see in others what one does not wish to become conscious of in oneself: projection, which is most marked in certain mental diseases, but is also present in normal people; think of the crusader against homosexuality, who is really fighting against his own repressed homosexual impulses. We believe that the Jew appears to the antisemite as murderous, dirty and debauched so that he should not become aware of these same tendencies in himself. He sees the Jew as the lust to kill, as the low sexuality in general. We will see later on how this projection is facilitated. But we already understand why riotous impulses are so easily deflected against the Jews. The Jew not only unconsciously represents for the rioters the authorities whom they do not dare to attack, but also their own repressed instincts which they themselves hate and which are forbidden by the authorities against whom they are directed. Antisemitism is indeed a condensation of the most contradictory tendencies: the instinctual rebellion, directed against the authorities and the cruel suppression and punishment of this instinctual rebellion, directed against oneself. The Jew is unconsciously for the antisemite at one and the same time the one against whom he would like to rebel, and the rebellious tendencies inside himself. Now to come back to the question why is a racial minority like the Jews particularly suitable to act as the carrier of such a projection of the forbidden instinctual impulses; this becomes clear because of the already mentioned archaic, and at the same time superior foreignness.

One can put it in one sentence: One's own unconscious is also foreign. Foreignness is that which the Jews and one's own instincts have in common. At this point I may remind you how Freud explains the phenomenon of that which is "uncanny" psychologically. The feeling of uncanniness comes over us whenever something which we once believed to be true, later giving up this belief, proves itself to be really true after all. All happenings are uncanny which seem to prove the existence of magical connections in the world, because we once thought magically, and later gave up this way of thinking in favor of the logical one. To the average person a murderer is uncanny, in particular a parricide or a person guilty of incest, because each one of us once felt such impulses and later one repressed them. And the other way round, a person or race which is in any way uncanny, is capable of murder and incest. The Jew with his unintelligible language and ununderstandable God appears uncanny to the non-Jews, not only because they cannot understand him and therefore can imagine all sorts of sins in him, but still more so because they can understand him very well somewhere in the depths, because his customs are archaic, that is contain elements which they once had themselves, but later lost. There is also a rational point which helps to strengthen the irrational side. The Jews as a racial minority were oppressed everywhere. It is clear that the ruling people must fear the possible revenge of the oppressed people, in particular where the oppression appears to be unsuccessful, when the oppressed people rise up again and again and, believing themselves to be a chosen people, refuse to give up their peculiarities under any torture. Jehova is considered to be a revengeful God. And there is no doubt, that he is described in many places in the Old Testament as a very revengeful deity. But there is also doubt that the command "love thy neighbour as thyself" does not come from the Christian religion, but from the Jewish, that the Jewish God also showed many loving and merciful traits. Why have these traits been forgotten by the other races, and why do they imagine Jehova, like the individual Jew in abstract, and the Jewish people, to be malicious and revengeful? And this conception being of an irrational nature is not to be changed by any real experiences with Jews. It is well known that every antisemite knows one Jew who is free of all abominable Jewish qualities, and yet this makes no difference in his antisemitism. There is an anecdote which illustrates this very well in Olsvanger's collection "Rosinkess mit Mandlen" and which I will translate from Yiddish into English.

Jews and antisemitism. The world cries— antisemites, antisemites, and really, antisemites. But let us see what is the difference between an antisemite and one of our Jews. If you ask a gentile: "Listen, what do you think of the Jews?", he will answer: "Jews, an abominable race, swindlers, criminals." "And what do you think of Todres?" "Ah, Todres is a fine man, he bought hay for me and we got on very well." "And how do you like Schmuel?" "Schmuel is one of the finest men I have ever

known." And the gentile will speak in the nicest way about every individual Jew. But try asking a Jew the question: "What do you really think of the Jews?" "Jews are the chosen people, the most perfect nation, an understanding and wise folk." "Now, what do you say to Berl?" "Oh, the dog, there was never such a loathsome man in the world, he bought corn from me for the squire, and swindled me from head to foot." "And how do you like Jizchok?" "The rascal, the low hound . . . ," and so the Jew will speak about every son of Israel.

The endless revengefulness of the wicked Jews is again a projection. The ruling people cannot imagine that the oppressed are not revengeful. They recognize archaic-deep features in their behaviour and they know how revengeful they themselves are at such depths. The rejected instincts and the rejected ancient times come back to them in these incomprehensible people who live as strangers in their midst. That which they had believed was overcome, appears to rise up again and again like a hydra, and they try to cut off its head. At the same time they despise it in the same way as they despise their own disavowed instincts. Contempt and disregard are meant to help them to overcome their fear. They try to refute their fear by proving to themselves how easy it is to attack someone defenseless. But even then this proof does not succeed. With a curious pride, even with arrogance, this defenseless one appears to rise again and again. The fear still exists and therefore they must always despise and humiliate more and more, to refute this fear. But they never succeed.

Apart from all this, there is one thing more which makes the position clearer, the effectiveness of the circumstance that the Jewish peculiarities and culture were centred almost exclusively round a common faith, the Jewish religion.

When the Romans conquered a nation they would erect a temple in Rome to the Gods of the conquered people to be on the safe side. Perhaps this God was powerful, then they would have to fear his revenge for oppressing his people, therefore it was better to be reconciled with him in any case. The revenge of the Gods of the oppressed nation is a dangerous thing.

Now it is a strange thing with the Gods. The religions of all peoples and all times work with the fear which comes from the "uncanny." In the images of God itself, or in the cult, are many "archaic" features, which appear to bring back that which is old and overcome, in order to fill the believers with fear or awe and so keep a hold on them. The Gods have always had not only supernatural, but also underground, animal and instinctual traits which one must fear. One thing seemed to raise their particular wrath, that was to look at them. In the Jewish religion, too, the sight of the Holy of Holies was reserved for the high priest once a year, and they had to turn away at the Day of Atonement when the priest threw himself on his knees before God. It is the same in other religions. The sight of God, among the primitive people the sight of the king, his representative, means death.

This digression has led us from the point. Therefore, I will not go further into the meaning and genesis of this prohibition of looking. It is sufficient to say that it is universal. And from this prohibition against looking it is only one more step to the idea that God is a terrible, horror-inspiring and ugly sight. And, as is well known, a number of the Gods of primitive races are incredibly ugly. In the higher religions they are concealed allusions of a similar kind, which only the psychoanalyst understands. It is interesting that also the un-

canniness of the ugly God is based on his bringing back something which had been overcome: The ugly features of a God are always animal features, and the first incarnation of the dead chief, the great ancestor, who was later made a God, was the totem animal, the totemism preceded religion. This awe inspiring part of the cult, where a dreadful being threatened to show himself, also exercised a strange charm. Today we see a degenerated residue in the shows at fairs. The fairs originated in connection with the worship of God, and were connected with this, like a satyr play with the seriousness of the tragedy, and is still called "Messe" in German, which also means "mass." Here dreadful sights are offered the people which are otherwise forbidden or inaccessible. And what does one see? Rare animals, deformities, criminals in wax, sexual secrets. Perhaps it seems like blasphemy to bring this into connection with the worship of God, but I will tell you of one connection where you will not have this feeling and which will lead us back to antisemitism: At the fair one does not see native but exotic animals; and one does not see native but exotic Gods. This double character of wonder and fear, of highest beauty and terrible ugliness, which belongs to God, condenses itself with the double character of wonder and fear, which belongs to foreigners — both are "sacer" —, in the feelings which one has for strange Gods, and which caused the Romans to erect temples to the conquered Gods. It is unbearable, in the long run, to have contradictory feelings for one and the same object. And in the same way as the fairytale makes it possible for the child to manage the contradictory feelings it has for its mother, in that it introduces two mothers, an entirely good mother, and an entirely wicked stepmother, so that the love and hate felt against the same person is divided between two people, so the perception of a strange God, too, has been used by all people and at all times to divide the love and hate felt for God between two objects: Their own God is only good and beautiful, the strange one only wicked and ugly.

Many religious systems are dualistic, and have a good and a bad principle, an Ahriman and an Ormuzd, apart from a God—a devil. Reik has shown in his book that the devil is the degenerated strange God, the God of the strange people, of the conquered people, whose revenge is feared. The devil is always more uncanny than God, always has more archaic characters, namely animal qualities, goat's feet, horns, tail and ugliness. Therefore, he is always suitable to be a carrier of the projection of one's own instinctual impulses, he is murderous, dirty, debauched, a tempter and a deceiver. It is clear for the antisemite that the Jewish God and so the Jew is the devil, the anti-Christ, the wicked principle directed against God, which crucified God. The devil, too, is characteristically despised and dreaded at the same time. And one thing more: This "degraded" strange God is not only animal and ugly,—he is usually crippled. The deformed, blind, lame and hunchbacked are "sacer" for the primitive people, as beings near to God, as seers, but also as dangerous; they are, altogether, uncanny for the ordinary mortal. An interesting point, which, however, does not belong to our theme, is that on the ordinary man the artist has a similar effect; he, too, has retained a more archaic character. This, he owes chiefly to the fact that he is strange. And in fact, we see that people who have longer noses and darker hair than the others, are therefore regarded by these practically as deformed. What is the rational essence of the special position of deformed people? The deaf, but also hunchbacks and in particular red-haired people are regarded as malicious and ill-natured. Why? Because they are really at a disadvantage compared with healthy people, and because the healthy people tend to despise and laugh at them, and they, therefore, tend to protect themselves by being aggressive themselves. The physically inferior are a "badly-treated minority" and, therefore, their revenge is feared. This fear condenses itself with the deep feelings of uncanniness which one feels for the devil and the cripple-God, and increases when the physical disadvantage or dissimilarity is combined with superiority in certain mental spheres (one is reminded of the uncanny, skillful, lame blacksmith of the sagas), which is thought to be proof of an alliance with supernatural powers, as magic (particularly when they themselves consider themselves to be a "chosen people").

But the sight of a cripple does not only arouse the fear of strangeness and revenge, but also the special fear that he will want to make one a cripple like himself. It would lead here too far to undertake a psychoanalysis of the burial and death customs of the various peoples. But we know that they all rest on the tendency to prevent an unconsciously feared return of the dead, who could revenge themselves for their dying, by fetching the living and so make them dead, too. Is there any reason to suppose that the people fear the Jews could want to make them Jews, too?

It is often mentioned that *Freud* once expressed the opinion that antisemitism is connected with the Jewish custom of circumcision! Now: my whole lecture shows that it is not my intention to maintain that antisemitism consists in the uncircumcised despising the circumcised as unmanly, and fearing that the circumcised will want to circumcise them in revenge. The matter is somewhat more complicated and circumcision is only one of many customs which are felt to be uncanny. But I would like to explain what Freud meant by this remark.

Circumcision is not a purely Jewish custom. Many other races have this custom, too, and it is only a problem why the Jews have remained in this respect, as in many others, so conservative. Apart from the oriental peoples, circumcision is practised among many primitive races —a proof for the age-old nature of this custom. Other primitive races do not, it is true, practise circumcision, but have other analogous customs, more or less sanguinary injuries to the genitals, or other parts of the body, which have become substitutes for the genitals. To be sure, such injuries are usually performed on the young people at puberty and not soon after their birth. This is the essence of the so-called "initiation ceremonies" whereby the young people are accepted in the adult community. It is certain that this is the older form of the custom, and that in the case of the Jews for some unknown reason this ceremony has been transposed from puberty to infancy. It is not easy to say what is the meaning of such holy practices. Perhaps one can guess it by their effect. The youth who has now become a man will be proud of his initiation into the adult community, and this feeling will be increased by his now being allowed, among other rights, that of sexual intercourse. But the circumstance that he has had to pay a price for this admittance, that he has had to endure pain, shows him drastically and hammers into him that he can only enjoy the protection of this community as long as he obeys its rules, and that he can expect unpleasant things if he does not adhere to certain

conditions. And in fact, such and analogous social measures are effective. Even today, we find deep in the unconscious of men the fear that his penis might be cut off if he sinned, a fear, which acts as the chief motor for the suppression of the instincts desired by the patriarchal society.

The drastic reminder of the sanguinary puberty rites of the primitives has been replaced by less drastic measures during the course of history. The Jewish circumcision, although practiced on the infant, is still comparatively drastic. It has remained a real sanguinary operation on the genitals. This knowledge on the part of the uncircumcised people undoubtedly increased the feeling of uncanniness which the Jew gave them. It helped to give a more precise form to the indefinite fear that a retaliation on the part of these curious people is imminent; this retaliation became a sexual one. They will do something to the little girls of other races in the same way they do something sanguinary-sexual to the little boys of their own race. We are of the opinion, therefore, that circumcision which is strange and familiar in unconscious depths, works in the same way as the other customs which make the Jew suitable for a devil-projection.

We can sum up: The antisemite arrives at his hate of the Jews by a process of displacement, stimulated from without. He sees in the Jew everything which brings him misery, and not only his social oppressor but also his own unconscious instincts, which have gained a bloody-dirty-dreadful character from their socially caused repression. He can project them on to the Jew because the actual peculiarities of the Jewish life, the strangeness of their mental culture, the bodily (black) and religious (God of the oppressed peoples) peculiarities and their old customs make them suitable for such a projection. Perhaps there will be one objection to this formula: If it is true that there must be unconscious motives which complement the effectiveness of the anti-semitic displacement, and that it is a pre-requisite for these unconscious motives that the Jews live as strangers among their hosts, separated, and living in their own cultural circle, then—one could say—this could be valid for the old and even for the Czaristic antisemitism; but is this the case for the modern German antisemitism? Does not this contradict all our theories? Were not the majority of the Berlin Jews without any Jewish connection and tradi-tion, a fact, which the Prague and Vien-nese Jews who are nearer to the East Jews, often used to make fun of—were they not extensively assimilated, did they not feel themselves as Germans? Where was the archaic foreignness which was said to be the prerequisite for the purpose of projec-tion?—Now, it appears to me that the suc-cess of again using the Jews and not the red-haired men as scapegoats (so far as the success really is there, may be that anti-semitism does not really have such deep roots in the German people as previously in the Russians, who can judge the quan-tity?) proves that the foreignness, or at least the memory of it, is still there. Some Jews may not have felt this. But obviously, a large percentage of the Germans did. One cannot completely destroy a tradition and the memory of it in one, or even sev-eral generations. Let us look at any mod-ern German antisemitic literature, and we will see that not only aggression and destruction are demanded in the service of the ruling powers and of the good God, that not only have foreigners been shut out by their race theories, but accusations are made against the Jew which make him appear as the representative of their own low, greedy, dirty sexuality. "One often says," it is written in "Mein Kampf," "that the Jews are human, too. But if someone violated your mother, would you then say that he, too, was human?" And the Jew, it is maintained, violates the mother Ger-many. Streicher's "Stuermer" is filled with rape, castration and murder stories. And if one knows how to interpret the race-mysticism, one sees how in it the pure ideal is contrasted with the unclean instinct. "Mein Kampf" also terms the spread of syphilis among the Germans as a "judaisation of their soul." And so we have got back to where we began, to an admission of the limitation of the psycho-logical explanation. In order that this displacement, which seems to us psycho-logically to solve the secret of antisemi-tism, can take place, there must be in addition to the Jews with their qualities which make them suitable as scapegoats,— the instinct-repressed average man, the wish to destroy, arising from actual mis-ery, which has to be deflected, and the external motive which we termed "stimu-lant from outside" in our previous form-ula. The full utilization of the psycholog-ical facts which we have studied so that they become a real and politically effec-tive power is only possible under certain economic and political circumstances. We did not wish to speak about these conditions today. This does not mean that they are of secondary importance. We only need to look at the facts around us, and to consider these facts in the light of the psychological basis of antisemitism, in order to see what this complicated phenomenon, antisemitism, really is, in the present-day world: A weapon in the class-warfare dominating the present civilized world.

Like Otto Fenichel, GORHAM MUNSON (1896–1969), who had a varied career as teacher, journalist, editor, and author of more than a dozen books including *Waldo Frank: A Study* (1923) and *Sense and Sensibility* (1928), recognizes that antisemitism stems from "certain psychological peculiarities" as well as other factors. Unlike Fenichel, however, Munson emphasizes the economic roots. He notes that tolerance expands in times of economic security and contracts as jobs become scarce. His conclusion, therefore, is that "a flanking attack on racism through an improvement of economic life is the most hopeful way—perhaps the only way —of checking and reducing the malignant disease." In reading this selection, see if there is some type of antisemitism omitted from Munson's discussion. Does he account for the antisemitism of the rich and wellborn?*

Gorham Munson

Antisemitism: A Poverty Problem

Of all attitudes opposed to anti-Semitism the one most exploded today is liberalism. The younger liberals the writer associated with twenty years ago regarded anti-Semitism quite simply: it was atavistic. It was not studied—not very much, at any rate—as a religious, political or psychological problem, although some consideration was given it as an economic phenomenon. The general feeling was that anti-Semitism would yield and disappear before the spread of enlightenment. This crude survival from the past would be routed by ridicule and infectious tolerance and the spirit of modernity. True, there was a revival of anti-Semitism fostered by Henry Ford

but his propaganda was "absurd," and sure enough it failed to make progress against the liberal temper, and eventually Ford repudiated it in a splash front page announcement. In the nineteen-twenties, as the novels of Sinclair Lewis swept the country and syndicated columnists like Heywood Broun became the rage, it seemed that liberalism was sufficiently potent to beat down the liberalism of racial antagonism in its grosser manifestations. Was not the Ku Klux Klan hurled back with mocking laughter? Incidentally, the nineteen-twenties were prosperous.

Today, when anti-Semitism has become an instrument of the foreign policy of the nazi-fascist states, it would be hard

---

to discover a single person who believes in the efficacy of the liberal temper for dissolving racial hatred. Today it is terribly easy to see that our post-war liberalism adopted too short a view altogether. It had in America no historical sense of the problem of anti-Semitism. Its optimism was extremely shallow and it waged only a paper warfare with anti-Jewishness.

Liberalism twenty years ago did not know enough about the problem. It does not know enough today about the history of anti-Semitism from the Middle Ages to the pseudo-scientific racialism of nazi writers. Liberalism had no feeling for the epical character of anti-Semitism in time and geography. Here was a vast knotted historical drama of hate, outrageous lies, ignorance and crimson outbursts of violence, and yet liberalism thought that a happy ending, a sort of pageant featuring the Spirit of Progress, could be tacked on. Especially was there failure to notice that anti-Semitism was invulnerable to facts and reason because of certain psychological peculiarities.

If ever a case has been thoroughly armed with facts to disprove myths, it is the case against anti-Semitism. Facts have been overwhelmingly marshalled against the accusations of "ritual murders" and secret world conspiracies and commercial domination. But unimpeachable data have so often lost the contest against the "propaganda of the lie" as to shake, though not to destroy, one's belief in the existence of a canon of truth in the universe.

The best that can be said for facts and reason arrayed against racial irrationality is that they have occasionally converted individual anti-Semites to sanity. Wilhelm Marr, for instance, was a famous Jew-baiter after the Franco-Prussian War but later turned away from his writings with a disgust that actually made him sick. Count Heinrich Coudenhove-Kalergi, a leading opponent of anti-Semitism, was once a rabid anti-Semite. Nietzsche during his friendship with Wagner had anti-Jewish tendencies but after the break he declared that "to meet a Jew is a blessing, especially if one has lived among Germans." Henry Ford withdrew from circulation and destroyed the remaining copies of *The International Jew.* These examples prove that the appeal to fact and reason is not as hopeless as we are sometimes tempted to believe. But we must add that such an appeal converts only the best types among anti-Semites, those who through some idealistic vagary have strayed into the camp of persecution.

The anti-Semitism of the mob, however, appears unshakable by the appeal to reason. "The most effective appeal to the multitude," observed Benjamin Kidd in his unjustly neglected book, *The Science of Power,* "is the emotional appeal through the spirit of combativeness." Hitler has understood this too well, and although he is a leader of civilized men, his oratory is deliberately debased to the level of an appeal to an audience of savages. His secret is the arousing of collective emotion against *imaginary enemies.* The hateful Jew of nazi propaganda does not exist, although it is practically certain that Hitler believes in the flesh-and-blood actuality of his fiend. It is most difficult to shoot down a phantom with the bullet of a fact. The haters of the imaginary Jew either do not know actual Jews, or if they do they often make exceptions of Jews personally known to them—and continue to denounce the Jew of their fantasy. One of the toughest educational problems in dealing with anti-Semitism is how to make the imaginary enemy which anti-Jews cherish collide with the shattering world of reality. Our technique for coping with the unreal is undeveloped. Unfortunately the suffering of the Jews is not unreal.

The problem is greatly aggravated by the sad and curious fact that the hater is devoid of any wish to be rid of his hatred. Seized by hatred, a man feeds on it, draws intoxication from it. Nothing in him cooperates with the efforts of those who would relieve him of the emotion. Statistics, facts, arguments, enlightening literature—these cannot reach the depths of his psyche where he sucks on hatred. This trait of man is the jungle heart of the whole problem of anti-Semitism, and it does not seem susceptible to a direct psychological approach.

It is crises—economic and war—that bring out the hate in man and produce waves of zenophobia, of which anti-Semitism is a special example. War propaganda, as we all know, creates an inhuman image of the enemy upon which a blind hatred is projected. The propaganda against the Jews is akin to war propaganda. There are atrocity stories, inhuman caricatures, the deliberate incitement of hate, and the victims of this anti-Jew propaganda defy the gentler ministrations of psychology. So long as the crisis lasts, their zenophobia is invulnerable.

Liberalism then is discredited as a dissolvent of anti-Semitism; good will is not enough. And psychology can only explain the inner mechanisms of the persecutors, it cannot cope with and act upon the evil conditions that are favorable for the development of the germs of racial antagonism. Is there any doubt that those conditions are primarily economic? It is most significant that tolerance grows during periods of economic amelioration and intolerance springs up in hard times. After one has looked hard and long at anti-Semitism from various angles, it finally seems indisputable that a flanking attack on racism through an improvement of economic life is the most hopeful way—perhaps the only way—of checking and reducing the malignant disease.

Whatever else it is, anti-Semitism is a poverty problem. In its advanced form, there is psychological compensation for those in poor circumstances when they see the Jews worse off, starving, deprived of gainful occupation, stripped of civil rights; the comparison makes their own hunger and indignities easier to bear. There is a more tangible compensation in the loot taken from the defenseless Jews: loot in the form of jobs and physical wealth and money, loot that is all too welcome in the frantic scramble to pick up half a living.

The socialists had an economic interpretation of anti-Semitism, and it was a good one as far as it went. Anti-Semitism was engendered, they said, by competitive jealousy. In the struggle to avoid insolvency the business man came to focus jealousy upon successful Jewish competitors. In the professions it was the same. Competitive jealousy likewise was inevitable among the millions looking for jobs and not finding them. The socialists blamed the capitalist system for the almost universal feeling of economic insecurity and warned that a scapegoat would be found to mislead the masses. They foretold that the "ruling class" would attempt to change the class-war into a race-war. This was their sound interpretation.

Their remedy was the classless society to be achieved by socialization of the means of production, distribution and exchange. Some thought that reformism was the road to the classless society;

others insisted upon an interim of transition during which there would be dictatorship. The world has concluded that there was some miscalculation in the remedy. Faith has been lost in the promises of socialism, although we did not realize how completely faith had gone until the other day. We lived through much between Munich and the German-Russian pact.

The attempt to put socialism into practice in Russia turned out to be merely a new version of the old revolutionary riddle so succinctly stated by the Marxist scholar, Benjamin Stolberg. "How can revolution," Mr. Stolberg asks, "avoid a Thermidorean end? How can a revolutionary dictatorship keep from evolving into a privileged bureaucracy? Why do the Robespierres and the Saint Justs, the Lenins and Trotskys lose to a directory or an apparatus; and finally to bourgeois or proletarian Caesarism? . . . Why does the left always make the revolution and the right always write the constitution?"

The Russian experiment with its protracted ruthless dictatorship, its totalitarian features, its inequalities of income and privilege, its witch trials, and finally its enigmatic foreign policy has disillusioned the masses and the intellectuals. Nor has it borne lightly upon the Jews in the Soviet Union. Of the plight of Russian Jews, Simon Dubnov, the historian, wrote: "Two and a half million men and women are placed between an appalling present and an even more appalling future, faced by the choice between a red and a white dictatorship, between dying out and dying a violent death. Never before has the Jewish people been confronted with a more terrible alternative."

European observers report, however, that loss of faith in the promise of social-ism by no means leads to a renewal of faith in capitalist democracy. The people do not swing back and believe again that capitalism can provide jobs, security, freedom, dignity, equality for them. Just as the Russian experiment has ended hope in socialism because the socialist ideal failed to materialize after fifteen years of Bolshevik rule, so the Great Depression has corroded the old hope of capitalism. It ate too deep, lasted too long, generated too much despair. Only recently have we realized the profundity of the shock to people's trust as capitalism staggered and reeled year after year. Something (what?) seems to prevent capitalism from recovery and a higher development; something (what?) seems to have deflected the socialist advance and created a new bureaucratic class society where a classless society had been intended. The result was that where belief in some kind of new social order should have been, there came to be a vacuum. "Since nature abhors a vacuum," says Silone, "society was forced to create a substitute—fascism."

If we state that anti-Semitism is a poverty or economic problem to be relieved and cured by economic measures, we are seemingly pitched into a quandary as black as if we had taken any other approach to this thousand-year-old scourge. For capitalism clearly has not conquered poverty, and socialism, as Silone writes, "has defeated itself." Initiative, power, *élan* are with fascism, and to most people there appears to be no really new social order in prospect, even in conception, that would be an alternative to onrushing fascism. Where are the economics for the conquest of poverty?

A hint of a new direction in which to search for an economic solution was recently given by Stuart Chase in a plea for real unity in the American people. "If we can find an invention, or a series of inventions," said Mr. Chase, "to conquer unemployment without piling up a mountain of debt, we shall be as immune to foreign isms and ideologies as an iron dog is to rabies. . . . In simplest terms, the inventors must find a method which will permit Americans to buy back what they can make. . . . Like Alice in Wonderland, they [Americans] can just stand and look at the beautiful garden without being able to get into it."

Mr. Chase's finger points in the direction of financial reform, and it is just the *social possibilities* of financial reform that have been overlooked by leaders of public opinion. No better illustration of this neglect can be given than Mr. Chase's article in which, after calling for new economic inventions, he fails to mention or consider the series of economic inventions offered twenty years ago by Major C. H. Douglas which were designed to overcome the curse of unemployment ("unempayment") without piling up new debt.

It is as if intellectuals snobbishly did not wish to soil their minds with financial studies, just as once upon a time gentlemen refused to soil their hands with trade. A study of money, for instance, is not considered an essential duty of our intelligentsia although some acquaintance with anthropology is obligatory. Money reformers are widely considered crackpots—many of them are —but the interested banking propaganda that all unorthodox monetary thinkers are cracked is unfair.

Again it is felt that money reform is a narrow subject, and there is some justification for the feeling. The "100 per cent reserve" plan of Irving Fisher, now talked about somewhat, certainly has no social body; it is a banking mechanism

argued on its technical merits, divorced from a social or political philosophy. On the other hand, there is the Douglas social credit scheme which is integrated in a democratic philosophy, has an extensive sociological literature attached to it, and is developing its own unconventional politics. Its adherents, who came originally from the National Guilds movement in England, even speak of it as a "third resolvent factor," a new world theory in the sense that socialism and fascism are world theories.

It is not the writer's present purpose to argue for any one set of proposals for redesigning our money system to achieve certain social objectives. What the writer does insist upon is that no possible method of stopping dictators and combating their anti-Semite technique should be left uninvestigated, and the social possibilities of money reform— or monetary radicalism, as the writer prefers to say—are unexplored by anti-fascists and anti-anti-Semites.

The incontrovertible facts are that no essential change in the money system has taken place in the history of capitalism, and socialism proposed no essential change. (Marx took his financial economics from the banker Ricardo and fully believed that production automatically financed consumption, which is the cornerstone-belief of financial orthodoxy.) As our appalled eyes have seen, the masses in Europe are turning toward nazi-fascism out of despair over capitalism and socialism. But in doing so, they find themselves still imprisoned within the old financial system, working like helots on capital goods production, suffering cut after cut in personal consumption, flayed by tax-gatherers, and prodded toward war because their governments still find it necessary to wage trade wars exactly like the capitalistic democracies.

There are no fundamentally new financial economies operative in the Third Reich or in Italy. The proof is Hitler's "Export or die!" exclamation some months before the Danzig crisis boiled over into war.

It would seem only common sense therefore to say that it is just this element common to capitalism, socialism and nazism, namely financial orthodoxy, that needs to be critically examined by those hopeful of breaking out of the vicious circle. It would further seem that opponents of nazism and anti-Semitism would turn eagerly to the social blueprints of monetary heretics in a zero hour search for a new basis for democracy, a new economic order capable of catching popular imagination as an alternative [to] totalitarianism. There are, it happens, monetàry reforms of high standing in the "countries of the mind" that advance serious proposals for abolishing poverty. Dare we neglect the study of them in this hour of darkest crisis?

Unlike those who see antisemitism resulting from realistic deprivation, ARNOLD ROSE (1918–1968) stresses the symbolic use of the scapegoat, which allows the prejudiced person to obtain *"substitute satisfaction for some great need which cannot be satisfied normally or even openly."* Rose, whose sociological investigations into the political process, minority problems, and problems of the aged resulted in such works as *The Power Structure* (1967), *The Negro's Morale* (1949), and *Aging in Minnesota* (1963), which he edited, acknowledges that "correlation between hatred of city life and hatred of Jews has not yet been empirically established. . . ." Nevertheless, he suggests that there are indirect indications of such a relationship. What are these indications? What, if any, additional pieces of evidence are not discussed here?*

Arnold Rose

Antisemitism's Root in City Hatred

Students of prejudice have usually analyzed it from the standpoint of the objective outsider: they note that prejudiced beliefs deviate sharply from fact, and they try—by pointing out fact—to bring belief closer to fact. They fail to realize that the typically prejudiced person is likely to be quite familiar with the objects of his prejudice—Negroes or Jews—the falsity of his prejudices being daily demonstrated by the plain evidence of his senses. As a matter of fact, he even knows that his beliefs are false: "some of my best friends are Jews," he says, and he knows many "good Negroes." Yet he will continue to say "All Jews are Communists," or "Niggers can't be trusted."

Yet, however false as to fact, prejudice has a certain logic, a logic not of reason but of the emotions. Prejudice is not an eccentric whim or fancy; it has psychological roots which can be traced.

Prejudice is more than false belief; it is a structure of false beliefs *with a purpose,* however unconscious. In analyzing prejudice, it is important to discover the false beliefs, but it is more important to discover their purpose. Similarly, in fighting against prejudice, it is important to puncture the false beliefs factually, but it is more important to weaken the purpose. The false beliefs are the symptoms of prejudice, but the purpose is its root cause.

*Arnold Rose, "Anti-Semitism's Root in City Hatred," *Commentary,* vol. VI (1948), pp. 374–378. Reprinted from *Commentary,* by permission; Copyright © 1948 by the American Jewish Committee. Footnotes omitted.

How do we find out the purpose of a prejudice? There are no infallible ways, but the social scientist has some good clues; in the first place, he reasons that a structure of false beliefs that lasts for hundreds of years, as in the case of anti-Negro prejudice, or for thousands of years, as in the case of anti-Semitism, must represent a *substitute satisfaction* for some great need which cannot be satisfied normally or even openly expressed. The prejudices have what he terms a "symbolic significance." The symbolic significance of flat dresses and flat bobs for women during the 1920's seems to have been that women felt a need to look like men, and yet did not wish to admit that need openly. This is a very simple example, but on a far more complex level we have warrant for believing that "Jews" and "Negroes" have similar symbolic significance for prejudiced persons.

It has become common to say that Jews and Negroes are hated and feared because they have become the "scapegoats" onto which aggressions against frustrating conditions can be displaced. For instance, many well-meaning people who have thought about the position of the Negro in the South have come to believe that the hatred of the Negro stems solely from the economic deprivations of the whites. Because the poor white is kept down—by the rich Southern plantation owner, by the rich Northern industrialist, or simply by the undeveloped physical environment—he is frustrated, and vents his aggressions against the Negro, feeling helpless to revolt against the dominant groups. Similarly, it is said that German Jews were made scapegoats for all the frustrations due to political instability, inflation, and the Versailles Treaty. There is much truth in this "scapegoat-displacement" or "frustration-aggression" theory. It

does explain why a group with a common and major dissatisfaction with which it cannot come to grips feels a need to hate and fear a substitute symbol. But the scapegoat theory does not explain *why one group and not another is always chosen* to be the scapegoat. It does not explain why those who are not frustrated are frequently almost as prejudiced as those who are.

The major charges against Jews are that they are sneaky, dishonest, selfish, domineering, too clever, too ambitious, clannish, vulgar, noisy, and inclined to radicalism. The major charges against Negroes are that they are unbridled, passionate, violent, immoral, animal-like, untrustworthy, and lazy. There are some peculiar inconsistencies in these popular assertions. For example, Negroes are believed to be lazy and unambitious, yet they are said to be seeking political domination over whites in the South. Evidence of individual Negroes becoming "intelligent," proud, ambitious, self-confident, provokes the most violent reactions in the South. Jews are said to be clannish, yet they are also said to be always trying to push into circles where they are not wanted. Jews are held to be domineering, yet any evidence of Jews becoming servile or seeking sympathy stimulates only sadism on the part of those prejudiced against them.

Some of the distortions of fact are significantly peculiar. For example, a group of persons who had already volunteered the information that they objected to Jews because they had too much power, were asked what types of businesses they thought Jews dominated. They said that Jews dominated finance and politics. Few said that Jews dominated the movie and radio industries or the manufacture of clothing—which happen actually to be the only types of businesses in which Jews are disproportionately represented.

One of the most fascinating facts about statements of prejudice is the constant repetition of certain "reasons" in any and all contexts. When one argues with a prejudiced Southerner on the basis of fact and reason that no harm could come from letting Negroes use the regular restaurants and hotels, or suggests any measure, however mild, to reduce segregation and discrimination, he almost invariably ends up with the equivalent of "Would you like your daughter to marry a Negro?" These are the types of raw facts we pick up about prejudice. How can we interpret them? Looking at the stereotypes about Negroes, it is obvious that most of them picture the Negro as uninhibited, with special emphasis on the absence of sexual inhibitions. Then, we may ask from what premises do prejudiced whites draw the conclusion that their daughters would marry Negroes if they were to sit at the next table in a restaurant? Logically, we must infer that there is a repressed sexual attraction. When we check into Southern folklore we find that there are myths about Negro males having unusually large sexual organs, and tales about the greater passion and sexual adeptness of Negro females. Several of the stereotypes about Negroes —that they are uninhibited, rhythmic, passionate—further indicate their sexual attractiveness. We need not go into all the reasons which lead us to believe that the Negro is a symbol of free and passionate sex—which is desired by white Americans but still not felt to be proper in our society, with its codes of sexual expression.

The emotions which form the basis of prejudice are, on the one hand, hate and fear, and, on the other hand, envy and desire. Envy is created not only by the white male's desire for the Negro female, but also by his belief that the white female would prefer the Negro male to him if she had equal access to both. Similarly, the white female must suppress her desires for the Negro male, and she envies the Negro female her superior attractiveness for the white male.

In the United States, at least, there is little association of Jews with sexual desirability. Rather, the Jews are associated with economic success, political radicalism, and quick adaptiveness to a rapidly changing world. Historically such traits are connected with life in cities, and so are the Jews. The Jews are the urban people *par excellence*. In the Middle Ages they engaged in the then-despised commercial and financial occupations and were not allowed to live outside of cities. When capitalism grew and the cities expanded, the Jews had a head start, and became successful in terms of the new values despite the hurdles put in their way. Historical trends transformed what was intended to be a punishment into a reward. Non-Jews came to be envious of that reward. Envy generated hate—and there was already the initial hate arising from the Jews' rejection of Jesus as God.

It is worth noting how the popular image of the Jew is related to the city in many ways. (In much of America, "New York" and "Jew" are almost interchangeable epithets.) It is not simply that the Jew adapts to city life and makes a success of it. The Jew is willing to submit to the repression of the "free instincts" which is required by the city. The Jew is also thought of as rootless, as unattached to the "community" with its meaningful values. The Jew is mysterious; he might be the manipulator of all those forces which seem to control the life of the little man in the big city.

The Jews are hated today, I would suggest, primarily because they serve as a symbol of city life. Residents of cities as well as farm or village people can, and do, hate cities and what they stand for. An overall correlation between hatred of city life and hatred of Jews has not yet been empirically established, but there is indirect evidence that further study would find one.

In the first place, there is among the masses of urban residents, from whom anti-Semitism gets its most violent expression in America, a nostalgia for country life and the rural virtues. Sometimes it takes the form of a desire for ease and for avoidance of hustle-and-bustle, but always it includes a wish for a simple, straightforward existence. The wealthy classes are not exempt from this, but are rather especially prone to it, perhaps in unconscious moral revulsion against the sharp and devious ways in which their own fortunes were often built up. The ideal picture of rural life is, of course, unrealistic, in terms of the actual life of an average farmer—an unrealism buttressed by the experiences of the city dwellers who can afford to take vacations in the country. Nevertheless, city dwellers are so taken in by their picture of country life, and the supposed virtues of honesty, clear-thinking, and altruism which that life is supposed to engender, that this may be a factor in their acquiescence in the political dominance of farm blocs and "downstate" or "upstate" political machines, as well as the special legislation that exists for the farmer: artificial support of high prices for his product, guarantee of a minimum income without the need for proving indigency, special exemption from the draft law.

The glorification of rural life has real historical roots, of course. The early history of our country took place largely in a rural setting, and many of the great heroes of America, as well as of other countries, had a rural origin. Children in schools are drilled in the glories and virtues of rural life until it becomes the nearest thing to heaven on earth. The rural people, on the other hand, are schooled in distrust of the city, and they can never quite understand its economic basis, or the competitive, disinterested character of its relations with them.

It is not without significance that the city man's picture of country life excludes the Jew. He knows that Jews are not farmers, and every evidence that Jews ever have been or might become farmers is greeted with astonishment. Urban non-Jews who do not object to residential proximity to Jews in the city, are yet likely to protest vehemently against the presence of Jews in or near their summer resorts. Jews remind them of the city, whose ways they try to forget when they take their mental and moral, as well as physical, vacation.

Thus, perhaps, the host of contradictory antipathies toward the Jews can be explained by the association of these antipathies with another one—an antipathy toward city life. Jews are called sharp businessmen (capitalists) and are hated for that; Jews are called Communists and are hated for that. Both capitalism and Communism are urban products, which are hated because they are too complex to be understood by the little people and because they "make trouble" for them. Yet there is no point in hating such impersonal phenomena as capitalism and Communism; it is much easier to hate their symbols—the Jews.

Jews are blamed for being successful

and for being low class. But it is only by rural standards that they are successful — all city people are successful when they have to work only eight hours a day and can have so many of their household duties taken care of by other people. It is also by rural standards of an older day that Jews are low class. Farmers today may be just as dirty, just as concerned with striking a good bargain, and just as noisy (when they have a chance to talk) as lower-class city people, but gentlemen farmers or rural Puritans of an earlier day may not have been — at least in myth.

Jews have been blamed at the same time for being both narrow-minded and so cosmopolitan as to put their general human loyalties above their national loyalties. These are urban traits. The typical city dweller lives such a compartmentalized existence and is forced to avoid so large a portion of the stimuli that bear down on him from all sides that he must be narrow in terms of the possibilities of his world. Yet the city-dweller is often also forced to become aware of the wider currents of opinion and of problems outside his province or nation.

Similarly, the Jew is blamed for being at the same time cliquish and "pushy." The urbanite must make a selection of those to whom he chooses to respond among all the thousands with whom he comes in contact every day. The urbanite does, however, want to get ahead, and to cultivate those acquaintances that he believes will be enjoyable or profitable. The rural person, on the other hand, has a limited number of human contacts, and it is taken for granted that he will be "pushy" — that is, make friends with all he meets and learn as much about his acquaintances as he can.

The Jew is feared because he is believed to be superhumanly wise, and yet viewed with contempt because he is thought to be weak and "unhandy." The "city slicker" stereotype has merely been extended in the first instance, out of the truth that a wide range of social contacts sharpens the wits. On the other hand, the helplessness of the city man in the fact of any breakdown of the complicated services that usually support him is notorious. He does not have the knowledge or the tools to improvise in his physical environment, and when the web of interdependence he assumes is broken, he is helpless. This extends into his social, intellectual, and emotional life as well.

For understandable reasons, many urban and rural persons hate the characteristics of city life — the impersonality, the sharpness, the weakness, the cosmopolitanness, the narrow-mindedness, the pushiness, the cliquishness, the "capitalism" and the "Communism" which it creates. Yet these haters retain at least an unconscious recognition that the city is also necessary and good. They know that the many desirable products of modern life presuppose cities, and that much of what we are so proud of in "modern civilization" is a consequence of cities. They admire cities, at the same time as they fear and hate them. They hate cities because they cannot adjust to them, or — as in the case of the successful — because they feel that they have been immoral in adjusting to them. But just as they unconsciously admire the city, so they envy the Jews.

The symbolic projection of hatred of the city onto the Jews allows the prejudiced person to destroy the city and to escape the city, and at the same time to keep it and live in it. Prejudice, we have said, is a way of finding relief from a mental conflict about something; a particular group becomes identified as a symbol of that thing, so that the group can be hated and the thing itself left untouched. Of course, the conflict must be deep and important to the minds of the prejudiced persons, and the symbolic group must be associated over a long period of time with the thing in question —sex and cities, in our analysis—about which there is mental conflict. The conflict must be felt by most of the members of the society, and the symbolic association must occur for practically all of them before there can be prejudice.

Further evidence of the basis of prejudice in the symbolic substitution of a group of people for a thing which is both feared and admired, hated and loved, emerges when people who were once critical of uninhibited sex and of city life, or who come out of a background of such criticism, have a radical conversion in their favor. Those who rebel against the straightlacedness of their childhood into bohemianism are the ones who go into ecstacies over all things Negro—they love the Negro because he is so uninhibited, so natural, so "African." They are not concerned with the rights of the Negro *per se,* nor with his participation in a common humanity. They would put the Negro on a pedestal to love and admire—still a symbol of sex, now freed from puritanical restrictions. They have become converted, from both sex restrictions and anti-Negro feelings, but their symbolic identification of the two remains.

Similarly—although not nearly so often in American society—one can see that persons who radically break off from the anti-urban attitudes of their youthful environment and become enamoured of city life, who become Communist, or completely sophisticated, often can't do enough for Jews, for Jews as Jews. For these people, Jews are still the symbol of the city, or Communism, or of the pursuit of expensive pleasure they are now embracing.

The symbolic interpretation of prejudice allows for an explanation of group self-hatred. It is natural for a group of people who must participate in a culture to absorb aspects of that culture even when the latter work to the detriment of the group. Thus, Jews too hate the city; some of them fear it because they have not been able to make a satisfactory adjustment to its complexities. Unconsciously accepting the identification of Jews with the city, they hate the Jews and are ashamed of any manifestation of Jewishness (urbanness) in their own family. Though Negroes are perhaps less susceptible to this group self-hatred today, the severe criticisms by middle-class Negroes of the sex freedom displayed by lower-class Negroes offer an obvious example.

What suggestions for the treatment of prejudices come out of this diagnosis? Since symbolic identification is only one of the requirements of prejudice, its disappearance could not eliminate prejudice completely. The neurotic whose compulsive behavior is a symbolic manifestation of a repressed childhood desire or fear, may not be able to rid himself of this behavior even when the symbolic significance of his neurosis is made clear to him and he accepts it.

But understanding might help to dispel prejudice. Obviously, among the major psychological needs of the prejudiced person would be his realization of the conflict in his motives and values. He would need to be shown that he both wants more pleasure in sex and that he thinks that sexual pleasure is reprehensible. The puritanical "ideal" of the South would need to be weakened, and the myth of the sexual superiority of Negroes dispelled. If the preoccupation of the South with the Negro in general, and with the sexual habits of Negroes in particular, were eliminated, prejudice would be reduced. The Southerner needs first to be taught not to envy Negroes before he can learn not to hate and fear them. An open admiration, if it has a reasonable basis, is mentally healthy, but a secret, ungrounded envy—especially when it deals with so fundamental a general human desire as sex—is not.

Similarly in the case of the anti-Semite, the conflict of desires must be resolved before prejudice can be reduced. He needs to be shown that he likes and needs cities, and yet that he hates and fears them. He needs to learn to accept cities as a necessary part of modern civilization, and he needs to learn how to adjust to cities or to join movements for the elimination of their undesirable features. The Jews and the city should be disassociated in his mind—possibly by public emphasis on every effort of the Jew to regain a position on the land. Movies on the Palestinian settlements might be a soul-stirring revelation to anti-Semites well-intentioned enough not to dismiss it immediately as propaganda.

Of course, one must not exaggerate the effect of such measures. After all, a large part of anti-Semitism is based on envy of the Jew, and envy is not to be reduced by making the envied object—successful urban adjustment, that is—less enviable, but by making it more attainable.

This relates to the "frustration—aggression" theory. Frustration may be conceived of as supplying the energy, the motive force, for prejudice: symbolic association directs it against certain suitable groups. It would be naive to suggest that frustration can be reduced or symbolic associations dissolved simply by the *presentation* to consciousness of the real sources of frustration and the real meaning of the symbolic association. Both are products of long and complex historical developments, both require long and complex developments to eliminate them: just as getting over a neurosis may be as long and painful a process as acquiring it. Nevertheless, the attack on prejudice, like the analysis of it, must work on the basis of the desire of all sane men to be rational—albeit rational in their own peculiar way rather than in the view of the impartial observer.

OSCAR HANDLIN (b. 1915), professor of history and
director of the Charles Warren Center at Harvard
University, is the author of numerous works, including
Boston's Immigrants (1941), which won the Dunning
Prize from the American Historical Association, and
The Uprooted (1951), which received a Pulitzer Prize.
Handlin argues that the upheavals of the 1890s turned
Americans from a primarily positive attitude toward
Jews to a negative one. Does he substantiate his case?
Does he omit any material that would mitigate the
impact of this essay? Finally, can real events *create*
prejudice? Or do they merely allow latent attitudes
to surface?*

Oscar Handlin

American Views of the Jew at the
Opening of the Twentieth Century

In the portentous period between 1913
and 1920, years which brought so many
other changes to the United States and to
the world, anti-Semitism became a factor
of considerable importance in this country. As the years went by between the
Frank case and the publication of Henry
Ford's version of the forged Protocols
of the Elders of Zion, great numbers of
Americans became obsessed with fear of
the Jew. Ominous hatreds began to take
form in economic and social discrimination and even in political action. Shortly,
the Klan would draw for part of its armory
upon those hatreds.

These hostile sentiments were quite
new to American society. Indeed the
favorable prevailing temper of tolerance
had produced a great willingness to accept
the Jew as a desirable and equal participant in the emerging culture of the nation. The steady disappearance of political disabilities early in the century and
the opening of all sorts of political and
social places as the immigrant Jews adjusted to the New World were the signs
of that acceptance.

It is possible to find occasional slurs
such as those in General Grant's Order
Number 11; there are instances of exclusion as when Joseph Seligman was refused
accommodations at Saratoga's fashionable
Grand Union Hotel; and a handful of
obscure pamphlets were explicitly hostile.

---

*Oscar Handlin, "American Views of the Jew at the Opening of the Twentieth Century," *Publications
of the American Jewish Historical Society*, XL (June, 1951), 323–344. Reprinted by permission of the American
Jewish Historical Society and Oscar Handlin; copyright 1951 by the American Jewish Historical Society.
Footnotes omitted.

But the shocked public repudiation of the slurs and the exclusion indicated how exceptional such instances were. It would be a mistake to treat them as the same in meaning with the anti-Semitism that did emerge after 1913. After all, in 1899, Tom Watson, later of the Frank case, was still vigorously condemning medieval prejudices against the Jews.

The factors that produced anti-Semitism in the twentieth century are well known and have been abundantly discussed. Competition for places generated economic discrimination. The movement to restrict immigration gave rise to a chain of arguments in which Jews, like other newcomers, were blamed for pauperism, vice, crime, and every other social evil. The growth of racist thinking allowed men like Madison Grant and Lothrop Stoddard to foster the Aryan myth. Most important, perhaps, the xenophobia of the war years and after led many Americans to reject every kind of tie with Europe.

There was, in addition, another factor that has not been as well evaluated, the disappointment of many radicals and reformers who somehow came to blame the Jews for their failure after 1900. The great populist, Tom Watson, was only the most striking of many figures who felt the world was plunging hell-ward and who held the Jews responsible for the descent. And significantly the mass of decent folk who joined the Klan and who read the *Dearborn Independent* came from areas that had in the 1890's been strongly moved by radicalism.

Yet these later prejudices were not inscribed upon a *tabula rasa*. They were overlaid on attitudes toward the Jews that had already taken form before the turn of the century. An examination of those anterior conceptions will throw light both on the general American view of the Jew in the 1890's and on the nature of radicalism in that decade.

The ten years after 1890 were not only free of anti-Semitism; they were actually marked by distinct philo-Semitism. The picture of the Jews I am about to reveal existed in the minds of people who were horrified by the Dreyfus Case, people who condemned pogroms in Russia, ritual murder charges in Hungary, and the distorted propaganda of the Stoeckers and Drumonts in France and Germany.

To a certain extent that picture was based on real contacts with Jews. As the number of Jews in the United States grew through the nineteenth century, they became familiar figures in every part of the country. From dealings with them emerged a distinct stereotype, the features of which were dictated by the condition of the Jews as immigrants.

Like other immigrants the Jew was a strange and easily recognized character in American society. He could be distinguished from the mass of his fellow citizens physically, in visual or auditory terms. In mid-nineteenth century, there was still a good deal of vagueness about his particular features however. What seemed then to mark off the Jew most prominently was language and accent. Yet to untutored American ears, his sounds were quite like those of the generality of Germans; often he was counted simply a kind of German.

In the writings of the New England humorist Charles Follen Adams are the most characteristic expressions of this early image. The central personage of these popular poems bore the unmistakable name, Yawcob Strauss and spoke an outlandish dialect in which the humor seemed to lie. But Yawcob was not recognizably different from any other German. A shopkeeper, he was pictured in a wholly kindly light, sentimental and good-hearted, preoccupied with his beer and his pipe. The same lack of differentiation was evident in such minor characters as Shonny Schwartz "mit his hair so soft und yellow und his face so blump und mellow."

By the 1890's however, the stereotype was much more clearly delineated. In the comic magazines of the decade it appeared fully drawn in all its lights and shadows. Occupationally, the Jew was more distinctive than ever. He had by then been identified as a peddler, as an old clothes dealer, and as a pawnbroker; indeed the three-ball sign and the title "uncle" were synonymous with him. Distinctive names also set him off; Isaacs or Cohen, Ikey, Jake, or Abie. His appearance was familiar too, pack on back, or holding a basket, or pushing a cart. His garments were either old and shiny with an inevitable black derby hat, or else they were ludicrously new and flashy. His hooked nose stood prominently forth from his bearded face and his accent was thick. Finally he was invariably concerned with money; the words put into his mouth dealt always with finance and reflected a stingy, grasping temperament. Some Jews were just on the edge of dishonesty like the Bowery shysters, Katch & Pinch. But even a likeable chap like Old Isaacs from the Bowery, in the popular play, tells his daughter,

Vhy, I vould trust you mit my life, Rachel. But vid mein money, ach, dot vas different.

There are undoubtedly antecedents of this figure in the older Shylock image. But its specific form came from the contemporary scene. A dispute over closing hours could bring the charge from a labor leader that the "hoggish Jews" were always after "their pound of flesh."

Whatever its source, by the end of the century the stereotype was clear. Repeated in popular novels, in the press, on the dramatic and vaudeville stage, it made Americans acquainted with a distinctive pattern of physical features, clothing, forms of expression, and language associated with the Jews. Most important, it ascribed to that figure a pervasive concern with money.

These caricatures in the perspective of their later uses have the appearance of anti-Semitic insults. But there is evidence that they were not meant and not taken as such. In the first place, no such intent was involved. A public school teacher in New York could affectionately give *Oliver Twist* to a little Jewish boy as a reward. And as late as 1913, Maurice Levy would unreflectively be described in like terms in Booth Tarkington's popular Penrod stories without derogatory intent.

Here was the critical departure from the Shylock image; the American stereotype involved no hostility, no negative judgment. In a popular story, repeatedly reprinted throughout the century, Moloch, a money-lender thirsty for revenge, plots to compel a duke's son to marry his niece. The duke's response is not anger, but compassion. In the denouement, he declaims:

Take her my son and wear her close to thy heart, for she is a jewel worthy of thy high position. . . . Moloch where is now thy revenge!

"Thou hast conquered it, my noble Duke," answered Moloch, overcome with surprise and admiration.

And everyone lived happily ever after. Indeed, a Jew detective with "the stamp of his race, indelibly traced on the features of all his blood" could, in another romance, win the beautiful Anglo-Saxon heroine, who in assenting declares, "to you I now turn for happiness in life, for your people shall be my people, your creed my creed, and your God my God."

The stereotype of the Jew is more comprehensible when we recall that it was, in the 1890's, only one among many. The notion that physical appearance was a sign of national identity was so widely held that a dime novel could speak, as a matter of course, of the New York detective who disguised himself as an Englishman. In the comic magazines the Jew was joined by the drunken, shiftless Irishman, by the sinister Catholic priest, by the gaudy or ragged Negro, by the stupid, soggy German, and by the avaricious Yankees, Mandy and Aminadab. Identified in outward aspects and in dialect as decisively as the Jew, these were intended to be as funny, but no more hostile, than the Mr. Dooley of the same period. Significantly, the Jews themselves accepted the caricature: *Der Yiddischer Puck,* a comic magazine edited and published by the well-known journalist N. M. Schaikewitz, often sketched the identical picture of the Jew as its English counterparts. In neither case, did the picture reflect a depreciatory attitude.

In the 1890's, an additional element took a place in the American picture of the Jew. The conception of Jewish interest in money deepened into the conviction that Jews controlled the great fortunes of the world. Although the Jews are still sometimes miserly Shylocks, more often they are princes wielding power through their gold.

In part the newer image was a shadow cast by the prominence of certain Jewish banking houses in Europe. Every American had heard of the Rothschilds and of Lazard Frères. If they had not, an English edition of Drumont's *La France juive,* published in the United States, gave them long lists of names, even if its conclusions

were rejected. Articles in popular magazines devoted considerable space to Jewish millionaires. The exotic figure of Disraeli, "the Empire-making Jew" seemed large in significance; and travelers in England, like James Russell Lowell, were quite ready from what they saw, to believe Jews were coming to control the whole world.

By a variety of means, the notion of limitless Jewish wealth gained wide currency. Already in Henry Adams' anonymous novel of 1880 there appeared the opulent Hartbeest Schneidekoupon "descended from all the kings of Israel and . . . prouder than Solomon in his glory." In dime novels, the fabulously rich Jew was a stock character. In the midst of depression in 1894, the notion was so commonplace that a magazine seriously suggested that the unemployed of the United States would be relieved if only "the trustees of the magnificent fund that Baron Hirsch entrusted to a band of Wall Street bankers" would "loosen the cords about . . . [their] money bags."

The wealth of the Jews was ascribed to the fact that they were

a parasitical race, who, producing nothing, fasten on the produce of land and labor and live on it, choking the breath of life out of commerce and industry as sure as the creeper throttles the tree that upholds it.

Like the American Jew in a serialized novel, who stayed at his telephone speculating while the world was threatened with destruction, these people were credited with the capacity for profiting from every contingency.

Again, such judgments were not intrinsically hostile. So a tract that warned "you should not be prejudiced against any race," went on to point out the Jews were naturally money changers through no fault of their own, but simply "on

account of their excessive shrewdness."
Even laudatory accounts praised the
Jews' ability to make money. One of the
books to defend the group boasted:

In finance the Jew has for four hundred years
been the factor that supplied the nations of the
earth with money. The financial system of the
world, its inventions and perfection, we owe
to the Rothschilds.

A little later, a compilation published by
the American Hebrew Publishing Company casually remarked:

Of all the nations, which the world has known,
the commercial instinct is strongest and most
fully developed in the Jew. He never sacrifices
future opportunity for present gain.

If an occasional commentator did point
out that the great American bankers were
Christians, that only seemed to stress the
internationalism of the Jews.

To some extent, the lines of socialist
thinking that connected capitalism with
the Jews strengthened these conceptions.
So, the foremost exponent in this country
of revisionist socialism in a widely-read
volume pointed out:

Our era may be called the *Jewish age*. The
Jews have indeed, had a remarkable influence
on our civilization. Long ago they infused
in our race the idea of one God, and now they
have made our whole race worship a new true
God: the Golden Calf. . . . "Jewism," to our
mind, best expresses that special curse of our
age, *Speculation*.

Even more important, the growing preoccupation of many Americans with the
money question fixed the tie between Jews
and finance. In a period of falling prices
disaster was close at hand for great numbers of farmers who, despite mounting
production saw their situation deteriorate
steadily, particularly after the depression
of 1893. The temptation was well-nigh
irresistible to seek a solution in terms

of monetary reform. There were still some
calls for greenbacks, but increasingly
those who agitated for a change in the
currency thought of silver, demanded
bimetallism, the free coinage of silver in
some established relationship with gold.

In the 1890's these wishes met with an
uninterrupted succession of defeats. The
rate of silver coinage was not expanded
but contracted. President Cleveland's
arrangement with J. P. Morgan strengthened the hold of gold and the election of
1896 confirmed the trend. What was more,
silver in that decade was abandoned by
almost every other country that still used
it — Tunis in 1891, Austria-Hungary in
1892, China in 1896, Japan and Russia in
1897.

Frustrated, the reformers acquired a
sense of religious intensity about their
cause; their speeches became profuse with
Christian images. Unable to see any flaw
in the rationality of their arguments, they
could explain their defeats only by the
intervention of some external power. The
blame was not in themselves, nor in the
people in whom they had faith; it must be
outside, in England, among the international bankers, or — with growing frequency — among the Jews.

The prominence of Montefiore Levi
and Alfred de Rothschild in the Brussels
Monetary Conference gave the silver men
one ground for their suspicion; the activity of Perry Belmont among the gold
Democrats gave them another. But they
hardly needed evidence. By 1894, the
famous *Coin's Financial School* included
a map entitled, "The English Octopus.
It Feeds on Nothing but Gold." Where
England belonged was the simple in-
scription, Rothschild. In a novel, William
Harvey traced the monetary difficulties
of the whole world to a plot by "Baron
Rothe" to demonetize silver for the sake
of English world mastery. In 1895 a silver

tract noted as a fact that the Rothschilds owned "one-half the gold in the world, available for use as money, and their aids and satellites own nearly all the remainder."

What could have been in the minds of the delirious audience at the Democratic national convention the very next year when Bryan ascended to his blood-stirring peroration, "You shall not crucify mankind upon a cross of gold!" There is an indication of the answer in the explanations advanced by the silver men in the next few years to explain their defeat.

They had been beaten, they explained, by the power of an "invisible empire," an "oligarchy" centered in the "mysterious money power," which had bound "the hands of the United States" and had then "proceeded . . . with marvellous rapidity to enslave the human race." Although there was a vagueness in identifying the members of the oligarchy, the Rothschilds are often mentioned and occasionally Shylock openly reveals himself. Thus, one of the reformers, J. C. Ridpath, has Shylock confess his fear of the radicals, and has him point out that the

insurgents will presently turn upon me and my tribe and destroy our business. I must keep my influence with these contemptible Christian nations, else they will cease to support me and my enterprises. My business is to live by the labor of others.

The use of such terms was perhaps figurative to begin with, but they certainly received a more literal reading as time went on.

The radicals' suspicions of the designs of the financial oligarchy gained strength from the sense of mystery within which Americans had long enveloped the Jew. The elements of the conviction in the United States that there was a strangeness

to the Jew were quite different from those of the demoniac character that persisted into nineteenth century Europe from its medieval past. The emphasis in this country was upon interpretations of the mission of Israel which went back at least two hundred years to the reflections of Cotton Mather on the subject.

The visible evidence of mystery was the persistence of Jewry itself. Wonderful in their past achievements, the Jews were "still more wonderful in their preservation." Scattered among the nations they held to their identity. Like the gulf stream in the ocean of mankind, endless movement did not alter their essential quality; found throughout the world, they were everywhere alien.

The strangeness discernible in Jewish ritual and belief might extend to many unknown realms. The rabbi initiate in the lore of the kabbalah might possess the power of divination. By the same token the detective with a Jewish name might uncover a murderer with the aid of "second sight." All sorts of practices might have hidden significance. "The Jewish people don't believe in taking life," testified a social worker, "so to all sorts of vermin they use a whisk brush and out it goes out of the window." The functionings of their institutions were likewise obscure. *The Century Magazine* exposed the practices of the Kahal through which Jews

have always succeeded in driving alien elements from the town . . . where they have settled to get into their hands the capital and immovable property of those places.

There was a purpose to the survival of the group and to the persistence of these differences. In one sense, the Jew retained his identity to serve as the eternal witness of the truth of Christianity. To one Christian advocate of the Jewish return to Palestine, these people were "Jehovah's ever present answer to the innuendoes against the absolute credibility of the Inspiration of the Old Testament."

But there was a larger purpose still, one involved in the whole Christian conception of salvation. For it was in the whole scheme of things that the mass conversion of the Jews would herald the second coming. While practical efforts to induce Jews in the United States to change their religion seem to have fallen off in this period, their Christian fellow-citizens were still eager to read about such conversions and looked forward with anticipation to ultimate total success. The Reverend Joseph Ingraham dedicated three of his immensely popular novels to "the daughters of Israel," to the "Men of Israel," and to "all American Hebrews" in the hope they would see the light.

In a more rationalistic form, the mission of the Jews was sometimes described as the task of disseminating among all mankind their own peculiar cosmopolitan spirituality and sense of ethics. But that still left a distinctive purpose to their strangeness. If Americans then continued avidly to read Sue's *Wandering Jew,* it was in part at least due to the hold on their minds of its very title.

The vogue of popular novels with a biblical setting added to the atmosphere of mystery that surrounded Jews. Lew Wallace's *Ben-Hur* was only the best known of an enormous number of books the scenes of which were set in ancient Palestine or Babylonia, books which took their readers back in everyday language through the incidents of the bible. In these stories, Jewish characters appeared in a variety of forms, generally sympathetically portrayed, but in any case, in close connection with the most sacred and most mysterious events.

The attributes of mystery were naturally transferred to the present since Jews had retained their identity from the most ancient times and since their strangeness gave continuing evidence of inexplicable characteristics. This mysterious strain explains the beautiful Jewess who appears so often in the novels of these years. She has antecedents of course in Scott's Rebecca and in Shakespeare's Jessica; but she is no mere copy. The American heroine is exquisitely beautiful and distinguished by great nobility of character. Some taint, curse, or fateful misfortune involves her in intricate difficulties which however lead to a happy ending. Often she is juxtaposed with a mean and miserly father, who is, in a sense, her taint, the source through his paternity of her troubles. The mysterious element here is hereditary, in a way, racial.

These mysterious racial ties can also take other forms. In 1872 Lynn Linton, a popular English writer of romantic stories, described in a novel the life of a revolutionary who attempted in modern times to pattern his acts upon those of Jesus. To heighten the analogy, the author gave her hero the English version of the name of Jesus, Joshua Davidson. The novel was well-known in the United States.

Twenty years later, Jesse Jones, a radical New England minister who had his own doctrines of social reform to expound, labored on a novel that used the same device. However Jones felt the compulsion to secure for his protagonist a Jewish ancestor, one of "Israel's sacred race," a grandfather, from whom Joshua could learn "as a 'son of the Law.' the sacred Lore of Israel." The injection of this element was significant for it suggested that there was a mysterious body of knowledge available only to "one of the blood."

In this review of the American image of the Jew, I have attempted to isolate three elements, the stereotype of the immigrant Jew, the relationship to finance, and the sense of mystery. In the writings of the populist leader, Ignatius Donnelly, one may trace the combination of those elements into a pattern that markedly influenced many of the earnest radicals of the period. In *Caesar's Column,* a utopian novel, Donnelly looked ahead to a period when

the task which Hannibal attempted, . . . to subject the Latin and mixed-Gothic races of Europe to the domination of the Semitic blood

had been accomplished

by the cousins of the Phoenicians, the Israelites. The nomadic children of Abraham . . . [had] fought and schemed their way, through infinite pains of persecution . . . to a power higher than the thrones of Europe.

At that future date, "survival of the fittest" had made the aristocracy of the world "almost altogether of Hebrew origin." Christians had earlier subjected the Jews

to the most terrible ordeal of persecution. . . . Only the strong of body, the cunning of brain . . . the men with capacity to live where a dog would starve, survived the awful trial. . . . Now the Christian world is paying, in tears and blood for the sufferings inflicted by their bigoted and ignorant ancestors upon a noble race. . . . The great money-getters of the world . . . rose from dealers in old clothes and peddlers of hats to merchants, to bankers, to princes. They were as merciless to the Christian as the Christian had been to them.

Under the leadership of Prince Cabano, born Jacob Isaacs, the Jewish oligarchy was pushing the world toward destruction.

In this anticipation of things to come is a tone of fear. The radical urging changes yet dreads the effects of change. For Don-

nelly was no facile optimist as to the possibility of reform. His revolution degenerates into an orgy of destruction in which the whole civilization is consumed.

Significantly, the brains of the revolutionary organization was "a Russian Jew, . . . a cripple, driven out of his synagogue in Russia, years ago, for some crimes he had committed." With the success of the uprising, he fled to Judea, taking with him one hundred million dollars of public funds, with this vast wealth intending to "re-establish the glories of Solomon, and revive the ancient splendors of the Jewish race, in the midst of the ruins of the world."

There were specific reasons for the distrust of revolutionary violence. The labor rioting at Homestead, at Coeur d'Alene, and at Pullman in these years, the activities of the anarchists at home and in Europe had the substantial citizens eager to build armories in the middle of the cities and had even the radicals worried about the dangers of unrestrained socialism.

But more interesting for our purposes is the implication in *Caesar's Column* that there were hidden organizations, conservative and radical, working toward hidden Jewish ends. To that suspicion would later be added confused impressions of what the Zionist Basle Congress of 1897 was up to, hazy recollections of European charges, and the explicit accusation of the *Protocols of Zion* that the gold standard was the Jewish tool of world domination. The sum total would be the conspiracy of the international Jew. Millions of well-intentioned Americans would find the later anti-Semitic libel credible because they had already accepted its ingredients in a form that was not anti-Semitic.

There still remains the task of accounting for the sense of fear from which the idea of conspiracy grew, a sense that was repeatedly expressed in other connections as well. The apocalyptic visions of the radicals in these years were often stated in terms of imminence of doom. They envisaged great eras of ruin and destruction that would precede the final redemption and reconstruction of society. The conviction that suffering was inevitable was fed by memories of the commune of 1870, by scientific descriptions of lost worlds or of the end of this one, by the analogy with the reign of anti-Christ that was to precede the second coming, and by the figure of Christ himself.

Thus in both the English and the American *Joshua Davidson* the martyr hero is killed by the very people to whom he preached and for whom he suffered. Donnelly's novel of revolt ended in disaster as did Jack London's a few years later.

These uneasy conceptions of the future were judgments of the unhappy nature of the present in which they were written. Certainly in the unhappy decade of the 1890's there was much that seemed to be changing—and for the worse. For the class in which Edith Wharton grew up, the changes appeared to be a deterioration of culture and the reaction of that class was fastidiousness in speech and manners. But for the mass of Americans, change took another form.

Through the period change centered in the city, an object of dread and fascination. To the city, and particularly to New York, whole regions of the South and West felt themselves in bondage. Yet to the people of those regions, the metropolis was altogether strange; often their only source of information was the lurid detective story. The farmers' view of the city was therefore based less on knowledge of it than on its impact upon them.

The cities were unnatural. They worshipped Mammon, not God. They could all burn down, Bryan declaimed, and the great heart of America would still beat. "Embodied paganism," the city was "composed of the people of this world . . . seeking the ends of this world, . . . satiating the animal man with the riches, with the lavish luxury of things." The city,

Babylon the great, the mother of the harlots and of the abominations of the earth . . . drunken with the blood of the saints, and with the blood of the martyrs of Jesus . . . reigneth over the kings of the earth

and feeds off peoples and multitudes and nations.

This literal fear of the city was not altogether surprising in a period which, despite its rationalism, still found the occult, spiritualism, mesmerism, theosophy, astrology, mental healing popular, even among the intellectual reformers. Nor is it unexpected that some men should transfer the blame for their tribulations to these alien places. In the same years, others were blaming the Pope or secret societies, and one ingenious author even demonstrated that the Jesuits had infiltrated the Masonic societies in order to spread atheism in the United States. The city was indeed a likely butt for the hatred and resentments of disappointed people.

In the United States, the Jews were particularly connected with the city through commerce which was its lifeblood. Coming back in 1907, Henry James was impressed by the alien quality of American cities. He noted "the extent of the Hebrew conquest of New York," a new Jerusalem, and felt a certitude that the culture of the future in this country might be beautiful in its own right, but would inevitably be totally strange.

This was the opinion of a widely-traveled man of the world. But what did the farmers think in the populist areas while the mounting burden of debt loosened their hold on the land? In the years of populism's mounting strength, William Allen White was reaching maturity in Eldorado, Kansas. The children of the few Jews in town mixed freely with the adolescent elite of which White was himself a member, just as Maurice Levy was one of the boys. When White thought of the Jew he thought of the wealth of the tradespeople, of the luxury of their weddings. Himself well off, his impressions were favorable.

But there were others, many others, who believed "all trade is treachery," who believed that commerce "by the manipulation of Satan" has become "a curse to humanity" dominating all the people of the earth. To those people every Jewish storekeeper was in the advance guard of the new civilization, bore the standard of all the dread forces that threatened their security.

Two decades later, a boy who had grown up in Donnelly's Minnesota, who had come to New York and never adjusted to the change, gave explicit statement to that sentiment. Down the street, the hero of his novel

read a dozen Jewish names on a line of stores; in the door of each stood a dark little man watching the passers from intent eyes — eyes gleaming with suspicion, with pride, with clarity, with cupidity, with comprehension. New York — he could not dissociate it now from the slow upward creep of this people — the little stores, growing, expanding. . . . It was impressive — in perspective it was tremendous.

In those formative years of the 1890's, the injured groups of American society, in agony, had issued the cries of an infant that has no words to express its pain. Searching vainly for the means of relief, they could scarcely guess that the source of their trials was a change in the world in which they lived. And groping toward an understanding of that change, some perceived its instrument, the Jew. If all trade was treachery and Babylon the city, then the Jew — stereotyped, involved in finance, and mysterious — stood ready to be assigned the role of arch-conspirator.

It was this suspicion that transformed the conception of the Jew after 1900, replaced the older images with that of the Elder of Zion.

RICHARD HOFSTADTER (1916–1970) won the Pulitzer Prize in history for *The Age of Reform* (1955) and in nonfiction for *Anti-Intellectualism in American Life* (1963). His views about Populism and its antisemitic components inaugurated a major controversy among American historians and generated numerous reexaminations of agrarian attitudes at the end of the nineteenth century. In reading this selection, try to evaluate the evidence that Hofstadter marshals to substantiate his views. Is it convincing? How much weight is given to the expressions of southern Populists who were so important in the agrarian crusade?*

Richard Hofstadter

The Folklore of Populism

. . . Populist thought showed an unusually strong tendency to account for relatively impersonal events in highly personal terms. An overwhelming sense of grievance does not find satisfactory expression in impersonal explanations, except among those with a well-developed tradition of intellectualism. It is the city, after all, that is the home of intellectual complexity. The farmer lived in isolation from the great world in which his fate was actually decided. He was accused of being unusually suspicious, and certainly his situation, trying as it was, made thinking in impersonal terms difficult. Perhaps the rural middle-class leaders of Populism (this was a movement of farmers, but it was not led by farmers) had more

to do than the farmer himself with the cast of Populist thinking. At any rate, Populist thought often carries one into a world in which the simple virtues and unmitigated villainies of a rural melodrama have been projected on a national and even an international scale. In Populist thought the farmer is not a speculating businessman, victimized by the risk economy of which he is a part, but rather a wounded yeoman, preyed upon by those who are alien to the life of folkish virtue. A villain was needed, marked with the unmistakable stigmata of the villains of melodrama, and the more remote he was from the familiar scene, the more plausibly his villainies could be exaggerated.

It was not enough to say that a conspir-

*Composite of excerpts from *The Age of Reform,* by Richard Hofstadter. © Copyright 1955 by Richard Hofstadter. Reprinted by permission of Alfred A. Knopf, Inc., and Jonathan Cape Ltd. Pp. 73–81. Footnotes omitted.

acy of the money power against the common people was going on. It had been going on ever since the Civil War. It was not enough to say that it stemmed from Wall Street. It was international: it stemmed from Lombard Street. In his preamble to the People's Party platform of 1892, a succinct, official expression of Populist views, Ignatius Donnelly asserted: "A vast conspiracy against mankind has been organized on two continents, and it is rapidly taking possession of the world. If not met and overthrown at once it forebodes terrible social convulsions, the destruction of civilization, or the establishment of an absolute despotism." A manifesto of 1895, signed by fifteen outstanding leaders of the People's Party, declared: "As early as 1865–66 a conspiracy was entered into between the gold gamblers of Europe and America. . . . For nearly thirty years these conspirators have kept the people quarreling over less important matters while they have pursued with unrelenting zeal their one central purpose. . . . Every device of treachery, every resource of statecraft, and every artifice known to the secret cabals of the international gold ring are being made use of to deal a blow to the prosperity of the people and the financial and commercial independence of the country."

The financial argument behind the conspiracy theory was simple enough. Those who owned bonds wanted to be paid not in a common currency but in gold, which was at a premium; those who lived by lending money wanted as high a premium as possible to be put on their commodity by increasing its scarcity. The panics, depressions, and bankruptcies caused by their policies only added to their wealth; such catastrophes offered opportunities to engross the wealth of others through business consolidations

and foreclosures. Hence the interests actually relished and encouraged hard times. The Greenbackers had long since popularized this argument, insisting that an adequate legal-tender currency would break the monopoly of the "Shylocks." Their demand for $50 of circulating medium per capita, still in the air when the People's Party arose, was rapidly replaced by the less "radical" demand for free coinage of silver. But what both the Greenbackers and free-silverites held in common was the idea that the contraction of currency was a deliberate squeeze, the result of a long-range plot of the "Anglo-American Gold Trust." Wherever one turns in the Populist literature of the nineties one can find this conspiracy theory expressed. It is in the Populist newspapers, the proceedings of the silver conventions, the immense pamphlet literature broadcast by the American Bimetallic League, the Congressional debates over money; it is elaborated in such popular books as Mrs. S. E. V. Emery's *Seven Financial Conspiracies which have Enslaved the American People* or Gordon Clark's *Shylock: as Banker, Bondholder, Corruptionist, Conspirator.*

Mrs. Emery's book, first published in 1887, and dedicated to "the enslaved people of a dying republic," achieved great circulation, especially among the Kansas Populists. According to Mrs. Emery, the United States had been an economic Garden of Eden in the period before the Civil War. The fall of man had dated from the war itself, when "the money kings of Wall Street" determined that they could take advantage of the wartime necessities of their fellow men by manipulating the currency. "Controlling it, they could inflate or depress the business of the country at pleasure, they could send the warm life current through the channels of trade, dispensing peace, happiness, and prosperity, or they could check its flow, and completely paralyze the industries of the country." With this great power for good in their hands, the Wall Street men preferred to do evil. Lincoln's war policy of issuing greenbacks presented them with the dire threat of an adequate supply of currency. So the Shylocks gathered in convention and "perfected" a conspiracy to create a demand for their gold. The remainder of the book was a recital of a series of seven measures passed between 1862 and 1875 which were alleged to be a part of this continuing conspiracy, the total effect of which was to contract the currency of the country further and further until finally it squeezed the industry of the country like a hoop of steel.

Mrs. Emery's rhetoric left no doubt of the sustained purposefulness of this scheme—described as "villainous robbery," and as having been "secured through the most soulless strategy." She was most explicit about the so-called "crime of 1873," the demonetization of silver, giving a fairly full statement of the standard greenback-silverite myth concerning that event. As they had it, an agent of the Bank of England, Ernest Seyd by name, had come to the United States in 1872 with $500,000 with which he had bought enough support in Congress to secure the passage of the demonetization measure. This measure was supposed to have greatly increased the value of American four per cent bonds held by British capitalists by making it necessary to pay them in gold only. To it Mrs. Emery attributed the panic of 1873, its bankruptcies, and its train of human disasters: "Murder, insanity, suicide, divorce, drunkenness and all forms of immorality and crime have increased from that day to this in the most appalling ratio."

"Coin" Harvey, the author of the most popular single document of the whole currency controversy, *Coin's Financial School,* also published a novel, *A Tale of Two Nations,* in which the conspiracy theory of history was incorporated into a melodramatic tale. In this story the powerful English banker Baron Rothe plans to bring about the demonetization of silver in the United States, in part for his own aggrandizement but also to prevent the power of the United States from outstripping that of England. He persuades an American Senator (probably John Sherman, the *bête noire* of the silverites) to co-operate in using British gold in a campaign against silver. To be sure that the work is successful, he also sends to the United States a relative and ally, one Rogasner, who stalks through the story like the villains in the plays of Dion Boucicault, muttering to himself such remarks as "I am here to destroy the United States—Cornwallis could not have done more. For the wrongs and insults, for the glory of my own country, I will bury the knife deep into the heart of this nation." Against the plausibly drawn background of the corruption of the Grant administration, Rogasner proceeds to buy up the American Congress and suborn American professors of economics to testify for gold. He also falls in love with a proud American beauty, but his designs on her are foiled because she loves a handsome young silver Congressman from Nebraska who bears a striking resemblance to William Jennings Bryan!

One feature of the Populist conspiracy theory that has been generally overlooked is its frequent link with a kind of rhetorical anti-Semitism. The slight current of anti-Semitism that existed in the United States before the 1890's had been associated with problems of money and credit. During the closing years of the century it grew noticeably. While the jocose and rather heavy-handed anti-Semitism that can be found in Henry Adam's letters of the 1890's shows that this prejudice existed outside Populist literature, it was chiefly Populist writers who expressed that identification of the Jew with the usurer and the "international gold ring" which was the central theme of the American anti-Semitism of the age. The omnipresent symbol of Shylock can hardly be taken in itself as evidence of anti-Semitism, but the frequent references to the House of Rothschild make it clear that for many silverites the Jew was an organic part of the conspiracy theory of history. Coin Harvey's Baron Rothe was clearly meant to be Rothschild; his Rogasner (Ernest Seyd?) was a dark figure out of the coarsest anti-Semitic tradition. "You are very wise in your way," Rogasner is told at the climax of the tale, "the commercial way, inbred through generations. The politic, scheming, devious way, inbred through generations also." One of the cartoons in the effectively illustrated *Coin's Financial School* showed a map of the world dominated by the tentacles of an octopus at the site of the British Isles, labeled: "Rothschilds." In Populist demonology, anti-Semitism and Anglophobia went hand in hand.

The note of anti-Semitism was often sounded openly in the campaign for silver. A representative of the New Jersey Grange, for instance, did not hesitate to warn the members of the Second National Silver Convention of 1892 to watch out for political candidates who represented "Wall Street, and the Jews of Europe." Mary E. Lease described Grover Cleveland as "the agent of Jewish bankers and British gold." Donnelly represented the leader of the governing Council of plutocrats in *Caesar's Column*, one Prince Cabano, as a powerful Jew, born Jacob Isaacs; one of the triumvirate who lead the brotherhood of Destruction is also an exiled Russian Jew, who flees from the apocalyptic carnage with a hundred million dollars which he intends to use to "revive the ancient splendors of the Jewish race, in the midst of the ruins of the world." One of the more elaborate documents of the conspiracy school traced the power of the Rothschilds over America to a transaction between Hugh McCulloch, Secretary of the Treasury under Lincoln and Johnson, and Baron James Rothschild. "The most direful part of this business between Rothschild and the United States Treasury was not the loss of money, even by hundreds of millions. It was the resignation of the country itself INTO THE HANDS OF ENGLAND as England had long been resigned into the hands of HER JEWS."

Such rhetoric, which became common currency in the movement, later passed beyond Populism into the larger stream of political protest. By the time the campaign of 1896 arrived, an Associated Press reporter noticed as "one of the striking things" about the Populist convention at St. Louis "the extraordinary hatred of the Jewish race. It is not possible to go into any hotel in the city without hearing the most bitter denunciation of the Jews as a class and of the particular Jews who happen to have prospered in the world." This report may have been somewhat overdone, but the identification of the silver cause with anti-Semitism did become close enough for Bryan to have to pause in the midst of his campaign to explain to the Jewish Democrats of Chicago that in denouncing the policies of the Rothschilds he and his silver friends were "not attacking a race; we are attacking greed and avarice which know no race or religion."

It would be easy to misstate the character of Populist anti-Semitism or to exaggerate its intensity. For Populist anti-Semitism was entirely verbal. It was a mode of expression, a rhetorical style, not a tactic or a program. It did not lead to exclusion laws, much less to riots or pogroms. There were, after all, relatively few Jews in the United States in the late 1880's and early 1890's, most of them remote from the areas of Populist strength. It is one thing, however, to say that this prejudice did not go beyond a certain symbolic usage, quite another to say that a people's choice of symbols is of no significance. Populist anti-Semitism does have its importance—chiefly as a symptom of a certain ominous credulity in the Populist mind. It is not too much to say that the Greenback-Populist tradition activated most of what we have of modern popular anti-Semitism in the United States. From Thaddeus Stevens and Coin Harvey to Father Coughlin, and from Brooks and Henry Adams to Ezra Pound, there has been a curiously persistent linkage between anti-Semitism and money and credit obsessions. A full history of modern anti-Semitism in the United States would reveal, I believe, its substantial Populist lineage, but it may be sufficient to point out here that neither the informal connection between Bryan and the Klan in the twenties nor Thomas E. Watson's conduct in the Leo Frank case were altogether fortuitous. And Henry Ford's notorious anti-Semitism of the 1920's, along with his hatred of "Wall Street," were the foibles of a Michigan farm boy who had been liberally exposed to Populist notions.

JOHN HIGHAM (b. 1920), professor of history
at The Johns Hopkins University and author
of *Strangers in the Land* (1955), which won the
American Historical Association's Dunning Prize, has
written the best historical synthesis of American
antisemitism. He sees antisemitism primarily as a
Gilded Age phenomenon although he also notes its
earlier roots. Higham's analysis contains arguments
both similar to and different from those espoused by
Handlin and Hofstadter. Which of Higham's
evaluations coincide with the findings of Handlin and
of Hofstadter, and which differ? What does Higham
mean by ideological antisemitism? How much weight
does he give to religious motifs in the development
of American antisemitism? How much to the Shylock
image? Would you agree with Higham's conclusion
that antisemitism "as a troublesome social issue" has
generally faded?*

American Antisemitism
Historically Reconsidered

To general American historians, anti-Semitism has never seemed a subject of major importance. No decisive event, no deep crisis, no powerful social movement, no great individual is associated primarily with, or significant chiefly because of, anti-Semitism. Accordingly, historians have shown scant interest in studying it. I myself became intrigued with the subject only in the course of examining the larger theme of nativism, and after I thought I understood the relation between the two, my attention turned elsewhere.

A single notable exception to the prevailing lack of interest occurred in the 1950s, but it was more apparent than real. A fierce little academic quarrel developed over the role of anti-Semitism in the Populist movement of the 1890s. Though everyone tacitly agreed that anti-Semitism was at most a minor aspect of Populism, no other aspect received such anxious scrutiny. The specific issue was to what extent Populists had activated the myth of an "international Jewish conspiracy." The scholars' real concern, however, was not with the nature of anti-Semitism; it was with the integrity of Populist democracy. Young historians born and bred in the city were re-evaluating the "agrarian radicalism" that an

*John Higham, "American Anti-Semitism Historically Reconsidered," from *Jews in the Mind of America* by Charles Herbert Stember and others, © 1966 by the American Jewish Committee, Basic Books, Inc., Publishers, New York. Footnotes omitted.

older, less urbanized generation had fondly chronicled, and the charge of anti-Semitism lent a melodramatic touch to this new criticism of the rural, Midwestern mind. Further inquiry took the sting out of the charge, and the quarrel subsided with no one much the wiser as to where American anti-Semitism had its sources. For answering that question, a preoccupation with an essentially democratic movement supplied too narrow a basis.

Unlike historians, social psychologists have found anti-Semitism in America enormously interesting and significant. A recent bibliography lists hundreds of research studies. One of the classics of American social science, *The Authoritarian Personality* (1950), puts anti-Semitism at the very center of its conceptual scheme, on the assumption that critical attitudes toward Jews emanate from—and enable us to identify—a personality type that threatens the very survival of democratic society. Confronted with this literature, a historian must wonder at the embarrassing gap between his own priorities and those of an allied discipline, from which he would like to draw aid and comfort.

Part of the difference is doubtless inherent in the natures of the two disciplines. Social scientists operate in closer proximity to current action and policy than do most historians, and are therefore more easily involved in the action-oriented research encouraged by such concepts as "prejudice." In contrast, historical inquiry does not lend itself to sharp value distinctions, and historians tend to distrust the element of prejudice that may enter into the designation of certain attitudes as "prejudices." Moreover, a prejudice that is primarily latent rather than overtly mobilized—surely the case with anti-Semitism in America—

seems more important to the psychologist than to the historian because the psychologist is far better equipped to deal with such phenomena. That which lurks in the hidden depths of personality offers him a special challenge and stimulus. The historian, having little access to the kind of material elicited through intensive interviews, must base his judgments largely on overt expression and behavior.

Yet the historian, with his more distant and impersonal perspective, need not shrink from criticizing social psychology's findings. Although the historical eye penetrates less deeply and registers categories less sharply, its angle of vision is wider. What counts in the long run in human affairs is not the latent potential of an underlying predisposition, but rather the visible impact of actual events. And of the long run, history most nearly provides a total assessment.

Recent events should help us put both anti-Semitism and the assumptions that have governed its study into clearer historical perspective. During the last decade, the Negro revolution has so vastly overshadowed the remnants of anti-Semitism in America that it is no longer easy to regard the latter as the representative type of prejudice. Rather than postulate a generic need to hate that fixates on any and all minorities, we now incline to interpret group prejudices as functions of specific conflicts. Indeed, the whole concept of prejudice, with its emphasis on the subtle, covert dimension of hostility, pales in the light of overt conflict between Negro and white today. It is now possible to suggest that the psychological approach to prejudice and the accompanying stress on anti-Semitism may have been outgrowths of a particular historical situation which is rapidly changing.

Pluralism and Its Alternatives

One of the great achievements of American social science in the second quarter of the twentieth century was its massive assault on racial thinking and ethnocentrism. Beginning perhaps with Walter Lippmann's elegant critique of stereotypes in *Public Opinion* (1922), with the sociological study of race relations by Robert E. Park and his associates and with the cultural relativism of Franz Boas and his disciples, social scientists discredited the value ranking of ethnic groups. In the 1930s, psychologists joined the campaign, showing that ethnic prejudice was commonly interrelated with other illiberal attitudes such as militarism, imperialism and economic conservatism. By the end of the 1940s, a standard encyclopedia defined race as an "obsolete division of humanity," and virtually the entire intellectual community had been converted to a stanchly egalitarian view of minority problems.

While avoiding explicit value judgments, the egalitarian intellectuals took a highly sympathetic approach to minority cultures. Uncomplimentary facts about a given ethnic group were traced to environmental conditions over which it had little control. Desirable characteristics, on the other hand, were credited to the group's own cultural heritage. Thus, any antipathies it encountered could have had little to do with its actual qualities. The group in such cases was an innocent victim, a "scapegoat." Hostile feelings toward minorities accordingly had to be explained as irrational; they were thought to flow from aggression and mental rigidity in the dominant culture.

The whole point of view was, in a word, pluralistic. The solution to ethnic problems was believed to lie in obliterating inequalities of condition, while fostering and praising differences of culture. Democracy was conceived as a system for conserving rather than liquidating cultural differences. Any expression of a specific ethnic hostility, such as anti-Semitism, was to be understood as a manifestation of a generally anti-democratic temper. One could therefore expect to find all nationalistic and racial antipathies interrelated in a characteristically authoritarian "syndrome."

The pluralist outlook has comprised a generous and humane faith. Drawing upon our best traditions, it has helped in no small measure to make the United States a better homeland for many of its people, and few men of good will would want to impugn its basic values. Some affirmation of diversity, some pleasure in the sheer variety of the American people, would seem to be an essential element in the receptiveness and fluidity of our open society. Yet the improvement of ethnic relations during recent years has not occurred entirely in the way the cultural pluralists anticipated.

Whatever its normative value, pluralism is no longer an accurate description of ethnic processes. The remarkable advance of tolerance, decency and justice in every dimension of American ethnic relations since the Second World War has been accompanied by a steady decline of cultural distinctions. To be sure, ethnoreligious activity flourishes, so that one may speak of "structural pluralism." But communal customs, beliefs and aspirations have become more and more homogeneous. The trend toward equality has involved a hybridization of behavior and values, which resembles the old melting-pot theory more than it does the pluralists' vision of permanent minorities. Indeed, the very term "minorities" —that proud badge of underdogs asserting themselves against the dominant culture—is heard less and less often. As the minorities of yesteryear participate increasingly in our mass society, they become more concerned about the quality of their own group life, and less able to maintain their identity by resisting a hostile majority. Prejudice, defined as a rigidly exclusionist frame of mind antagonistic to any and all "others," no longer seems to be the chief problem they face.

To put it differently, the concept of minorities as innocent victims of generalized prejudice had meaning only vis-à-vis an aggressive, insecure majority. In fact, this theory of prejudice—and the whole ideology of cultural pluralism—arose as a reaction against the inflamed racial nationalism of the early twentieth century. An immense, heterogeneous immigration, coinciding with war and other social dislocations, did indeed produce the highly generalized kind of prejudice that pluralists have described. On the eve of the First World War, and even more in the years immediately following, hostility toward various ethnic and religious minorities tended to coalesce into a sweeping rejection of all groups deviating from a conservative, Protestant, Northern European pattern. An unprecedented need for national unity and social conformity generated the spirit of "100-per-cent Americanism." Seeking to repress all deviant groups, the 100-percenters indiscriminately assailed Catholics, Jews, Negroes, Japanese Americans and foreigners. The Ku Klux Klan of the 1920s enbodied this convergence of anti-minority feelings, providing a single outlet for every racial and religious hatred and every defensive anxiety that festered among the nation's white Protestant majority. Instead of concentrating on a single adversary, the Klan proposed to "restore" the supremacy of the "old stock" and thus purify America of moral and racial pollution. In this milieu, anti-Semitism became part of a broader movement with a strongly racist ideology. And social scientists quite rightly began to conceive of anti-Semitism in terms of a larger pattern of prejudice.

During the 1930s and 1940s, events in Germany placed anti-Semitism in the very center of attention. Hitlerism seemed to indicate the direction in which the "100-per-cent American" impulse was heading; and by its monstrous irrationality the slaughter of the German Jews further encouraged the view of prejudice as a scapegoating process. Anti-Semitism became the "classic prejudice": a sure indicator of the authoritarian personality, and a litmus-paper test of the racial nationalism that liberals were fighting.

By 1950, liberal intellectuals had nearly forgotten that a different interpretation of anti-Semitism had once commended itself to men of good will. They hardly remembered that until the early twentieth century anti-minority sentiments were not always so illiberal, so interlaced with one another in an authoritarian syndrome. Yet through most of America's history, ethnic tensions had been relatively discrete, and the prevailing theory of nationality had been consonant with that fact.

In the nineteenth century, American democracy was viewed primarily as a means of overcoming cultural distinctions rather than preserving them. This vision of an ultimate oneness fostered the belief that frictions such as anti-Semitism arose from temporary or special maladjustments between particular minorities and the rest of the population. So diverse were these tensions that no one tried to subsume them all under a single explanatory pattern. True, a wide range of hostilities, known as nativism, swirled recurrently around newcomers from overseas; but even this anti-immigrant sentiment was more selective and diversified than we ordinarily appreciate.

Accordingly, no considerable variety of anti-minority sentiments was strongly felt at the same place and the same time. The Alien and Sedition scare of 1798 produced much hysteria over foreign radicals but none over foreign Catholics. A second nationalist crusade, the Know-Nothing movement of the 1850s, concentrated its fire on Catholics, ignored Jews and attracted many Northerners who sympathized with the plight of the Negro. The concurrent xenophobia of California, on the other hand, was racial and not at all religious. The anti-Chinese movement in that state hurt other minorities only in the sense that riotous Irishmen were often blamed for sparking the antagonism. A strong revival of anti-Catholic sentiment in the Midwest during the 1890s bore no direct relation to the Anglo-Saxon nativism simultaneously developing in the East; and neither agitation threatened the Negro, whose situation in the North was actually improving somewhat. While the Anglo-Saxon nativists of the East fretted about the Jews, the hard-hitting anti-Catholic movement ignored them. To avoid offending either the Protestant or the Catholic bloc, the Republican national convention in 1896 chose a rabbi to deliver the invocation. Indeed, throughout the nineteenth century, the great diversity of minority groups and the relatively specific nature of ethnic tensions kept the members of any one group from feeling greatly involved in the welfare of another. It was not uncommon for Jews to join Anglo-Americans in disparaging the Irish or the Negroes.

Under these circumstances, men of good will could consider anti-Jewish feeling in the United States to be in large measure a result of the Jews' real situation. It was thought that Jews encountered discrimination and prejudice partly because they were often foreign in manner and appearance, partly because their hard-driving pursuit of economic and social advancement made their foreignness especially salient. In 1923, this interpretation, still widely prevalent, was succinctly summed up by a contributor to the liberal weekly, *The Nation*. Anti-Semitism in America, Lewis S. Gannett argued, differed from the same phenomenon in Europe. Here it was largely an expression of a traditional dislike for newcomers. At the moment, nativist feeling concentrated on the Jews because of their prominence among the immigrants of recent years, and because of their distinctive ambition and assertiveness. The Jews' characteristic intensity, Gannett held,

. . . defeats us at our own game. Sometimes it leads new arrivals to intellectual or financial success before social adjustments have been made — while the voice is still uncouth, the accent strong, and the sense of tact and social relationship still in the stage of the suspicious push-cart peddler. The very rapidity with which the Jew adjusts himself to the primary conditions of life in America is his chief handicap.

Many Jews had long agreed that conspicuously alien traits occasioned most of the rebuffs they met. In 1855, for example, an American Jewish periodical predicted the rise of a new respect, once Jews as a group "overleap the trammels of ages and become again what we were in olden days, noble, independent, laborious, instead of submissive, over-polite and scheming, living more by our ingenuity to turn everything to advantage, than by well-directed labor and persevering industry in some industrial and economical pursuit." We need not accept this view literally to appreciate the urgent drive for assimilation which it reflects or the strong optimism with which Jews then looked forward to their future in America. They confidently expected the normal working of the melting pot to solve their problem; and they strove to adapt themselves to the process.

This assimilationist theory of anti-Semitism persisted into the 1920s, but in the following decade it collapsed. Jews now abandoned the hopeful idea that American anti-Semitism was a passing phenomenon, unlike the deep-rooted Jew-hatred of Europe. To attribute anti-Semitism in any considerable degree to the nature of the Jewish presence became, among decent and humane people, not just wrong but unthinkable. To do so was *prima facie* to proclaim oneself an anti-Semite.

This *volte-face* can best be understood as part of the larger revolt against racism and 100-per-cent Americanism which so profoundly affected the intellectual and political life of the 1930s and 1940s. Intellectuals identified themselves with all the underdogs, who were simultaneously gaining power through the New Deal. Cultural pluralism and the scapegoat theory of prejudice became banners behind which a loose coalition of liberal intellectuals, ethnic minorities and urban politicians united and triumphed over the conservative defenders of the old-stock, Protestant order. The defensive Anglo-Saxon Protestant majority of the 1920s was broken up, and in its place emerged an inter-ethnic establishment that has made tolerance an instrument of equipoise and adjustment.

The victory has had its ironies, however. In struggling to change American culture, the immigrant minorities have become increasingly integrated into it. No longer reinforced by substantial immigration, they are settling into a congenial new status quo and losing the distinctiveness they sought to defend. In particular, anti-Semitism as a troublesome social issue has so generally faded that we can now perceive the intense irrational anti-Jewish feeling of the early twentieth century as a transitory rather than a permanent phase of American experience. Moreover, American Jews have become so much assimilated that we can once more seriously entertain the old hypothesis associating anti-Semitism with immigration and conspicuously foreign traits.

These reflections on recent changes in American culture offer a point of departure for examining the earlier history of anti-Semitism in America. Now that social science must explain the rapid decline (rather than the intensity) of a prejudice supposedly anchored in personality structure, the specific historical circumstances under which the prejudice arose in the first place acquire a fresh significance. To what degree has discrimination against Jews resulted from a real conflict of interest and cultures? What further conditions temporarily magnified anti-Semitism into a highly charged ideology and linked it with a whole complex of irrational feelings? The following pages will first examine the record of social and economic discrimination, the areas where tensions have been most persistent and keenly felt. We will then consider the emergence of anti-Semitic ideology, and finally return with some concluding remarks to the contemporary scene. Throughout, this essay will bypass the not unimportant subject of anti-Semitism among ethnic minorities, in order to focus on the predominant national culture.

Social and Economic Discrimination

The very few Jews who appeared on the North American mainland in the seventeenth century—perhaps 250 in all —at first encountered sporadic restrictions on their right to vote and to engage in certain kinds of trade. In practice, however, these restrictions survived no better than any of the other efforts to transplant medieval patterns of control and stability to the American wilderness. The peopling of a new society by voluntary means allowed capitalistic competition to overwhelm traditional privileges and prescriptions. In early America, virtually from the beginning, there was no Jewish question.

By the middle of the eighteenth century, a regime of freedom flourished so profusely that intermarriage was frequent and socially acceptable. Well-to-do Jews joined the same clubs and private libraries as their Christian peers, attended the same dancing assemblies and sent their children to the same schools. Jews contributed to Anglican and Catholic undertakings and, on at least one occasion, solicited the aid of Christians for a synagogue. Full political rights lagged somewhat behind social integration: In a few states, religious tests for holding public office lingered into the early nineteenth century. These tests, however, were not distinctively anti-Jewish, and in any case they survived only where the absence of an active Jewish community left them unchallenged and inconsequential. "In all the various intercourse of social life," concluded an American writer in 1833, "we know of no uncharitable barriers between Jews and Christians in our happy community."

This is not, to say, of course, that unfavorable attitudes were unknown. In the folklore of Western civilization, the "Shylock traits" of avarice and dishonesty were too firmly associated with Jews to leave no imprint on the American consciousness. But such sentiments remained mild and often mixed with favorable stereotypes; they lacked the support of any real group antagonism. "Here you stand," a liberal Christian told American Jews, "on the same level with your fellow citizens of other sentiments; and if, in some cases, prejudices are still entertained against you, they are not stronger certainly than those which many denominations of Christians entertain against others." Among "fellow citizens of other sentiments" a small, well-established American Jewish community created no social discomfort.

A change for the worse became perceptible in the 1840s. It stemmed, quite simply, from immigration. The hitherto stable, middle-class Jewish minority, numbering about 15,000 in 1840, entered a period of rapid growth with a substantial influx from Germany. From the literature of that day, one might still cull more favorable than unfavorable comments; no general pattern of hostility was as yet emerging. But the raw Jewish peddlers who swarmed southward and westward made a mixed impression. Terribly poor and often not very clean, they looked unappealingly alien and untrustworthy to some. In the worst section of New York the immigrants opened squalid second-hand shops, hardly more than cowsheds, their little windows broken and patched with old newspapers. A popular description of the sights of New York in 1849 comments on these shops and refers casually to the typical proprietor's hooked nose, "which betrays the Israelite as the human kite, formed to be feared, hated and despised, yet to prey upon mankind." For many decades thereafter, assimilated

Jews anguished over the bad reputation the immigrants were giving to their whole people.

The spread of such unflattering stereotypes prepared the way for a basic shift in social relationships. But what finally set off this shift and precipitated a pattern of social discrimination, in the 1870s, was not the arrival of immigrants; it was their rise. Though a remarkable number had prospered mightily, evidently few had as yet acquired much education or polish. Discrimination began where Jews as a group pressed most heavily upon a limited field of opportunity: at the social clubs and summer resorts in and around New York City.

Such institutions were then becoming increasingly important determinants of prestige. In a materialistic society troubled by its own clamorous mobility, many possessors of privilege—the Brahmin gentry, the leaders of bar associations, the founders of art museums, social registers and country clubs—were endeavoring to formulate a hierarchy of authority. Unfortunately, the very exclusiveness of clubs and resorts made them attractive to outsiders as well as insiders. Social mobility was the essential mechanism of social assimilation in the United States; and Jewish immigrants, more than any others, were eager and able to pay for acceptance into prestige circles. Thus, wherever standards of admission were not clearly defined, a crush of Jewish applicants inspired fears of invasion. Efforts to bar the Jews—in effect to retard their assimilation—generated real ethnic strife in the 1880s and 1890s. One may imagine the mutual frustration that occurred when Jews bought the hotels that tried to exclude them, only to find that the non-Jews fled to less accessible precincts. In time, the Catskills and the New Jersey resorts of Lakewood and Long Branch passed into Jewish hands.

The crest of Jewish immigration, now flowing largely from Eastern Europe, came in the first two decades of the twentieth century. By its very size, the Eastern European influx obscured the increasing gentility of the mid-nineteenth-century immigrants' sons and grandsons. New kinds of resistance developed, notably in the areas of housing and education.

Even back in the 1880s, according to William Dean Howells, property values on a fashionable Boston street would drop after the first German Jew bought a house; but in the sprawling middle-income suburbs of that day, status rivalry had not yet become acute, and a heterogeneous ethnic democracy prevailed. Around the turn of the century, however, the newer Jewish immigrants began to break out of the great urban ghettos, the original enclaves of settlement, and poured into better neighborhoods. This massive exodus, so much more concentrated than the earlier dispersion of German Jews, produced tensions on an altogether new scale. Jews encountered restrictive covenants, refusals by landlords to rent apartments and even a wave of hoodlumism. In one way or another, segregation generally resulted.

Eastern colleges and universities became another seat of conflict when Eastern European Jews revealed an extraordinary passion for higher education. As early as the 1880s, fraternities at the College of the City of New York were blackballing Jews. At Columbia University, where student societies soon followed suit, the first Jewish fraternity in America was founded in 1898. Around the time of the First World War, some of the colleges with large numbers of Jewish applicants instituted covert enrollment quotas.

Discriminatory employment practices

first became troublesome during the years just before the war. Until that time, Jews had not competed prominently for white-collar jobs that were in general demand. The Eastern European immigrants were petty tradesmen or workingmen, employed for the most part in a largely Jewish environment. But they wanted their children to get out of the factories, and now great numbers of Jewish high-school graduates, the immigrants' sons and daughters, were looking for jobs as clerks, stenographers and secretaries in non-Jewish firms. Their widespread debarment from such openings came to light in 1916, when Jacob Schiff resigned from the board of directors of a large employment agency because its mercantile branch discouraged Jewish applicants.

The second-generation Jews' search for entry into urban middle-class life made its greatest impact between the two World Wars. All types of social and economic discrimination reached a corresponding peak. Stringent quotas regulated admission to medical schools. Public schools and colleges commonly hired only Protestant teachers; one study showed that during the 1930s Catholic colleges— with 3 per cent of their faculties Jewish —were considerably more receptive to Jews than were non-Catholic institutions. Even the Jewish-owned *New York Times* accepted "help-wanted" advertisements specifying "Christians only"; other newspapers ran ads asking explicitly for Anglo-Saxons. The Depression made job discrimination more acute than ever. It was generally understood in New York that a Jew stood no chance of getting a white-collar job if a non-Jewish applicant was available. This led to many painful subterfuges; some Jewish girls, for example, joined in the vogue of wearing crosses. A significant counterattack was now developing, but the intensity of conflict obscured the revitalization of ethnic democracy. Few could have predicted the advances that lay just ahead.

Anti-Semitic Ideology

To say that anti-Semitism in America sprang chiefly from the difficulties of integrating large numbers of first- and second-generation immigrants is, inferentially, to stress its similarity to other kinds of anti-immigrant sentiment—to put it in the same class with dislike of the Irish, Italians, Japanese, Mexicans and other transplanted minorities, while making allowances for the differential characteristics of each group. Likewise, this approach minimizes distinctions often made between different kinds of anti-Semitism, in that it relates all of them to a common root. Yet we must also consider the role of irrational anti-Semitic fantasies that had no direct connection with real problems of ethnic integration. The ideological hatreds spread by the agitator and the fanatic have had a place in American history, too.

Unlike the more ordinary social prejudices thus far discussed, ideological anti-Semitism condemns the Jews as incapable of assimilation and disloyal to the basic institutions of the country. In its more extreme forms, it portrays them as leagued together in a vast international conspiracy. The alleged plot usually centers on gaining control of the money supply and wrecking the financial system; sometimes it extends to polluting the nation's morals through control of communications and entertainment. The supposed eventual aim is to overthrow the government and establish a superstate. In America, anti-Semitism of this kind has not been so well organized or so productive of violence as other racial and religious phobias. But it has enjoyed an unusually rich and complex imagery.

Religious motifs, by and large, have not figured prominently in American anti-Semitic thought. Except among certain preachers spawned by the Fundamentalist movement of the 1920s (notably Gerald Winrod and Gerald L. K. Smith), one looks in vain for a clearly religious animus. Though not entirely lacking in references to the treachery of Judas, ideological anti-Semitism has always dwelled mainly on the power of Shylock. Whether the Jew appears in his traditional role as exploiter or in his later incarnation as Bolshevik, his subversive influence supposedly flows from an unwillingness or inability to abide by the existing economic morality.

Born and bred in Europe, this indictment insinuated itself into the American value system at one responsive point. Americans have always put an exceptionally high premium on productivity: on the work of the hand and the machine in mastering the wilderness, creating abundance and achieving industrial efficiency. Many American heroes, from Franklin to Lindbergh, have been men skilled in making things; few have been men skilled in manipulating intangibles like money or ideas. The tradition of agrarian protest, from Jefferson through Jackson to Thorstein Veblen and beyond, rested on a fundamental distinction between the "producing classes" (the "bone and sinew of the country," in Jackson's telling phrase) and the unproductive creditors, speculators and middlemen. The former group comprised the industrious makers of things; the latter the parasitic makers of money. Thus, in identifying the Jew as the essential parasite, anti-Semitic ideologues tapped a vein of indigenous thought. "He is not a producer," the argument ran, "but a buyer and seller, a profit taker, who makes his gains from the labor of others." Henry Ford launched his widely noted propaganda campaign against the Jews by picturing a basic struggle between two great forces in the modern world: "creative Industry" and "international Finance."

Significantly, this charge of non-productivity figures in the earliest faint foreshadowing of American ideological anti-Semitism that I have discovered. In 1820, exactly a hundred years before Ford's *Dearborn Independent* opened fire on the "international Jew," the editor of the famous news magazine, *Niles' Weekly Register,* discussed the need to eliminate office-holding restrictions from the Maryland Constitution. Wondering why the Jews in most countries were denied some part of the rights of other men, he concluded:

There must be some moral cause to produce this effect. In general, their interests do not appear identified with those of the communities in which they live, though there are some honorable exceptions to this remark. But they will not sit down and labor like other people—they create nothing and are mere consumers. They will not cultivate the earth, nor work at mechanical trades, preferring to live by their wit in dealing, and acting as if they had a home no where. . . . But all this has nothing to do with their rights as men. . . .

What *Niles' Register* said so tranquilly, with so noticeable an absence of fear, could become a cry of alarm after immigration made Jews more numerous and visible in the United States. But this happened only in moments of crisis, when war or depression sharpened resentment at the trader and the profiteer. The first instance of something approaching explicit ideological anti-Semitism occurred during the Civil War, when Jews were accused of exploiting the war effort and occasionally of trying to destroy the national credit. The next manifestation took place during the socio-economic crisis of the 1890s, a time of searing depression, intense class resentments and widespread fears of an end to individual opportunity. A third, probably the sharpest, outbreak of ideological anti-Semitism began around the time of the First World War, and culminated during its immediate aftermath of domestic turbulence and disillusion. At last flareup came in the 1930s, stimulated by the Great Depression and the example of European fascism.

In all these instances, the typical native American formulation of anti-Semitism may be described as pseudo-agrarian. The major anti-Semitic ideologues gave a special twist to the moral and economic biases deeply ingrained in the agrarian tradition. Shaped by the old producer ethic, they hated the soft materialism of an urban civilization and looked back longingly to a time when no idle exploiters lived in corrupting luxury. They had little understanding of the problem of industrial overproduction, attributing society's troubles primarily to the lords of finance and trade. Like other American agrarians, they turned their special animus against banks, moneylenders and bondholders. Where the pseudo-agrarian seems to have differed from his fellows was in a sourer view of human gullibility and a more cataclysmic vision of the future. The few Populists who gave vent to anti-Semitic diatribes were extravagantly susceptible to fears of anarchy, of a breakdown of the whole civilized order.

In sum, the prophets of anti-Semitism were alienated and often despairing critics of the power of money in American society. Some, like Brooks Adams and Madison Grant, denounced the rule of greed from an aristocratic or martial viewpoint. Others spoke as frustrated, embittered reformers, thwarted in various efforts to restore the imagined innocence of a Jeffersonian world. These included Tom Watson, the former Populist, John Jay Chapman, the quondam municipal reformer, and a succession of monetary cranks ranging from Henry Ford through the Reverend Charles E. Coughlin to Ezra Pound. Coughlin and Pound, like Ford, evolved into anti-Semitic agitators after fixing on international bankers as the despoilers of America. "We were diddled out of the heritage Jackson and Van Buren left us," wrote Pound in 1935. "The real power just oozed away from the electorate. The de facto government became secret. . . . The people grovelled under Wilson and Harding, then came the nit-wit and the fat-face."

With this kind of sponsorship, the "international Jew" as visualized from the 1890s to the 1930s was perhaps mostly a hobgoblin of the rural imagination, associated with all the insidious influences thought to emanate from faraway Eastern cities. Certainly the most concerted propaganda campaigns were aimed especially at rural and small-town folk. These were the people whom Tom Watson, in 1914, provoked to a spasm of race hatred during the struggle for justice to Leo Frank, a Jewish factory superintendent in Georgia, who had been accused of violating and murdering an adolescent girl in his employ. Anti-Semitism in this episode appears to have stemmed directly from popular indignation over the "outside interference" of influential northern Jews and urban newspapers in Frank's behalf. A few years later, Ford's agitation against Jewish influence went out to a similar audience in the rural Middle West, the center of his popularity. *The Dearborn Independent* dwelled on the needs of the farmer and the soulless life of the big cities, as well as on the alleged machinations of the Jews. Again, in the late 1930s, Father Coughlin's anti-Semitic tirades received their widest approval in the small towns and the countryside of the upper Middle West.

Thus, ideological anti-Semitism seems to have made its primary appeal to native Americans in areas of low Jewish density, where the supposed enemy was a remote and shadowy figure rather than a daily reality. This may be one reason why the agitation has never really amounted to much. The economic and status rivalries that strained Jewish-gentile relations in urban society did not ordinarily coalesce with the irrational fears of the hinterland. In fact, the rural dwellers' suspicions of Jewish power seldom attached to the few Jews who actually belonged to the local community. As a rule, the Ku Klux Klan's feeble efforts to boycott Jewish stores failed abysmally, because the townspeople were on good terms with the Jews they actually knew. Studies of small towns characteristically reveal complete acceptance of local Jews alongside negative stereotypes of "The Jew."

We must ask, then, why the subjective and the objective aspects of anti-Semitism never fused in a major political movement or in a significant wave of violence. Why, for example, did anti-Jewish feeling never develop the organized power that anti-Catholic crusades acquired in the 1850s, the 1890s and again in the 1920s? The question leads us back from projective fantasy to social reality. If a nation can have its enemies, it does so in terms of its own scheme of values. Between Jewish and American values, a general compatibility has always obtained. At the very outset of our history, the New England Puritans identified themselves with ancient Israel; later, Jefferson proposed for the seal of the United States a picture of the children of Israel fleeing from Egypt. In addition to specifically

Biblical images, Americans acquired a very strong attachment to religious freedom and a profound distrust of centralized ecclesiastical authority. The Jews had always had these values, and as a religious group they readily accepted the voluntaristic and pluralistic pattern of America.

Perhaps the most important symbiotic link between Jewish and American values, however, lies in the very economic sphere that modern anti-Semitism has tried to exploit. As an ethnic group, Jews have traditionally emphasized the materialistic, competitive values of business life that are so deeply ingrained in American culture. The prestige America confers on the businessman—the man of thrift, enterprise and rational calculation—has ordinarily encompassed the Jew. Nowhere does this deference appear more vividly than in the immense respect Americans felt for the House of Rothschild during a great part of the nineteenth century. Aware as we are of the anti-Semitic potentialities of the Rothschild stereotype, we may find it hard to credit how cheerfully rank-and-file Americans once attributed vast power to that family. In 1856, a Know-Nothing newspaper, patronized largely by lower-class readers, concluded a worshipful sketch of "The Money Kings" with the statement that the Rothschild family "for forty years past has controlled the destinies of our century more than any other power." Similarly, the conservative editor of *Harper's Monthly*, in the course of praising the Jews, wrote quite casually that Rothschild was "the most powerful man in the world." Rudolf Glanz has perceptively attributed the mythic scale of the Rothschild legend to a "need to express the essence of capitalism in one great human example, that was, moreover, no individual fortune doomed to extinction, but a family undertaking, continuing from generation to generation."

After the 1890s, admirers of the Jews no longer extolled Jewish wealth and power; yet the continued vitality of a capitalistic way of life has surely remained a major roadblock to ideological anti-Semitism in twentieth-century America. In fact, the increasing integration of rural America into a homogeneous national culture has largely dissipated the old hostility to the city, and the rise of a consumption ethic has helped to shatter the ideological distinction between "producing classes" and the idle rich. With the decline of agrarian protest, the pseudo-agrarian perversities have withered, too. Ideological anti-Semitism has lost the narrow basis it once had in American economic morality.

From Immigration to Integration

Although ideological anti-Semitism never cut very deep, antagonism to Jews as foreigners and *arrivistes* once did. The rise of social discrimination, beginning in the 1870s and reaching a peak in the 1920s, roughly paralleled the growth of national concern over unrestricted immigration; and the principal ideological outbursts against the Jew also occurred in an atmosphere charged with anxiety over foreign influence. Thus, the problem of anti-Semitism in America ultimately needs to be viewed in relation to mass immigration.

The same impulse propelled the movement to check immigration and the discriminatory drive to limit internal mobility and opportunity. Both types of restriction resulted from fear of being invaded and overrun. Both sought to stabilize a society caught up in bewildering flux. In the early twentieth century, the wildfire spread of discrimination and the mounting clamor for immigration controls reflected the increasingly beleaguered feelings of millions of Americans obsessed by fears of dispossession.

After the First World War, however, the parallel ended. Restriction of immigration now acquired the force of law and became a permanent feature of American institutions; domestic restraints on immigrant minorities for the most part did not. The measures that reduced Jewish immigration to a trickle acquired a legitimacy and respectability which anti-Jewish discrimination within American society never enjoyed. The reason, no doubt, is that practicing discrimination within a society is much more divisive than regulating admission to it. Americans wanted stability, but they wanted integration even more. Discrimination at home could only retard integration. Restricted immigration, on the other hand, though discriminatory in its own way, in the long run made for homogeneity at home. Indeed, it ultimately undermined the *raison d'être* of domestic discrimination. After secure barriers to immigration were finally erected in 1924, the strain and tempo of assimilation eased. The jerry-built structure of internal restrictions was destined gradually to crumble, as official restraints on immigration made informal restraints on assimilation superfluous.

To invest immigration restriction with the requisite legitimacy, it was essential not to carry the invidious ethnic distinctions in men's minds overtly into law. Although an ugly strain of anti-Jewish feeling ran through the restriction movement, it was seldom openly confessed. Even when restrictionists campaigned unabashedly for protecting the "Nordic race" from all lesser breeds, they devised a quota system cleverly contrived to rest on apparently impartial criteria. Only the

Asiatic exclusion clauses made a frankly racial discrimination, and these were later repealed by Congressmen intent on strengthening the basic law. If the laws had been more explicitly discriminatory, they might never have been enacted, and they surely would not have survived into the 1960s.

Only once was a serious effort made to strike especially at Jewish immigration, and the embarrassed slyness of the attempt reveals the powerful sanctions against any such scheme. In the winter of 1896–97, Congress passed by huge majorities a bill excluding adults unable to read and write their own language. (This literacy test, while looking impartial, would chiefly obstruct the "new immigration" pouring in from Southern and Eastern Europe.) At the last minute the restrictionist leaders, captained by Henry Cabot Lodge, tried to alter the proposed test so that it would fall with special severity on Eastern European Jews: The sponsors quietly changed the pending bill to require literacy, not in the immigrant's own tongue but in that of his native or resident country, so as to take advantage of the fact that few of the Yiddish-speaking Jews from Russia or Rumania could read the national language. The maneuver came to light. Lodge resorted to bland double talk, but other Congressmen took alarm. To save the bill from possible defeat, the original formula was restored.

Congress never again tried to discriminate specifically against Jews; in all likelihood, it seldom wished to do so. As a strong group consciousness crystallized among old-stock Americans, concrete hostilities fused into a broadly racist ideology. The great problem was not just the Jews but the outsiders of all kinds, alien in blood and heritage. In the early twentieth century, the United States was becoming so heterogeneous that every social strain could be interpreted in terms of ethnic subversion; and "100-per-cent Americans" tried desperately to impose unity and social stability by asserting against all intrusive groups their own sense of possession and pre-eminence in the land of their fathers. In this situation, Jews learned to think of themselves as allies of all the other minorities in a common front against racism.

Now the great wave of immigration has passed, the ethnic majority that rallied against it has lost cohesion and the generic prejudice it inspired is subsiding. The Nordic ideology, by which super-patriots once sought to justify their traditional ascendancy, cannot sustain today's right wing. Lacking a sense of proprietorship and doubtless aware of their own disparate origins, the members of the new Right are little inclined to construe Americanism in ethnic terms. They rely instead on moral and constitutional dogmas. For them, the enemy is the "establishment" —an entrenched aggregation of power— rather than a rising tide of immigrants. Anti-Semitism has thus lost both its objective basis in the presence of the Jewish immigrant and its subjective support in the psychology of American nationalists.

Much the same account can be given of the decline of other prejudices since the Second World War: for example, the fading of "Yellow Peril" propaganda and of anti-Catholic crusades. These, too, have dissolved in the common process of ethnic assimilation. But the case of the Negro is significantly different. Although prejudice and discrimination against Negroes have also fallen markedly in recent years, the similarity in trend is somewhat deceptive. While social resistance to Catholics, Jews, Japanese Americans and even Puerto Ricans has been breaking down almost imperceptibly, with hardly any overt strife, the partial release of the Negro from oppression has excited the one live ethnic hatred of our time. The general weakening of ethnic barriers that has so greatly reduced conflict between groups of immigrant and of native white descent has intensified conflict between whites and Negroes. This difference between the experience of Jews, Catholics or Orientals and that of Negroes provides a final measure of the importance of immigration in defining the status of the Jew in America.

Cultural pluralists have taught us to think of all Americans, except possibly the Indians, as immigrants. Yet we have difficulty in so conceiving of early English colonists or African slaves. The difficulty, I believe, points to a fundamental sociological distinction. Colonists and their captive labor force constituted the original social order that took form in the seventeenth century. From the outset, it is now clear, prejudice and subordination marked out the Negro's sphere of life under this order; both law and mores positively forbade his assimilation. In contrast, other racial and religious minorities entered the new society voluntarily and with no such clearly defined status. Their extensive integration during the eighteenth century established the reality of a society open to new arrivals.

A presumption in favor of the assimilation of immigrants, whatever their race or origin, became embodied in the symbol of the melting pot. But neither the presumption nor the symbol included the American Negro.

Thus, the custom of the country sanctioned the aspirations of the peoples who arrived in the United States during the nineteenth and twentieth centuries. Any barriers to mobility and opportunity for immigrant groups had to be newly created, whereas resistance to the Negro had only to be maintained. No one told the Jew to stay in his place, for he had no historically appointed "place" in America. Typically, he was enjoined to become more "American"—*just not too fast.* Conflict arose when others moved to check his assimilation, not when they permitted it. In the case of the Negro, strife has typically come from efforts to make assimilation possible.

For Jews, we might say, the promise of America was never really lost, only temporarily deferred. For Negroes it has yet to be achieved. By one of the ironics of history, the breakdown of broad-spectrum prejudice—of the generalized hostility that taught Jews to think of themselves as a racial minority allied with the Negroes—is revealing the painful distance between the two.

FREDERIC COPLE JAHER (b. 1934) is the author of
Doubters and Dissenters (1964), editor of *The Age of
Industrialism in America* (1968), and coeditor of *The
Aliens* (1970). Jaher, who teaches at the University of
Illinois (Champaign-Urbana), claims that Populists did
not originate American antisemitism, that they were no
more hostile to Jews than toward other groups, and that
the Populist movement as a whole was not antisemitic.
In reading this selection, see if Jaher provides greater
substantiation for the views of Richard Hofstadter than
he does for his own position. Can one be only slightly
antisemitic? Although Jaher claims that the Populists
did not originate American antisemitism, does he cite
any other groups or movements in American history
that exhibited Judaeophobia?*

Frederic Cople Jaher

Were the Populists Antisemitic?

Current interpretations of Populism differ over the relationship between farmers and social change. Historians have divided on the question of whether the movement was a romantic-atavistic gesture to recapture the past or a realistic-progressive attempt to cope with modern times. Two aspects of the farmers' ferment—anti-Semitism and the conspiracy theory of history—have been the chief points at issue. Populist prejudice and fears of clandestine expropriation also found expression in predictions of doom. A study of these attitudes as manifested by the agrarian cataclysmists should therefore provide insights into agricultural insurgence in general.

An awareness of the varied and sometimes contradictory characteristics that constituted Populism must serve as a guide in analyzing any of its components. There is a fundamental division in Populism, as in all great movements, between the inspirational and the organizational, the idealistic and the pragmatic. To uncover all these strands and weave them into a coherent whole would take an intensive and extensive study of the various leaders and groups within the movement. A brief examination of the Populist élite will show the complexity of the task and the difficulty of putting agrarians into any one particular category. Some leaders, like Mary Lease and Pitchfork Ben Tillman, were given to prophetic poses, but there were also such practical and sober reformers as William V. Allen and William A. Pfeffer, who did not utter revolutionary imprecations or dwell on impending doom. Then there were men like Donnelly and Weaver, who dwelled in both camps. The Populists came from different regions; some were southerners, others western, and several were born in the East. These diverse geographical origins played their part in increasing of heterogeneity of the movement. Differences in education and occupation— many were lawyers and college graduates rather than simple sons of the soil—also caused cleavages in the ranks. Even disparity in age had an influence. Donnelly and his generation were reformers of pre-Civil War vintage for whom free silver was merely one article in a varied creed of dissent. On the other hand, Populists of Mrs. Lease's type had grown up in the agricultural depression, and their convictions were bound to differ from those who had known a youth of confident plenty. Finally, there were those who turned "soft" and embraced free silver, while the hard-core "middle of the road," represented by Donnelly, kept the earlier reform program and, after the brief Bryan interlude, controlled the party.

Since Donnelly shared both moods, since he was both an unrealistic seer and a hard-headed politico, it is rewarding to examine *Caesar's Column* as a product of these attitudes. Its conspiratorial, cataclysmic, and absolutist elements are irrationally idealistic. Donnelly suggests a conspiracy theory of history, brands the money power as absolutely evil, predicts complete destruction of a godless society, sees no discrepancy in achieving individualism through government interference, proposes a radical political framework to maintain a reactionary economic system—and offers as a twentieth-century panacea a Christ-domi-

nated, antebellum, rural paradise. Because Donnelly was more than a hysterical hayseed, however, his book is also more than the primitive response of an innocent rustic.

Donnelly's dualism is most apparent in his treatment of Jews. He uses many irrational anti-Semitic stereotypes. The Oligarchic leader, Prince Cabano, is a Jewish banker whose real name is Jacob Isaacs. In fact, the whole governing class, "the aristocracy of the world is now altogether of Hebrew origin." To be under the heel of an un-Christian foreigner is the ultimate degradation of traditional America. A Jew is also prominent in the Brotherhood. He is second in command and flees with the booty of victory to recover the kingdom of his people in Judea. These two leaders comprise the classic anti-Semitic image. The Jew is both rich banker and proletarian anarchist; he threatens society and its backbone, the independent middle class, from both above and below.

Another example of this type of bigotry is Donnelly's characterization of the Jew as a crafty coward—the typical anti-Semitic charge that the Jew makes up for his lack of straightforward manliness with supple shrewdness. Both commanders are physical failures. The revolutionary is crippled, and Prince Cabano is a coward, but they compensate for their inadequacy with great cunning. The "cripple" is "the brains of the Brotherhood," and Isaacs maintains his position by wit. They also exhibit the other attributes of superior intellect associated with Jews— mystery and treachery. The head of the Oligarchy tries to trick his military aide, and the other Jew sneaks away to Palestine with the Brotherhood's plunder. Both men surround themselves with mystery. Isaacs changes his name to Cabano and always acts secretly, and the

"Vice President" of the Brotherhood is "the nameless Russian Jew."

Uncleanliness and lechery are two more traits supposedly representative of Judaism. Accordingly, "the Cripple" in "his person was unclean," and Cabano lusts for the Anglo-Saxon Estella Washington. Another Semitic vice manifested by the two antagonists is an unscrupulous and infinite hunger for wealth. Isaacs is willing to slaughter millions rather than give up some of his riches to forestall an uprising, and the Jew of the Brotherhood absconds with its entire treasure. Finally, Donnelly manifests the basic anti-Semitic fear: the fear that the Jews, a people without a country, are ever-wandering aliens subversive to all societies. The cripple symbolizes this Jewish failure to assimilate by fleeing to recreate the only homeland to which the Hebrews have ever been loyal.

It is not difficult to find an explanation for Populist anti-Semitism. The Jew was alien to everything that the farmer held most dear. He lived in the city, usually did not perform ennobling manual labor, spoke a strange tongue, and dressed exotically. In addition, he was history's eternal criminal, a member of the sect that had been guilty of mankind's greatest betrayal. In view of his sinful past, he became a ready suspect for any horrendous conspiracy. Christ's murder had not sated the Hebraic appetite for evil, and now the descendants of Jesus's killers were plotting to wipe out those who still lived in His image. Farmers were sure that the international cabal of Jewish bankers, typified by Rothschild and his American agent, the Jewish banker and Gold Democrat Perry Belmont, were trying to crucify them economically, as their ancestors had done physically. Fortifying these suspicions of conspiracy was the aura of mystery through which Americans saw the

Jews. Rabbis were rumored to have powers of divination, Jewish detectives were supposed to have an occult "second sight" in trapping criminals, and the theme of the mysterious Jewess ran through much of American fiction.

The Jew became a man of mystery, part of a secret coterie aiming to steal the hard-earned property of the farmer. This belief alone would have been enough to stir agrarian anger. The villain's role in this rural drama, however, rested on far more than one evil. The Hebrew was foreign and unassimilable, as well as greedy. His refusal to be integrated into other cultures branded him an incurable alien. Surviving all assimilation schemes indicated superior powers—since he could resist change himself, the Jew had the power to change others. Thus, in *Caesar's Column*, he has transformed the United States. These superior powers, the means by which he conquers other societies, were associated with wealth, the East, the city, and business. Semitic strength was the power of the mind, or so thought the agrarians. Superior cunning was used to victimize the sturdy but simple yeoman. It mocked his upright virtues while using them against him. The farmer felt that he was being destroyed by such chicanery, and the Jew became the symbol of this duplicity. Since no American could be responsible for his decline, it must be a foreign conspiracy that was corrupting the nation and robbing the farmer of his birthright. Only Jews had the craft and the will to destroy the nation; only history's greatest betrayers could commit this greatest of betrayals.

Despite the plausibility of this explanation and the common use of anti-Semitic imagery, the facts are that Populists did not originate American anti-Semitism; that they were no more antagonistic toward Jews than toward other groups;

and that, even though individual Populists may have disliked Jews, the movement as a whole was not anti-Semitic.

Here is the evidence for the allegedly anti-Jewish nature of Populism. The New Jersey Grange in 1892 warned of candidates who represented "Wall Street and the Jews of Europe;" an Associated Press reporter noticed as "one of the striking things" about the Populist Convention at St. Louis an "extraordinary hatred of the Jewish race!" Coin Harvey and Gordon Clark slurred Jews in their free silver pamphlets; during the campaign of 1896, some Populists made anti-Semitic remarks; one foreign bigot did not deny that Bryan allegedly agreed with him; *Puck* and *The Police Gazette,* which contained unfavorable Jewish references, were widely read in the hinterlands; and Donnelly and Mrs. Lease frequently criticized Jews.

This evidence, sparse in quantity, looks even thinner when examined qualitatively. There were scarcely any Populist references to anti-Hebrew feeling before 1896. Thus almost a generation after its birth and several years after agrarianism had become a tidal wave of dissent, the movement showed no signs of hatred for Jews. There was some documentation of anti-Jewish attitudes during the campaign of 1896, but even a student seeking to prove that Populism was anti-Semitic apologizes for the paucity of "anti-Semitic references." Furthermore, most of the evidence for this feeling, except the statements by Donnelly and Mrs. Lease, was taken at second hand from Jewish periodicals, reform magazines, and the anti-Bryan press. If the Populists were indeed anti-Semitic and if they came from a region where such prejudice was welcome, it is indeed surprising that it did not appear in their own press. No other movement with an appreciable amount of anti-Semitic bigotry was ever so reluctant to express it.

A close look at the facts makes the allegation of Populist anti-Semitism seem even more specious. Citing anti-Semitism in the New Jersey Grange and alluding to the wide western circulation of *Puck* and *The Police Gazette* contradict rather than confirm the argument. All that these references prove is that this bigotry was not most at home in the West. New Jersey was hardly Populist territory, and *Puck* and *The Police Gazette* were published in the East, where they had a far larger audience than in the West. The same erroneous reasoning is evident in pointing to anti-Jewish remarks made by Populists in Louisville, Pennsylvania, Michigan, Indiana, and Florida. None was a center of agrarianism, and one looks in vain for evidence of such sentiments in Iowa or Kansas. As for Coin Harvey and Gordon Clark, they were Free Silverites, not Populists. Harvey was born in West Virginia; had mining and real estate interests in Colorado, Utah, and California; and was only briefly associated with the Populists in 1893–1894. Clark's anti-Semitic pamphlet, *Shylock As Banker, Bondholder, Corruptionist And Conspirator,* was printed, significantly, not by a Populist house but by the American Bimetallic League in Washington, D.C. It is not surprising that anti-Semitism existed among the bimetallists. This group, committed to the silver cure, would fear a "Jewish dominated gold conspiracy" much more than Populists whose diversified program was not tied solely to the money issue. It may be granted that agrarianism was temporarily allied with the bimetallists. The People's Party made many alliances, however, and in politics, virtue is rarely measured by one's bedfellows. Using Mrs. Lease and Donnelly, two of many Populist leaders, as evidence of the movement's deep vein of religious prejudice is typical of excessive generalization from scanty evidence. It proves only that some of the leaders were bigoted people, as are some individuals in any organization. To judge a group on the basis of a few members' personal traits smacks of guilt by association, hardly a valid historical method.

To ascertain what agrarians really thought about Jews, it is necessary to compare western feelings with national attitudes. Students of anti-Semitism place the upsurge of this prejudice about the time when Joseph Seligman was refused accommodations at the Grand Union Hotel in Saratoga Springs. Exclusion at summer resorts, numerous articles about the Jewish question in periodicals, and the barring of Jews from the Union League Club in New York City revealed burgeoning anti-Semitism in the 1890's.

These acts, showing that the East as well as the West was coming to look with disfavor upon Jews, indicate that this prejudice was not induced by Populism. Before 1890, when there was little bigotry, there is no proof that agricultural organizations disliked Jews. Afterward, when anti-Semitism became nation-wide, there is no evidence that it was greater in one area than in another, nor that one region spawned and another merely caught the disease. Indeed, some of Mary Elizabeth Lease's anti-Jewish statements were made in New York City and, according to the New York *Times,* were greeted with cheers.

One historian, claiming that there was significant anti-Semitism in Populism, has explained away the scarcity of unfavorable references toward Jews as stemming from lack of publicity because the country was not sensitive to tolerance. This explanation does tie in with the growth of religious prejudice at the end of the century, but it is a self-refuting argument: If the entire nation accepted bigoted campaigning, it can hardly be claimed that anti-Semitism was exclusively, or even predominantly, western. Furthermore, we may conclude that this insensitivity—far from being the reason why the greater number of such remarks went unpublicized—was actually the cause of many of these epithets. Insensitivity may imply lack of preoccupation with, as well as intolerance of Jews. When the farmers uttered the terms "Shylock" or "Rothschild," they may have unwittingly been using colloquialisms that had no real reference in their minds to the Hebrews. One Jewish magazine, commenting on slights in Populist rhetoric, observed that "ofttimes when attention is called to public speakers and the press of the injustice and wrong of thus creating religious prejudice, the offensive words are explained in other ways, withdrawn, and a promise given never to use them again; seldom is the virulence pressed." Prominent Populists like Pfeffer, Allen, Weaver, and the young Watson never, to this author's knowledge, expressed any anti-Semitism. They blamed their plight on the English and the East, more specifically on the money power in Wall Street and Lombard Street, but never were the Jews accused as culprits. If these men attacked other foes, would they not have singled out a group much feebler in numbers, resources, and political power? At worst, it can be claimed that farmers were beginning to use stereotypes that would eventually become the bywords of anti-Semitic groups. Certainly, hatred of Jews was neither a Populist obsession nor part of its basic ideology.

An analysis of anti-Semitism is important because it throws much light on Populism and its cataclysmic thinkers. In the case of *Caesar's Column,* for example, it would prevent the confusion of agents with causes of catastrophe. More significant, however, is what this prejudice reveals about Populism. Anti-Semitism has never been part of any widespread and respectable political movement in the United States. It has always been the creed of demagogues, like Gerald L. K. Smith and Father Coughlin, who hover on the fringe of American politics. Most Populists, on the contrary, were not rabble-rousers leading a half-crazed mob. They were sincere and sober men, many of whom had grown old, if not prosperous and wise, fighting for the underprivileged, and the party to which they belonged was not a quivering ganglion to be motivated by any irrational stimulus. Proof that the Peoples' Party was made of substantial stuff can be seen by a glance at its platform. Treasury loans on stored crops and federally controlled elastic currency are not the principles of a primitive political organization and do not suffer when compared with the Manchester mutterings of the gold-standard academicians. Populist ideology was much more than stale slogans mouthed by paranoid bigots.

Tolerance was not only due to the realistic, progressive side of agrarianism. Populism was an American agricultural crusade and differed from European peasant uprising in that religious prejudice was not a part of the traditional legacy of the middle-class American farmer. Tender-minded traditionalism, even more than tough-minded pragmatism, may very well have been the source of the farmers' tolerance. Certainly Populists were traditionally oriented. Donnelly, to take one example, hoped that God would "give us back the simplicity, the purity and the prosperity of the early days." This group, like the Jacobins, was economically conservative and sought

to protect small property-owners, yet it found itself forced into radical political action. Unlike the Jacobins, however, Populists hungered for the old days and remembered best the old values—values of an independent and prosperous era, of an ascendant middle class that was confident of itself and the nation. Populist prejudices can be traced to the insecurity born of crushed hopes, vanishing opportunities, and declining status. But America before 1865 was the land of promise with plenty left over for alien groups. In those days, there had been little bigotry among farmers; people cared more where you were going than where you came from. If that was the past the farmer desired, if that was part of the agrarian myth, did it not have a mighty influence on his thinking? Would not the old faith of tolerant democracy be more a check than a spur to anti-Semitism?

The conspiracy theory of history is another idea that revealed both perceptive and paranoid elements in Populism. Although this vision sprang from suspicions of intrigues aimed at destroying the farmer, it also inspired intelligent suggestions for alleviating his plight.

Agrarian writers saw society dominated by a vast cabal seeking to transfer wealth from the laboring classes to parasitic bankers. Conspiratorial phantasies rose from suspicions of being victimized by a great swindle. Singling out a mysterious and evil coterie was a convenient defense mechanism to externalize feelings of failure associated with loss of prosperity and status, and it justified socially unacceptable reactions like violence and revenge.

The conspirators supposedly directed the Wall Street and Lombard Street international "money power," which gathered the world's wealth while crushing its producers. In 1895, Party leaders William V. Allen, James H. Kyle, Jerry Simpson, and James B. Weaver stated, in the "Populist Manifesto," that "as early as 1865–6 a conspiracy was entered into between the gold gamblers of Europe and America to . . . fasten upon the country the single gold standard of Britain, and to [give] . . . banking corporations . . . the sovereign control . . . for the issues and volume of all supplemental paper currency." The signers found "every device of treachery, every resource of state craft and every artifice known to the secret cabals of the international gold ring . . . being made use of to deal a blow to the prosperity of the people and the financial and commercial independence of the country."

The conspiracy theory was based on the idea that a parasitical minority had seized the reins of government and was digging its golden spurs into the mass of producers. This "money power" embodied all that the farmers feared and despised in the new industrial era. It was foreign (British) and urban (London and New York); it achieved wealth and status through mental rather than physical labor, and it represented the remote and mysterious world of finance, commerce, and industry. The alien nature of the gold cabal made the struggle between producers and parasites seem deeper and far more dangerous than any previous contest. On its outcome rode the future of the republic. "The contest opening in the United States," thought Farmers' Alliance member Leonard Brown, "narrows down to the individual contending against corporate power for the 'rights of life, liberty, and the pursuit of happiness'—the inalienable rights of man."

Convinced that the gold bugs threatened national prosperity and republican institutions, the farmers concluded that catastrophe could be averted only by immediate action. Dismal prognostications by such agrarian leaders as James B. Weaver and Tom Watson have been alluded to above. Other powerful voices joined the chorus of doom. Leonidas Polk, President of The Southern Alliance, said that "retrogression in American agriculture means national decline, national decay, and ultimate and inevitable ruin." W. Scott Morgan, author of one of the most widely read accounts of the Alliance, felt that the machinations of the government produced "cracks in the foundation," which revealed "the whole substrata of the social structure . . . in commotion." Morgan reminded bankers that in 1776 and 1789 "the wrongs of the people [were] wiped out in the blood of the patriot." Revolution, he warned, would happen again "if our statesmen persist in ignoring the encroachments of organized capital upon the rights of the people."

Despite the frequency of its expression in Populist thought, belief in conspiracy was no more restricted to agrarians than was anti-Semitism. Other reformers, even those who identified with the established order, were haunted by visions of wily subversives. There was, however, a distinction between Populist suspicions and the immigrant, anarchist, or Populist conspiracies imagined by defenders of dominant groups. Agrarians and other disaffected critics regarded conspiracy as a symbol and cause of evil trends that were destroying society. Ruling élites and their spokesmen, on the other hand, saw conspirators as foreign obstacles impeding the normal harmony of social forces. They blamed evil individuals who sought to wreck a sound social system. Their conspiracy fears, instead of inspiring reform measures became an argument for conservatism. These conservatives explained away grievances by attributing them to agitators and substituted moralizing for reform.

Fears of conspiracy were more than persecution phantasies that distorted reality. Feeling that he had been duped by a malignant and brilliant cabal enabled the farmer to face his own weakness. To be vanquished by a superior and unscrupulous foe made defeat less humiliating. By shifting responsibility for his failure, the yeoman could admit his inability to cope with modern forces. Recognition of his decline led the farmer to devise remedies to redress the imbalance of strength. Although the conspiracy theory of history distorted the farmer's analysis of his plight, it also provided a foe against whom to rally. "Gold bugs" and "Rothschild" may not have been the chief sources of agrarian troubles, but focusing on these enemies forced farmers to examine their situation and even inspired some sound monetary policies that were later adopted by the major parties.

Keeping the Populist dualism between realism and distortion in mind, we return to Donnelly. Certainly Donnelly fired his share of emotional broadsides at a stronghold that could be taken only by modern organizational methods. His ideological flabbiness is apparent. It manifested itself in his use of stereotypes, theories of conspiracy, and predictions of doom. The epithet "Prince of Cranks" was not totally unmerited by him. This Prince of Cranks had another name, however, which signified another aspect of his character. Ignatius Donnelly, the "Sage of Nininger," was respected for his learning, his sympathy for the unfortunate, and his experience as a reformer. Because of these qualities, *Caesar's Column* does not represent the raving of a demagogue; it is not surface without substance. In

place of the free silver elixir, Donnelly suggests a diversified program in which fiscal policy is only one of several remedies. The same touch of realism conditions his belief in a conspiracy theory of history. The accusation of conspiracy in *Caesar's Column* is no mere accusation of deviltry charged to men who are evil incarnate, nor does it rationalize the simple revenge of the outraged rustic. Experience and wisdom made Donnelly go deeper than aimless vilification. He sought the system, not the man. "There were some among these men whose faces were not bad," says Donnelly when he introduces the reader to the Oligarchy. "Under favorable circumstances they might have been good and just men. But they were the victims of a pernicious system."

Donnelly's attitude toward the Jews best brings out the process of a complex and intelligent mind coping with its prejudices and emotions. Donnelly, who portrayed the Jews unfavorably only in *Caesar's Column,* had a reputation for minority tolerance. He had many of the character attributes associated with bigotry, however. His life was a long, painful record of humiliation, frustration, and failure. He reached his pinnacle before forty, then watched his career waste away. Hence, his natural sympathies for the downtrodden conflicted with the very human desire to find a scapegoat for his own misfortune. Out of this conflict came ambivalence toward Jewry. It is an attitude full of Jew-baiting on the one hand, but, on the other, it reflects dissatisfaction with the easy epithets of anti-Semitism. Having undergone hardship himself, Donnelly sympathized with a people that was persecuted, humiliated, and denied respectability. In these passages, the Jew is the yeoman of yesteryear; his history foreshadows the destiny of the western farmer. He is persecuted rather than persecutor, victim not victor. The Hebrews, "originally a race of agriculturists," were turned into rootless and ruthless capitalists by centuries of oppression. "Christianity fell upon the Jews, . . . and forced them for many centuries, through the most terrible ordeal of persecution the history of mankind bears any record of. . . . Only the strong of body, the cunning of brain, . . . survived the awful trial." Now "the Christian world is paying, in tears and blood, for the suffering inflicted by their bigoted and ignorant ancestors upon a noble race." The Jews had become oppressors, but they would suffer the fate of all oppressors. History was a cycle, and oppression always brought with it a thirst for revenge to be sated only by cataclysm. Soon the Jews would be destroyed, but they would be sacrificed as the victims rather than the creators of the evil society over which they ruled.

Caesar's Column is a book of contrasts. It demonstrates, as did its author, all that was good and bad in Populism: doubt and despair conjuring up scapegoats and conspiracies; bitterness and frustration dwelling upon envy and revenge; the futility of the present half-concealed in the shrouds of adoration for the past; and the once brave words of the noble yeoman turned into the somber tones of a dirge. But there is more to *Caesar's Column,* as there was more to the author and the group from which it came. There is the sense of justice and equality, the ingenious proposals for mankind's hope and happiness. But most valuable is the throbbing pulse of humanity beating through the book, its writer, and his movement—the idealism that envisioned a world where innocence would triumph and virtue rule.

Ignatius Donnelly and Mary Lease were only two figures in the Populist gallery, a collection of many faces revealing a multitude of thoughts and expressions. More accurately, we can say that there is really only one portrait—an image more faceted and shaded than many observers perceive, a mind dwelling on reforms, and a heart longing to retreat into an eden-like past. We can discern a line of radicalism here and a stroke of reaction there. A glint of hatred merges into a glow of humanity, and a smile of victory becomes a grimace of defeat. But there is one central element in this sketch: Tragedy is etched in it so deeply that no eye can miss it. It is the tragedy of all failures that have a touch of nobility in them: the tragedy of great expectations that are not realized.

LEONARD DINNERSTEIN (b. 1934), who published an in-depth study of *The Leo Frank Case* (1968), attempts in the following essay to give the background necessary for an understanding of why an antisemitic outburst occurred in Atlanta in 1913. Note how much weight he gives to the findings of Handlin and Hofstadter. Is there any indication that antisemitism in the South predates the 1890s? Does Dinnerstein emphasize social tension or Christian teaching as the prime reason for the attack on Leo Frank? Moreover, can this case really be considered an example of antisemitism? Is it possible that the public merely reacted to a heinous crime with intense anxiety? Finally, are the facts presented in sufficient detail to allow a definitive conclusion to be drawn?*

Leonard Dinnerstein

A Dreyfus Affair in Georgia

Frustration and disillusionment with the rapid social changes caused by the industrial transformation at the end of the nineteenth century set off racial attacks in the United States and Europe. Alfred Dreyfus, Mendell Beiliss, the Haymarket anarchists, and Sacco and Vanzetti were all aliens victimized by societies undergoing rapid conversion. Jews, Italians, Germans, immigrants, anyone, in fact who deviated from the ethnic norm easily served as a scapegoat for the turmoil accompanying industrialism. Barbara Tuchman attributed anti-Semitism in France to "building tensions between classes and among nations. Industrialization, imperialism, the growth of cities, the decline of the countryside, the power of money and the power of machines . . . churning like the bowels of a volcano about to erupt." To a considerable extent, many of these same forces—in greater or lesser degree—also applied in Kiev, Chicago, and Boston. In Russia, Maurice Samuel tells us, "the Beiliss case was mounted by men who hoped by means of it to strengthen the autocracy and to crush the liberal spirit that was reviving after the defeat of the 1905 revolution." In Chicago, fear of foreigners, social revolution, and labor ascendancy triggered the vigilante response to eight immigrant anarchists charged with the bomb-throwing incident in Haymarket

Square. "A biased jury, a prejudiced judge, perjured evidence, extraordinary and indefensible theory of conspiracy, and the temper of Chicago led to the conviction. The evidence never proved the guilt." Sacco and Vanzetti, atheists, labor agitators, and "Reds" of Italian birth, were convicted of robbery and murder in Dedham, Massachusetts in 1920. The case made by the prosecution led many observers to believe in the innocence of the defendants, but the jury foreman allegedly concluded, "Damn them, they ought to hang anyway."

Social bias played a crucial role in obtaining the convictions described above. The industrial transformation of society uprooted too many too quickly, and made those caught up in the whirlpool of change cling all the more tightly to their old ways. Situations that might have been tolerated or handled differently in more stable societies seemed like conspiratorial attempts to undermine civilization. Dreyfus, Beiliss, the Haymarket anarchists, and Sacco and Vanzetti symbolized unwelcome innovations. So, too, did Leo Frank, a Jew upon whom Atlantans would vent their unveiled nervous tensions in 1913.

Atlanta was not spared the problems that industrialism brought to other cities. Indeed the traditions of southern culture intensified the burden of social change. Typical of most American cities during the Progressive era, Atlanta's population practically doubled between 1900 and 1913 (89,870 to 173,713). The population in other urban areas in the United States also increased at an impressive rate during the first decade of the twentieth century. In the South, though, of cities with populations over 100,000, only Birmingham outpaced Atlanta's population spurt between 1900 and 1910. Newly established industrial enterprises offered jobs to all

comers. Although urban conditions were better than rural squalor, the city fell far short of the industrialists' promise of the good life. Large groups of recently displaced Georgia crackers mingled uneasily with each other and with the foreign immigrants who wore strange costumes and spoke unintelligible tongues. In the concrete jungle, the newcomers worked together in the most menial jobs and congregated in the least desirable housing. Although foreigners comprised less than 3 per cent of the city's residents, the few Europeans loomed as a great menace to those many Southerners who retained strong feelings about racial purity and community homogeneity.

Working conditions in Atlanta compared unfavorably with those in other parts of the country. Despite a periodic shortage of workers, factory wages were low and hours long. The normal work week lasted sixty-six hours, and, except for Saturday, the working day generally extended from 6 A.M. to 6 P.M. with only a half hour for lunch. In 1902, the average wage-earner took home less than $300 a year. Atlanta's Commissioner of Public Works commented that the prevailing wages did not enable the men in his department to provide even the minimum necessities for their families. By 1912, when average earnings rose to $464 living costs had increased correspondingly and Atlanta's relief warden reported a record number of public assistance applications. "Even where women and children worked," he observed, "the money they rec⁀ve is not enough for their support." "There are too many people on the ragged edge of poverty and suffering," the warden concluded. A year later, some children still earned 22 cents a week for their labor in the city.

Atlanta's unplanned growth plagued officials and created problems similar to those in other cities at the time. Health hazards abounded, educational facilities were found wanting, and recreational outlets could not increase fast enough to service the burgeoning population. As late as 1912, for example, Atlanta provided no public swimming pools or parks for its Negro citizens. An overabundance of gambling dens, dope dives, and brothels, on the other hand, beckoned both whites and Negroes who sought to escape from factory drudgery and dingy tenements. On a number of occasions, in fact, the Mayor of Atlanta, James G. Woodward, "disgraced the city . . . by public drunkenness." His private conduct, however, proved no political liability. Woodward received a third renomination after being "found in a state of intoxication in the red light district of the city. . . ."

Living conditions were no better than public facilities. In 1910, there were only 30,308 dwelling units for 35,813 families. Eighty-two miles, or more than half of the city's residential streets, existed without water mains and more than 50,000 people —over a third of the population—were forced to live in areas of the city not served by sewers. A continuous fog of soot and smoke irritated people's lungs and eyes, and an appalling number of urban dwellers suffered from ill health. Ninety per cent of the city's prisoners in 1902 were syphilitic. Wherever records were kept, the statistics indicated that the problems grew worse during the next decade, rather than better. A comparison of the number of residents afflicted by disease in 1904 and 1911, when the city's population had increased by only 64 per cent, showed the following:

Table I

	1904	1911	% Increase
Dyptheria	114	396	347
Typhoid Fever	85	315	307
Tuberculosis	37	223	602

Atlanta also suffered an above average death rate. A United States census report for 1905 noted that of 388 cities in this country, only twelve had more deaths per thousand persons than Georgia's capital. In 1911, Atlanta's figures still exceeded the national average by almost 40 per cent (13.9 to 18.75 per thousand). A year earlier, sixty-nine people had died from pellagra, a vitamin deficiency prevalent among the poor. This was more than triple the figure for any other city in the country. Birmingham and Charleston, S.C., the two cities that ranked second to the Georgian metropolis, reported only seventeen deaths from the illness in 1910. The situation did not improve much in succeeding years. In 1914 the United Textile Workers complained that far too many Atlanta children still fell victim to the disease. Although exact statistics for all ailments are difficult to obtain, industrialism provided its share of fatal illness. One Georgian official reported in 1912, "occupational diseases are much more common than is believed true. Lead, arsenic and phosphorous poisoning has caused much suffering and many deaths."

The crime rate in Atlanta highlighted the stresses of the new urbanites. In 1905, Atlanta policemen arrested more children for disturbing the peace than did those in any other municipality in the United States. Two years later, only New York, Chicago, and Baltimore, cities with considerably larger populations, exceeded Atlanta's figure for children arrested. That very year, the police booked 17,000 persons out of a total population of 102,-702. The Mayor found the statistic "appalling." "It places Atlanta," he said, "at or near the top of the list of cities of this country in criminal statistics."

The police force, another city institution overwhelmed by the population spurt, proved unable to grapple with the new problems thrust upon it. The major reasons for its incapacity were inadequate staffing and facilities. In 1912, the Mayor acknowledged that two hundred men were unable to protect the city, "and, as a result, the residential sections cannot be effectively policed." Atlanta, alone among American cities whose area exceeded twenty-five square miles, existed with only one police station and no substations.

Besides the pathological conditions that menaced the growing city, the southern heritage also conditioned the "Crackers" reaction to the enormous differences in urban living. Of all the sections in the country, none has been so tied to the past as has the South. W. J. Cash characterized this southern revulsion by change as "the savage ideal—the patriotic will to hold rigidly to the ancient pattern, to repudiate innovation, in thought and behavior, whatever came from outside and was felt as belonging to Yankeedom or alien parts."

The race riot that erupted in Atlanta in 1906 was an example of the periodic explosions of violence that occurred when transplanted rural dwellers rebelled against the drudgery and disruptiveness of their new urban existence. Rampaging white mobs attacked Negroes with abandon. Before the National Guard successfully quelled the rioters several days later, twelve people had been killed (two white and ten Negro) and seventy had been injured (ten white and sixty Negro). The riot had been incited by sensational newspaper reports exaggerating Negro assaults upon white women. These incendiary statements were published a few weeks after Hoke Smith had whipped up popular passions in his racist campaign for the gubernatorial nomination. Subsequent explanations blamed the newspapers for the outburst, but the press could not be held responsible for the

poverty and squalor of the new urban masses. One "educated negro" shrewdly noted that recently arrived rural whites resented the relative prosperity of Negro business people in the city. A national reporter spoke more bluntly in calling Atlanta "one of the very worst of American cities" filled with the "riff-raff that the mining towns of the West used to relieve us of." In either case, the exacerbated race relations in Atlanta focused national attention upon the city. The upheaval was obviously an admission that discontent with city life had become unbearable for the erstwhile rural folk.

The conservative nature of the dominant religious groups in the South compounded the difficulties of adjustment to urban life. No secular influence of any kind, C. Vann Woodward has attested, had the power to sway men's thoughts with as much vigor as did those who allegedly spoke with the authority of God. Baptists and Methodists, the two largest denominations in the South since colonial times, have, for the most part, preached a Fundamentalist creed that opposed change, glorified the past, and uttered invectives against aliens of any stripe. During the nineteenth century, these sects "became centers of conservative political sentiment and of resistance both to the invasion of northern culture and to the doctrine of the New South." Their allegiance to the past and fundamental theological beliefs continued well into the twentieth century.

The great bedrock of Fundamentalist support came from the rural population. When these people moved into the towns and cities, they brought their ministers along with them. Many of the Fundamentalist preachers, who had earlier railed against urban wickedness, "continued to regard the great city centers as 'jungle areas' no less pagan than the

Congo, and looked upon themselves as life-saving missionaries." Southern ministers also eyed the new industrialists with great suspicion. Among Methodists, both "pulpit and press inveighed against corporate wealth for denying labor a living wage," while Baptist objections "to industrialization arose from the fear that industry would lead to rapid urbanization which in turn would corrupt the morals of the people and hinder the spread of Christianity."

The Fundamentalists stressed the godliness of maintaining the homely virtues and living a simple, agricultural life. They also believed in a literal obedience of God's word. In fact, they considered adherence to scriptural instruction as man's most sacred duty. Their preachers continually railed against modern innovations and warned parishioners that dancing, card-playing and theater-going undermined Christian teaching. The Fundamentalists also abhorred the alteration of woman's traditional role. She belonged in the home, they believed, and any changes in her position must invariably lead to a loosening of Christian morality.

The Fundamentalists hoped to stem the floodtide of progress by condemning social change as blasphemy against God's revealed word. This resistance, although unsuccessful, complicated and delayed adjustments to modern times. Anyone and anything that violated their own literal interpretation of the Bible became subject to assault. Violence frequently accompanied accusations. The self-righteous crusade to restore the simple, godly life often justified the use of weapons against those who dissented.

Southern Baptists also considered the influx of immigrants one of the great dangers of modern times. During the 1880s, southern Baptist periodicals expressed concern with the foreigners whom they regarded as "a threat to American customs and traditions." Many Baptist editors attributed the moral corruption of the nation to the newcomers and felt that national good demanded a cessation of our traditional open-door policy. One spokesman enunciated his anxieties at the Southern Baptist Convention in 1895.

Foreigners are accumulating in our cities, and hence our cities are the storm centers of the nation. But the great misfortunes of all of this is that these foreigners bring along with them their anarchy, their Romanism, and their want of morals.

In his analysis of southern mores, W. J. Cash perceptively summarized the Fundamentalists' demands. They wanted "absolute conformity to the ancient pattern under the pains and penalties of the most rigid intolerance; the maintenance of the savage ideal, to the end of vindicating the old Southern will to cling fast to its historical way."

Despite the pervasive influence of the Fundamentalist creeds and the inherent southern hostility toward innovation, the leaders of the new South—the railroad magnates and the owners of cotton mills and factories—endeavored to build an industrial community patterned after the North. To a considerable extent they succeeded and "by 1900 the industrialization of the South had become largely a case of capital seeking labor supply." Atlanta's *Journal* succinctly expressed the prevailing need: "The Southern States have reached a point in their industrial progress where the work necessary . . . can not be done by the present force of workers. . . . The South needs more folks—folks for the farm, folks for the factory." In Georgia, for example, it was said that without immigrant labor, the development of the iron and cotton mills and the building of the railroads would have to be halted.

The desperate plight of industry forced southern state governments to establish immigration bureaus in the hope of attracting suitable laborers. But most southerners were quite specific as to whom they would welcome. Senator Ben Tillman of South Carolina announced, "We do not want European paupers to come to the South." Tennessee's Governor Ben Hooper expressed his opposition to receiving the "motley mass of humanity that is being dumped upon our shores. . . ." And Georgia's Federation of Labor "objected to 'flooding' the South and Georgia with a population composed of the scum of Europe. . . ." Atlanta's two major newspapers stated their preferences clearly. The *Journal* desired persons of Teutonic, Celtic, and Scandinavian origins, "peoples near akin to [our] own by blood, and capable of full assimilation. . . ." And *The Constitution* editorialized, "The German makes a splendid citizen."

Unfortunately for both the South and the arriving immigrants, most of the newcomers were from eastern and southern Europe. They were treated, for the most part, with conspicuous inhospitality. In some sections, Italians, or "'dagoes' were regarded as about on a par with 'niggers,' and the treatment of them corresponded." In 1891, eleven Italians were lynched in New Orleans after three of them had been acquitted of murdering the police chief. Five years later, three Italians suspected of homicide were strung up in Hahnville, Louisiana. In 1899, five Italians were lynched in Tallulah, Louisiana after injuring a doctor in a quarrel over a goat. The twentieth century had hardly begun when three more Italians were mysteriously shot in Erwin, Mississippi. Czechs and Slovaks

established a colony south of Petersburg, Virginia, in the nineteenth century, yet forty years after their arrival, the "natives" still resented their presence.

In Atlanta, the single largest influx of immigrants was 1,342 Russian Jews who comprised 25 per cent of the city's foreign-born in 1910. Although this group made up less than 1 per cent of the population, it was well-known that they ran a large percentage of the saloons, pawnshops, and restaurants catering to Negro trade. The Jews were viewed contemptuously by other whites. One reporter wrote, "as to the white foreigners who cater to negro [sic] trade and negro [sic] vice . . . it is left to the judgment of the reader which is of the higher grade in the social scale, the proprietors or their customers." Sensual pictures of nude white women allegedly decorated the walls of the saloons, and some people even thought that the liquor bottle labels aroused the Negroes' worst passions. Many Atlantans thought that the beer parlors "served as the gathering and hatching place of criminal negroes." When the patrons got drunk and caused social disturbances, the nearby whites blamed the saloon owners for the mischief. One analyst of the 1906 riot, for example, observed, "It was the low dives where mean whiskey was sold to Negroes by whites that bred the criminality which furnished an excuse for the outbreak of the mob; and it was from the doors of the saloon that the ruffians of the mob poured forth to do their deadly work on the innocent."

Although Jews had been in the South since colonial times, they had never been accepted by the dominant Protestant community. To be sure, opportunities to assimilate existed, but those who desired to retain their faith suffered restrictions upon their political and religious liberties. Denial of the trinity, for example, had subjected Jews to imprisonment in Virginia and Maryland in the colonial era. Therefore, Jews did not settle in Maryland until after the American Revolution. Virginia, on the other hand, did not permit Jews to enter the colony without express permission. Georgia granted Jews political and religious equality in 1798, but not until 1826 were Jews allowed to vote in Maryland. Although John Locke's original Constitution for the Carolinas provided for toleration, both North and South Carolina deprived Jews of their political rights. A South Carolina law of 1759 barred non-Protestants from holding office and the North Carolina Constitution of 1776 forbade them to vote. A Jew elected to the North Carolina Legislature in 1809 was challenged, upon taking his seat, but defended himself successfully. A Constitutional Convention, however, banned all Jews from holding office in the Tar Heel State in 1835, and the restriction remained in effect until 1868. In 1818, in a letter to the Jewish editor of a New York City newspaper, Thomas Jefferson acknowledged "the prejudice still scowling on your sect of our religion. . . ."

Despite restrictions on office holding, concerted anti-Jewish prejudice did not occur in the South until the Civil War era. During this period, however, Jews did become scapegoats for Confederate frustrations. They were accused of being "merciless speculators, army slackers, and blockade-runners across the land frontiers to the North." One southern newspaper observed, "all that the Jew possesses is a plentiful lot of money together with the scorn of the world."

Some Georgia towns specifically singled out the Jews as the cause of their woes. In 1862, 103 citizens of Thomasville resolved to banish all Jewish residents and a grand jury in Talbotton found the Jews guilty of "'evil and unpatriotic conduct.'" Talbotton prejudices, in fact, forced the Lazarus Straus family—later to become famous for its development of Macy's department store in New York City—to leave Georgia during the Civil War.

The next major anti-Semitic eruption occurred in the 1890s. The Populist crusade, the severe economic depression of 1893, and the squalid living conditions in urban slums all helped to intensify hostility toward those who loomed, on the one hand, as the seeming monopolizers of material possessions, and on the other, as the manipulators who unfeelingly deprived the people of their purchasing power. In Georgia, for example, it was "quite the fashion to characterize the Jew as exacting his interest down to the last drachma."

Accusations of financial manipulation gave rise to suspicion of a vast Jewish international conspiracy. One writer, in fact, concluded that the "Rothschild combination has proceeded in the last twenty years with marvellous rapidity to enslave the human race." In North Carolina, Elias Carr, Governor from 1893 to 1897, frequently reiterated his point that "Our Negro brethren, too, are being held in bondage by Rothschild."

When rural southerners flocked to the cities at the end of the nineteenth century, their impressions of the Jew combined traditional stereotypes of financial wiliness with the time-worn southern prejudices. In 1906, Horace M. Kallen, the Jewish philosopher, observed that "there is already a very pretty Jewish problem in our South. . . ." William Robertson, author of *The Changing South*, later noted, "It was enough for Jews to prosper right under [southern] noses, without affording the added insult of being the descendants of the murderers of Christ."

A lack of scholarly studies makes it risky to generalize about anti-Semitism in the South or to suggest regional differences. The two most prominent historians who have investigated American attitudes towards Jews in the nineteenth and twentieth centuries—Oscar Handlin and John Higham—have found evidence supporting positive and negative judgments. Both historians, however, dealt primarily with northern experiences and provided relatively few examples from southern states. Studies about alleged Populist anti-Semitism, moreover, have concentrated almost entirely on the expressions of northern and western agrarians. There are no indications, for example, that Tom Watson, the Georgia leader, engaged in any anti-Semitic diatribes in his Populist heyday.

A significant clue to southern attitudes may be garnered, however, from Higham's findings. He noted that American anti-Semitism was deeply ingrained in the agrarian tradition—which was suspect of urban prosperity based upon the toil of others—and cropped up most frequently in times of crisis. "The prophets of anti-Semitism," Higham continued, "were alienated and often despairing critics of the power of money in American society," and frequently attributed their own woes to the "lords of finance and trade": banks, moneylenders, and bondholders. He discovered, moreover, that hostility toward Jews in this country was strongest in those sectors of the population where there were relatively few Jews and where "a particularly explosive combination of social discontent and nationalistic aggression prevailed." Finally, he found nationalistic fervor "most widespread and in many ways most intense in the small town culture of the South and West." The South was the least urbanized and most discontented region in

the United States. Consequently, if Higham's conclusions are accurate, the South must figure as the most anti-Semitic area in the country.

Certain aspects of southern culture—aside from the squalor that existed in Atlanta and other fledgling urban areas—tended to make the natives react more violently to Jews than did residents of the North and West. Southerners were more inbred than were northerners and were, therefore, more concerned with the purity of their Anglo-Saxon heritage. Religious fundamentalism, another force that encouraged anti-Semitism, was more widespread in the South than the North. According to William J. Robertson, most southern Methodists and Baptists were advised by their spiritual leaders that the Jews were "Christkillers." Social instability accompanied by personal anxiety was the final factor that intensified regional hostility toward Jews. Throughout history, the position of the Jews has reflected the degree of security prevailing in a given society. They have frequently been blamed for defeats, depressions, and other disruptive crises. Southerners, notoriously insecure and continually on the defensive, seized upon hatred for Jews as one outlet for the frustrations of their existence.

The above mentioned factors existed, to some extent, in different parts of the North as well, and anti-Semitism appeared among different northern groups. But despite temporary interludes of cataclysm and depression, most northerners expected progress to improve the conditions of life. Many southerners, however, clung to fantasies of past heroics to compensate for a forbidding contemporary life, and looked upon change as subverting cherished values.

It is against this complex background of social change and the resistance it engendered that the murder of a thirteen-year-old girl, in 1913, triggered a violent reaction of mass aggression, hysteria, and prejudice. Leo M. Frank, the Jewish superintendent and part owner of the National Pencil Factory where the dead girl, Mary Phagan, had been employed, became the prime suspect. It was to be Frank's misfortune that he symbolized the alien institutions about which the South had always had the greatest apprehensions.

Mary Phagan had been found dead and disfigured in the basement of the National Pencil Factory by a Negro nightwatchman at 3 A.M. on April 27, 1913. Near her body lay two notes, purportedly written by the girl while being slain. They read:

Mam that negro hire down here did this i went to make water and he push me down that hole a long tall negro black that hoo it wase long tall negro i wright while play with me.

he said he wood love me land down play like the night witch did it but that long tall black negro did buy his slef.

Georgia, and particularly Atlanta, newspapers milked every ounce of sensationalism that they could from the tragedy. One daily indicated that the "horrible mutilation of the body of Mary Phagan proves that the child was in the hands of a beast unspeakable," while the editors of another added: "Homicide is bad enough. Criminal assault upon a woman is worse. When a mere child, a little girl in knee dresses, is the victim of both, there are added elements of horror and degeneracy that defy the written word."

An aroused public demanded vengeance. One of the victim's neighbors remarked to a reporter, "I wouldn't have liked to be held responsible for the fate of the murderer of little Mary Phagan if the men in this neighborhood got hold of him last night." The minister of Atlanta's Second Baptist Church thundered, "The very existence of God seems to demand that for the honor of the universe the murderer must be exposed."

Atlanta's inadequate police force was under intense pressure to find the culprit. Aside from being understaffed, the force left much to be desired in terms of intelligent action. They had been accustomed to a slower pace and simpler life and their inability to handle the problems of an industrial metropolis made them rely increasingly on an irrational use of power. On one occasion, for example, when Atlanta had experienced a labor shortage, the police attempted to rectify the condition by arresting all able-bodied men found on one of the main streets. Employed and unemployed, black and white, were hauled into court, fined, and sentenced to the stockade without being given a chance to defend themselves. One man so punished had been in the city for only three days. Neither relatives nor employers were notified of the round-up or the sentencings.

The police also had a poor record for solving crimes. A few years before Mary Phagan's death, a national periodical had revealed that only one murder in one hundred was ever punished in Georgia. Atlanta policemen allegedly used brutality with those people who were picked up. In 1909, they were accused of beating one Negro to death and chaining a white girl to the wall until she frothed at the mouth. In 1910, a commission, investigating prison conditions in the city, uncovered "stories too horrible to be told in print." During 1912–13, more than a dozen unsolved murders tried the public's patience. Because these victims had been Negroes, there had been no great protestations over the constables' inefficiency. But Mary Phagan was, as a Georgian so characteristically put it, "our folks." Failure this time would not be tolerated.

A great deal of action seemed to be taking place at the police station. Seven people were arrested, and although four were quickly released, three were still held on suspicion, including the Negro nightwatchman who had discovered the corpse. Of the trio, the one upon whom suspicion quickly fell was Leo Frank, the superintendent of the National Pencil Factory where Mary Phagan had been employed and where her body had been found.

When the police had first questioned Frank, he appeared quite nervous and overwrought. From him, they discovered that Mary Phagan had come to pick up her pay shortly after noon on April 26— Confederate Memorial Day. The superintendent admitted having been alone in his office, and having paid the girl her $1.20 in wages for the ten hours that she had worked that week. Mary had then left his office, and no one else ever admitted to having seen her alive again.

The day after the corpse had been discovered, strands of hair "identified positively" as Mary Phagan's, and blood stains, were found in a metal workroom opposite Frank's office. The night watchman had also told the police that Frank had asked him to come in early on the day of the girl's death, but dismissed him when he arrived and ordered him to return at the normal time. Frank's uneasy behavior before the police and the pressure from an hysterical public led to his arrest.

Leo Max Frank was the Jewish superintendent and part owner of his uncle's pencil factory. Although born in Texas, in 1884, he had been reared in Brooklyn and educated at Cornell University. His first position had been with a firm in a Boston suburb, and he did not settle in the South until 1907. Once in Atlanta, however, he planned to stay. He married Lucile Selig, daughter of one of the more prominent Jewish families in the city, and was popular enough to be elected president of the local chapter of the B'nai B'rith in 1912.

The arrest of the northern, Jewish industrialist won the approval of Atlanta's citizenry. Rumors spread that the prison might be stormed and the prisoners, Frank and the Negro nightwatchman, Newt Lee, lynched. Street talk had it that one of the two must be guilty and killing both would avenge the murder. *The Atlanta Constitution* cautioned its readers to "Keep An Open Mind." "Nothing can be more unjust nor more repugnant to the popular sense of justice," its editorial read, "than to convict even by hearsay an innocent man." The advice went unheeded.

The furor that erupted after the murder can largely be attributed to the deed having rekindled the residents' awareness of the harshness of their lives; having reawakened traditional southern resentment toward outsiders who violated southern mores; and having, once again, dramatized the inherent iniquities of industrial life. "What was uppermost in the minds of those who were indignant," The *Outlook* reflected in 1915, "was the fact that the accused represented the employing class, while the victim was an employee." And the Jew, more than the Negro, provided a symbol for the grievances against industrial capitalism and its by-product, urbanism. The Baptist Minister of Mary Phagan's church made the conventional southern identification of Jewishness, evil, the stranger, and hated northern industrialism when he recalled:

[my] own feelings upon the arrest of the old Negro nightwatchman, were to the effect that this one old Negro would be poor atonement for the life of this innocent girl. But, when on the next day, the police arrested a Jew, and a Yankee Jew at that, all of the inborn prejudice against Jews rose up in a feeling of satisfaction, that here would be a victim worthy to pay for the crime.

The employment of minors in factories particularly aroused the ire of Atlanta's residents. A spokesman for those crusading to restrict child labor viewed Mary Phagan's death as the inevitable consequence of industrial perfidy: "If social conditions, if factory conditions in Atlanta, were what they should be here, if children of tender years were not forced to work in shops, this frightful tragedy could not have been enacted." The antagonism and venom harbored toward the entrepreneurs and their characteristically inhumane attitudes found expression in Atlanta's *Journal of Labor:*

Mary Phagan is a martyr to the greed for gain which has grown up in our complex civilization, and which sees in the girls and children merely a source of exploitation in the shape of cheap labor. . . .

The Southern Ruralist, Atlanta's largest circulating periodical, also interpreted the slaying as the product of a heartless and cruel society. It branded "every Southern legislator" who thereafter refused to vote for laws prohibiting the employment of children in factories, "as a potential murderer."

There were other reasons for resenting the factories. White females had always been placed on a pedestal, to be worshipped, exalted, and protected. To Southerners they embodied the purity and nobility of the South itself. Considered a "queen worthy of honor [and] deserving protection from the contamina-

tion of a man's world," the white woman had to be zealously guarded from the evils of society.

Industrialism, however, had inaugurated factory work for women. Since tradition dictated that women belonged in the home, southern society regarded the change as subversive of regional honor and family ties. Few white men accepted the alteration without qualms. They may have felt unmanned because they could not maintain their families without an additional income—a feeling particularly disturbing in a society that had always emphasized virility. Guilt was also aroused in the traditionalist southern conscience because the factory system forced wives and daughters to come in contact with strange men. The Southern Baptists, it is said, had an "abnormal fear of the intimate association of the sexes." An Atlanta judge later elaborating upon this argument claimed: "No girl ever leaves home to go to work in a factory, but that the parents feel an inward fear that one of her bosses will take advantage of his position to mistreat her, especially if she repels his advances." A factory owner expressed similar southern sentiments:

It was considered belittling—oh! very bad! It was considered that for a girl to go into a cotton factory was just a step toward the most vulgar things. They used to talk about the girls working in mills upcountry as if they were in places of grossest immorality. It was said to be the same as a bawdy house; to let a girl go into a cotton factory was to make a prostitute of her.

Given the nature of southern prejudices, Atlantans were particularly receptive to the devastating indictments the authorities apparently unearthed against Leo Frank. One newspaper reported that pictures of Salome dancers "in scanty raiment" adorned the walls of the National Pencil Factory. At the coroner's inquest, a thirteen-year-old friend of Mary Phagan's told his audience that the girl had confessed her fears of the superintendent's improper advances. Former factory employees recalled that Frank had flirted with the girls, that he had made indecent proposals, and that he had even put his hands on them.

Regardless of the veracity of the accusations, other witnesses at the inquest corroborated Frank's statements as to his whereabouts on the day of the murder which, if true, made it almost impossible for him to have been the culprit. Nevertheless the coroner's jury ordered Frank held on suspicion of murder.

Subsequent police disclosures incriminated the factory manager even more in the eyes of many Georgians. A park policeman swore that he had seen Frank and a young girl behaving improperly in a secluded section of the woods a year earlier, while the proprietress of a bordello confessed that the superintendent had phoned her repeatedly on the day of the murder in an effort to obtain a room for himself and a young girl. Both statements were eventually repudiated but not before an impact had been made upon the public. At the time of the madam's affidavit, newspaper readers were informed that her remarks constituted "one of the most important bits of evidence" that the state had against the factory superintendent.

The numerous suggestions dropped by newspapers and police gave rise to the wildest rumors, most of them concerned with the "lasciviousness" of the "notorious" Leo Frank. The Jewish faith, it was widely asserted, forbade violations of Jewesses but condoned similar actions with Gentiles. Frank had allegedly killed another wife in Brooklyn, had illegiti-

mate offspring too numerous to count, drank heavily, was about to be divorced by his wife, and finally, was a pervert. One man said he knew that Frank was a "moral pervert" because he looked like one. These tales, lacking any foundation in fact, suggest how concerned Atlantans were with the religious and social background of Mary Phagan's suspected slayer. Gossip magnified fears. The people, it seemed, wanted Frank to have the characteristics attributed to him.

The trial of Leo Frank for the murder of Mary Phagan opened on July 28, 1913, amidst great hullabaloo. It lasted until August 26. During the entire period, the temper of the crowd indicated the antipathy Atlantans felt toward the defendant. "The fact that Frank is under indictment today," one reporter explained the day before the trial began, "means to many minds that he is therefore guilty. . . ."

The state's case rested primarily upon the testimony of Jim Conley, a Negro sweeper who had been employed in the National Pencil Factory. He charged Frank with having committed the murder and acknowledged that he had helped his employer remove the body to the factory basement. There were no witnesses to corroborate any of the sweeper's statements.

The defense based its case primarily upon proving that Frank did not have the time to commit the murder. Witnesses were presented who corroborated the superintendent's account of his whereabouts on the fatal day. Frank maintained his innocence and characterized Conley's tale as "the vilest and most amazing pack of lies ever conceived in the perverted brain of a wicked human being."

The jury needed less than four hours of deliberation before finding the defendant guilty. The judge sentenced Frank to hang. Atlantans were jubilant with the verdict. A crowd outside of the courthouse, estimated at between two and four thousand, screamed itself hoarse. As he stepped out of the courthouse, the prosecuting attorney was lifted to the shoulders of two husky men and carried to his office amidst huzzahs and cheers. After what was perhaps one of the wildest celebrations in Atlanta's history *The Marietta Journal and Courier* observed, "It seems to be the universal opinion that Frank was guilty and that he was the cause of the demonstration when the verdict was announced."

Frank's lawyers appealed his case through the Georgia courts and ultimately to the United States Supreme Court. None of the tribunals ordered another trial. The Governor of Georgia re-evaluated the evidence in June, 1915, and commuted the death penalty to life imprisonment. Two months later, in August, 1915, a band of men stormed the prison, kidnapped Frank, and lynched him.

The joyousness with which Frank's conviction was received revealed the people's desire for a scapegoat for their deeper resentments. Georgia's Governor, John M. Slaton, explained the hostility toward Frank as "the prejudice of the employe against the employer. The fact that the head of a large factory is accused of attacking a girl, one of his employes, has been sufficient to give rise to this kind of prejudice."

The lynching of Leo M. Frank, August 1915. *(Courtesy, American Jewish Archives, Cincinnati)*

The anti-Semitism that erupted in Atlanta also suggested the need for a particular type of a villain. Manifestations of this sentiment are evident in the widespread acceptance of Negro Jim Conley's testimony; the numerous rumors that Frank's Jewish friends had collected a "fund of hundreds of thousands of dollars" to buy the jury; and tales to the effect that some defense witnesses had been bought with "jew money." In addition, Frank's lawyers had received anonymous phone calls with the cryptic message, "If they don't hang that Jew, we'll hang you." Crowds outside of the courtroom frequently hurled epithets like, "Lynch him!" and "Crack that Jew's neck!" The jury was also threatened with lynching if it did not "hang that 'damned sheeny!'" This passionate hatred disclosed the Atlantans' intense yearning for some culprit upon whom they could fix blame for the frustrations of their barren lives. "People haunted by the purposelessness of their lives," Eric Hoffer has written, "try to find a new content not only by dedicating themselves to a holy cause but also by nursing a fanatical grievance." This was especially true of the newly urbanized working classes in the South.

Ignorant, frustrated, and frightened, the workers sought a devil to exorcise. Moreover, their severe tribulations and limited education made necessary a dogmatic oversimplification. In such a situation, Leo Frank could easily be visualized as the diabolical perpetrator of savage crimes against society.

Reinforcing these cultural and emotional sources of prejudice is the herd tendency in human nature. Widely shared personal opinions are difficult to sway. People tend to absorb the knowledge to which they are exposed through the refraction of their own emotional needs and experiences and through the evalua-

tions prevalent among the groups with which they identify. Facts and opinions that differ from one's own or that are disturbing to convention are frequently not perceived. Psychologists have found a high correlation between belief and desire ($+.88$) but a negative one in regard to belief and evidence ($-.03$). In other words, factual information is insufficient to disturb established opinions. Ellen Glasgow, the Virginia novelist, has noted that in the South for people "to think differently meant to be ostracized."

Enthusiastic acceptance of Frank's conviction was further enhanced because people are conditioned to defer to those whom they have been trained to respect. Statements made by public officials are accepted as accurate unless there is some reason to suspect obfuscation. This was especially true in the South where the ruling classes "had extraordinary powers over the whole social body." Hugh Dorsey, the Georgia-born prosecutor, had announced before the trial: "the possibility of a mistake having been made is very remote." Southern Pinkerton and Burns detectives, who had conducted separate investigations, had also expressed their firm belief in the factory manager's guilt. Why, then, should the masses have assumed that the alien Jew was telling the truth while their own leaders were not?

The members of the jury, a representative cross-section of Atlantans, pleased their peers with the verdict. A spokesman for the jurors stated that they had all accepted the prosecution's arguments and conclusions. To be sure, they may have been convinced of Frank's guilt on the basis of the evidence presented in court. But even if the material had been less persuasive, the opinion of the Atlanta crowds would certainly have influenced those who had to decide Frank's fate. What would have happened to their jobs, their social relationships, and the position of their families, for example, if the jurors had voted to acquit the man who most of Atlanta assumed had ravished the little girl? More than a year after the trial had ended, one juror confessed to a northern reporter that he was not sure of anything except that unless Frank was found guilty the jurors would never get home alive.

A Boston newspaperman wrote in 1916 that had Frank been a native Georgian he would never have been convicted of Mary Phagan's death. More likely, had he been a respected member of the gentile community, no southern prosecutor would have staked his case on a Negro's accusations. Moreover, had the people of Atlanta not found the cares of life so great a burden, there would have been less demand for a scapegoat to pay for their accumulated frustrations. The coming of industrialism was not solely responsible for Frank's fate. But the technological changes in society, which uprooted people and set them down in strange, urban areas, aggravated whatever intolerance and anxiety the southern culture had already nurtured.

The murder of Mary Phagan stood out as a symbol of industrial iniquity. She was continually referred to as "the little factory girl" long after the focus of the case had shifted to Leo Frank. A newspaperman observed during the trial: "The little factory girl will be remembered as long as law exists in Atlanta." A Confederate War veteran contributed "a dollar for the erection of a monument to Mary Phagan, the little factory girl who recently laid down her life for her honor." And Georgia's patrician historian, L. L. Knight, narrating the events of the murder and the solution arrived upon, years later wrote, "Espousing the cause of the little factory girl, [Tom] Watson in a most dramatic vein of appeal, summoned the true manhood of the South to assert its chivalry in vindicating the child's honor." The "little factory girl's" death, and the factory owner's responsibility for it, had at last provided an acceptable outlet for the discontented. Employment of minors, unconventional association of the sexes, and the evils of the factory system deeply disturbed a conservative society uneasily confronting the beginnings of industrialism. Most Atlantans, having uprooted themselves from rural origins, were alienated by their work in the factory and by life in the city. The murder of an innocent southern girl by a northern, Jewish factory superintendent evoked the hostility latent in their unsettled existence and directed this hostility to the symbol of their fears and grievances.

Discrimination against Jews at American universities is primarily a twentieth-century phenomenon. MORTON ROSENSTOCK (b. 1929), associate dean of the faculty at the Bronx Community College of the City University of New York and author of *Louis Marshall, Defender of Jewish Rights* (1965), from which the following selection is taken, implies that the imposition of quotas designed to hold down the number of Jewish students at Harvard was a shocking and shameful policy. But perhaps this is only a contemporary view. What were the attitudes of the press, other institutions, and Harvard students and alumni when the restrictive policy was announced? Is the quota system inherently discriminatory? Is it either necessary or morally justifiable for universities to maintain a "balanced" student body? Can discrimination of any kind in university admissions policies be of a beneficial nature?*

Morton Rosenstock

Are There Too Many Jews at Harvard?

Educational discrimination against Jews, mostly of the *sub rosa* kind, was increasingly practiced after the [first world] war, but it did not become a national issue until public reference was made to it by the administration of Harvard College in June, 1922. The percentage of Jews at Harvard had grown from 10 per cent immediately after the war to over 15 per cent by 1922, and reports circulated that some faculty members were alarmed at the prospect of an even greater Jewish enrollment. Prof. Albert B. Hart declared that in one Government course, 52 per cent of the men were "outside the element" from which the college had been "chiefly recruited for three hundred years." President A. Lawrence Lowell, who had been an early supporter of the Immigration Restriction League, and its Vice-President since 1912, was quite concerned over the influx of Jewish students.

On June 1, 1922, a statement was issued by Frederick L. Allen, Secretary of the Harvard Corporation, confirming that the subject was under consideration:

The great increase which has recently taken place in the number of students at Harvard College, as at other colleges, has brought up forcibly the problem of the limitation of enrollment. . . . Before a large general policy can be formulated on this great question, it must engage the attention of the governing boards and the Faculty, and it is likely to be discussed by alumni and under-graduates. It is natural that with a widespread discussion of this sort going on there should be talked about the proportion of Jews at the college. . . .

The statement did not stress the Jewish question, but it implied that Jews might be the objects of restriction. When it was learned that a special meeting of Harvard's Board of Overseers had been called and that Judge Julian Mack, the Jewish member of the Board, was much exercised, suspicions deepened. At commencement, on June 22nd, President Lowell officially announced that the college had to face its problems and that a faculty committee had been appointed to consider a new admissions policy.

Most Harvard students approved President Lowell's sentiments. A Jewish student leader at Harvard reported that there was not so much a dislike of certain Jews as a feeling that, good or bad, there were too many Jews and, consequently, Harvard might turn into a New Jerusalem—a second City College. A survey of eighty-three upperclassmen in the Social Ethics course revealed that forty-one believed in the justice of restricted admissions based on race or religion, eight were on the fence, and thirty-four were opposed. The proponents of limitation were unanimous in their belief that the unprecedented increase of Jewish students threatened the Anglo-Saxon character of the college, that admission should be based on personality as well as scholarship, and that education was more than pure knowledge. Jews, they felt, did not assimilate, were selfish, and had no alumni loyalty. Harvard students shared the desire of many adults of their social class for a continuation of a homogeneous society in which ethnic groups other than the old American would be kept in their place.

Outside the Harvard campus, reaction to the proposed anti-Semitic admissions policy was negative. Other New England colleges, including Yale, Tufts, and Bates, publicly denied any intentions of limiting classes by discriminatory measures. Chancellor Elmer Ellsworth Brown of New York University denied the existence of discrimination at his institution, but President Nicholas Murray Butler of Columbia refused to comment. In Massachusetts, local politicians, perhaps relishing the opportunity to deliver a blow to Harvard, condemned the alleged discrimination. Representative George Webster of the Massachusetts legislature proposed a state investigating commission; Speaker B. L. Young summoned President Lowell to the State House for an explanation; the Boston City Council passed a resolution of censure; and Governor Channing H. Cox finally appointed a legislative committee to inquire into opportunities for higher education in the Commonwealth. The annual convention of the American Federation of Labor, then in session, ordered the Executive Council to take appropriate action against Harvard's proposals.

A minority defended Harvard's right to limit admissions as it saw fit. *World's Work,* the Doubleday publication, said that the problem concerned primarily urban Russian Jews rather than the aristocratic Spanish and German Jews, and that Harvard, if it did not deal frankly with the situation, would soon have a 40 per cent Jewish student body. President Faunce of Brown University claimed that restriction of admission was a necessity. "The idea that any shrewd boy that can by cramming 'get by' on written examinations must thereby be automatically admitted to college is anti-American." Faunce disclaimed discriminatory intentions, but if, he said, there were not enough places to go around, then, "Let us exclude the greedy and overbearing and inconsiderate and disloyal."

Generally, American press opinion was critical of Harvard's actions. This was especially pronounced after it was learned that the new questionnaire for Harvard admission raised, for the first time, the question, "What change, if any, has been made since birth in your own name or that of your father?" An article in the *Atlantic Monthly* called the policy of exclusion unwise, although the author pessimistically predicted that Eastern colleges, faced with the social problem of admitting Jews, or keeping them out and risking a storm of protest, would do the latter. The *Nation* disapproved of the trend toward discriminatory admissions policies and feared that Harvard might set a pattern for other institutions: "The very fact that Harvard is considering a Jewish 'problem' and taking steps that seem to look toward measures of exclusion will be reason enough for scores of lesser colleges more or less avowedly to put up the bars."

Possibly more important than opposition from the general public were signs that some Harvard alumni could not reconcile their alma mater's new attitude with its professed position of leadership in the American intellectual community. As Roger S. Greene, class of 1901, said,

Harvard is not meant to be a glorified private school for the socially eligible. . . . If elements previously strange to our community, elements which are not altogether popular, are beginning to appear at Cambridge in embarrassing numbers, it is because they are now important elements of the American people. We must accept the difficulties involved in our position as a national university or we shall sink to the grade of an insignificant parochial institution.

Rev. Dr. Percy Stickney Grant called on Harvard to become more democratic and John Haynes Holmes expressed outrage that anti-Semitism was "rearing its ugly head in the sacred precincts of this great institution of learning." The temper of Harvard alumni feeling was illustrated also by an incident at the meeting of the Associated Harvard Clubs in Boston. Dr. Clarence C. Little, the newly elected President of the University of Maine, and former Secretary of the Harvard Corporation, demanded an official retraction of reported plans for racial discrimination in admissions. President Emeritus Charles W. Eliot blunted the attack with a reassertion of Harvard's devotion to the principles of racial and religious equality. Eliot frankly admitted that some members of the faculty had become prematurely excited and that there had been a stir on the Jewish question. He advised the alumni to leave the matter in the hands of the faculty committee appointed by President Lowell.

In the meantime, Jewish public opinion had been greatly aroused by the news from Cambridge. Some Jews were satisfied that the national reaction to the Harvard proposals was a "tribute to the soundness of America," but many others agreed with the rabbi who characterized the situation as "the most disturbing manifestation of anti-Semitism in America up to date." The shock was most apparent among the more Americanized Jews; Rabbi David Philipson's comment was revealing: "Had the thing not happened, we would have said with confidence that such a thing could not happen here. It would not have occurred to us in our wildest imaginings." The implications of Harvard's proposals for the status of Jews in America were reinforced by the knowledge, as Rabbi Louis L. Newman wrote, that "If the Jew loses his fight to gain admission to the college campus, he is defeated in a far more significant battle, namely the right to entrance into the higher spheres of the professions and commerce."

Outrage led to invective, and one Jew called Harvard an "intellectual Ku Klux Klan." The Harvard affair led also to the usual self-criticism, with a Jewish fraternity leader calling on his fellows to show the gentiles that Jews were not "ostentatious, greedy or materialistic." Horace Kallen, however, observed that it was not "the failure of the Jews to be assimilated into undergraduate society which troubles them. . . . What really troubles them is the completeness with which the Jews want to be and have been assimilated."

Shortly after the Harvard proposals reached the press, A. A. Benesch—a Cleveland attorney and Harvard graduate, class of 1900—addressed a letter to President Lowell, protesting plans for discriminatory admissions. Lowell's reply offered an interesting explanation of the Harvard authorities' motivation. According to him, anti-Semitic feeling, imported from Europe, was on the rise in the United States. As the number of Jews on campus grew, anti-Semitic feeling grew in proportion, and if the percentage ever reached 40 per cent, feelings would be intense. Lowell concluded that limitation of the Jewish student body would "go a long way toward eliminating race feeling among the students." To this curious argument, Mr. Benesch retorted that anti-Semitic restriction of Jews in order to overcome anti-Semitism could logically be carried to the extent of getting rid of Jews completely. President Lowell, how-

ever, stood his ground, once more alluding to the inescapable "problem of race."

Lowell further clarified his ideas in a letter of declination addressed to a sisterhood in St. Louis:

To some of us it appears that the conditions are drifting in the direction that they have been in for centuries in central and eastern Europe. . . . Some of us here at Harvard feel that this prospect is real, and that something could be done to prevent, in part at least, that segregation of the Jewish race.

He expressed disappointment that Jews had not approved of this worthy object by supporting his plan for restricted admissions.

The controversy grew more heated; a Jewish alumnus of Harvard reported that he had engaged Lowell in conversation during a train trip. According to him, Lowell spoke with great bitterness on the subject of Jews, predicting that in twenty years Jews would be treated as Negroes were in the South, and that the same conditions that existed in central Europe, with Jewish blood being spilled, might reach the United States. He was happy to see that Columbia and New York Universities were reducing their Jewish student quotas. As a way out, he suggested that Jews adopt complete assimilation, including religious conversion and intermarriage. Finally, he was quoted as having remarked that there was no need to complain about Harvard, because at some other colleges "the students duck the Jews in the river." Lowell issued a denial that these views were accurate, but the alumnus vouched for them and offered to produce witnesses who participated in the conversation.

American Jews reacted negatively to Lowell and his ideas. The *American Hebrew* termed his proposal "probably the most humiliating suggestion regarding the Jews that has been made in America," while the *Jewish Tribune* asked for the resignation of Lowell and his staff and for their replacement by men whose Americanism had not been "clouded with Fordism or Ku Kluxism."

[Louis] Marshall[1] was greatly concerned about the Harvard affair. He viewed discrimination by private preparatory schools as relatively insignificant, and in the N.Y.U. affair he had shown displeasure at the behavior of some Jewish students; but the Harvard case, to Marshall, appeared differently. Writing to his sister-in-law, he spoke of a serious outbreak of anti-Semitism in the United States, specifying that he meant Harvard, not Henry Ford. As for President Lowell,

He has played with fire, and has given the sanction of his great office to what, after all, is a vulgar expression of Jew-baiting. . . . We must insist upon equality of right and of treatment. We cannot concede that there is any social aspect to the question. . . . The only tests that we can recognize are those of character and of scholarship. . . . If President Lowell wishes to . . . ally himself with the vilest of European politicians, let him do it. We shall not make the way easy for him to accomplish his disgraceful purpose.

Marshall was informed of the Harvard situation long before it received public attention. His major informant was Judge Julian A. Mack, with whom he continued to work closely in behind-the-scenes maneuvering for a peaceful settlement. In this work, Marshall was fearful that some "Jewish snobs" might be willing to go along with Lowell's proposals. He was even more concerned about the tendency of each Jew to act as a spokesman for the entire people, rushing into print with

platitudinous nonsense, intemperate speech, or unfortunate generalizations. When the *Forward* expressed disappointment that Marshall and the "wealthy west side Jews" were apathetic on the college question, Marshall defended himself by challenging the usefulness of public agitation. "Arguments and persuasion and an appeal to their sense of right and justice are more likely to prove successful." Colonel Isaac Ullman, a leading American Jewish Committee member, remarked that brass bands were not needed.

Mack, Marshall, and the other Jewish leaders preferred to concentrate on the Faculty Committee designated in June, 1922, by the Board of Overseers to investigate and report on "principles and methods for more effective sifting of candidates for admission to the university." The committee consisted of thirteen professors, including three Jews—Paul J. Sachs, Harry A. Wolfson, and Milton Rosenau. It was charged with consulting alumni and prominent Jews throughout the country. Professor Charles H. Grandgent, chairman of the committee, issued an opening statement that supported Lowell's position:

The proportion of Jewish students at the university is greater than that of any other race. Consequently, the problem of restricting Jews, if it is necessary to restrict, is the greatest. The committee will devote a year to the investigation. . . . Today Jews are practically ostracized from social organizations. This prejudice is reflected in the college. If there were fewer Jews, this problem would not be so. I believe this is a racial rather than religious prejudice. . . . Just how to make a sifting of students seeking admittance to the college is most difficult. It seems plain that a college entrance examination would not solve the problem. The Jew is a remarkable student. He is intelligent. The Jewish race as a whole is intelligent. It is astounding the number of Jews from

---

[1] President of the American Jewish Committee. —Ed.

poor districts who enter Harvard and become remarkable students. They are very industrious.

Grandgent's remarks were hardly encouraging, but the committee proceeded to its task with scrupulous fairness. On August 23, 1922, Marshall was visited at his home by members of the Harvard Faculty Committee, including Professor Sachs. Frankly, Marshall told them that if Harvard established a *numerus clausus* for Jews, it might be "responsible for a new group of pogroms and for stimulating anti-Semitism in the United States, as well as abroad, to an extent that can scarcely be estimated." The college had every right to apply scholarship and character tests for admission, but nothing else. If it excluded applicants on racial or religious grounds, the result would be "a calamity to the United States and a menace to the Jews of the world." The impact of Marshall's warning is hard to measure, but he believed he made an impression on the committee. At the same time, Marshall and his friends busily steered the committee members to other prominent Jews, including the Straus family.

On April 9, 1923, the Harvard Faculty Committee on Admissions presented its report to the Board of Overseers, which unanimously endorsed it. The Committee recommended that Harvard maintain its policy of "equal opportunity for all, regardless of race or religion," that admissions policies be continued free of all forms of discrimination, and that no "novel process of scrutiny" be adopted. The report was a sharp repudiation of the proposals originally made in June, 1922.

The Harvard Committee's report was hailed by the press and most observers as a great moral victory. Defeated in its most blatant form, Lowell's restriction of Jewish enrollment nevertheless was accomplished indirectly through the use of differential standards on entrance examinations and other technical methods. Candidates attaining 75 per cent on Harvard's entrance examinations were admitted automatically, but those who scored between 60 and 75 per cent were admitted at the discretion of the admissions board. In 1926, Harvard announced a new admissions policy, limiting the freshman class to 1,000 and instituting careful screening procedures, including photographs, character testimonials, and personal interviews. The *Harvard Crimson,* while admitting that "Harvard's most precious quality" was its heterogeneity, editorially supported the new policy with a veiled reference to Jews: "If non-assimilable elements in the college tend to choke the freedom of the rest, their numbers should be reduced. Commuting students are an example of this class, racial groups another." President Lowell refused to repudiate these new procedures, despite the intervention of Judge Mack.

Similar conditions prevailed at many other universities. Columbia was reported to have maintained its proportion of Jewish students at no more than 20 per cent. In 1927, commenting on the existence of considerable anti-Jewish prejudice among Cornell students, Marshall remarked, "these conditions exist quite generally in most Eastern colleges and universities." There was some prejudice in the Syracuse public schools when he was a boy, Marshall recalled, but it was a trifle compared to the college situation in the post-war years.

Within colleges themselves, the problem of social exclusion continued to demand attention. Jewish students, for example, had experienced fraternity difficulties even before the war, and the problem was aggravated during the 1920's. In general, Marshall was strongly opposed to fraternities, for "booze and sex and their concomitants seem to constitute the be-all and end-all of their mental lucubration." He was, therefore, not particularly disturbed by the fraternity question:

College fraternities are a curse, and . . . more good men have been ruined by their association with these silly organizations than from any other one cause. While it is always unpleasant to be the subject or object of discrimination, I have entertained the belief that it has been rather fortunate that the Jews are not readily admitted to Fraternities. It will not injure their habits or their diligence or their scholarship if they are kept out. There is just one misfortune in this regard and that is that it has brought about the organization of Jewish fraternities which, so far as my observation goes, are even worse than those of the other creeds.

Joining their own fraternities, however, seemed to many Jewish students the only effective answer to exclusion from other groups. The twenties, therefore, saw the formation of many new chapters of these segregated fraternities.

When President Faunce of Brown University refused to grant permission for the establishment of a Jewish fraternity because it might kindle racial antagonism, Marshall became quite incensed. His opinions of fraternities, in general, and the Jewish kind, in particular, had not changed, "but to have it declared from high places that the Jewish students shall not have the right to form their frats that has been accorded to non-Jewish students, is a doctrine which cannot be accepted by self-respecting men." Marshall did not want to engage in a public campaign on this question, but he wrote to Faunce, asking him if Jewish fraternities were "dimming the light of learning, or muddying the stream of knowledge, or interfering with the flow of goodwill, by seeking a more limited brotherhood because a broader spirit of fraternity is denied to them." Faunce, however, refused to be moved, even after Marshall spoke to him personally in Washington. Eventually, a compromise solution was worked out, allowing the formation of an unofficial Jewish fraternity.

One reaction to the Harvard affair and the increase of academic anti-Semitism was a renewal of appeals for the creation of a Jewish university in America. Rabbi Louis I. Newman, one of the foremost advocates of this idea, pointed to a growing intolerance in American life, and argued that a university would be no different from the segregated camps, clubs, and fraternities which already existed. Although he had some support, most Jews rejected the proposal as a cowardly surrender and a compromise of the principle of Jewish equality.

Marshall was greatly annoyed by talk of a separate Jewish university. A Jewish university, he predicted, would be an "unqualified misfortune"; it would be a glorified ghetto, eliminating the advantages of contact with the outside world, and would stimulate hostility to Jews and give an excuse for continued discrimination at other universities. Marshall was also opposed to the foundation of a Yeshiva College in New York, because it might convert the Jew into a "self-created alien," and would undoubtedly "do much to harm the best interests of the Jews in America."

Father Coughlin was the best-known American antisemite in the 1930s, but millions of his countrymen, including, as DAVID J. O'BRIEN (b. 1938) indicates, many Catholics, shared his attitudes. Catholic periodicals like *Commonweal* and *The Catholic Worker,* as well as a significant proportion of Catholic laymen and church officials, opposed both Coughlin and his antisemitic views, but their objections received less publicity than the opinions of the celebrated priest. O'Brien, who teaches history at Holy Cross College, has written extensively about various aspects of American Catholic history, including *American Catholics and Social Reform* (1968). He contends, in the essay below, that Catholics were convinced that communism was a greater evil than fascism. Furthermore, he maintains that they deplored the fact that German atrocities toward Jews received so much condemnation while Russian and Mexican treatment of Catholics was all but ignored in American periodicals. O'Brien believes that large numbers of Catholics were—and are—"susceptible to demagogic appeals" because of their "largely self-imposed minority consciousness." Can you think of any other reasons for their susceptibility to antisemitic propaganda?*

David J. O'Brien

American Catholics and Antisemitism in the 1930s

The current reassessment of the Catholic record during the Third Reich has been relatively unmarred in the United States by the self-conscious defensiveness and emotionalism surrounding such affairs in the past. While many contemporary spokesmen have taken sharp issue with Rolf Hochhuth's characterization of Pope Pius XII and his treatment of historical materials, few have charged him with bigotry or with seeking to weaken the Catholic Church. Guenter Lewy's study of *The Catholic Church and Nazi Germany* (McGraw-Hill, 1964), far from being condemned as anti-Catholic, has been widely admired for its scholarship and impartiality.

Amid the goodwill and ecumenical spirit governing discussion of the issues raised by Hochhuth, it is easy to lose sight of the rancor which dominated such controversies in the recent past. Criticism

* David J. O'Brien, "American Catholics and Anti-Semitism in the 1930's," *Catholic World,* 204 (February, 1967), 270–276. Reprinted by permission of the author and the publisher.

of Vatican or ecclesiastical policy in the 1930's, for example, was interpreted by Catholic leaders as tantamount to direct attack upon the Church, the pope and themselves. Father Francis Talbot, writing during the Spanish Civil War, concluded in *America,* October 23, 1937, that the nation's liberals were always "Catholic baiters" anxious to divide and weaken the Church, while Cincinnati's Archbishop McNicholas in *Catholic Mind,* April 8, 1937, charged that they had "no real convictions and no real stamina of character." Patrick Scanlan of the Brooklyn *Tablet* echoed the feelings of many of his fellow Catholics when he wrote in the January 17, 1931 issue of the *Tablet* that American liberals "hate the Church just as bitterly, just as ignorantly and just as unfairly as any Klansman."

Similarly the new spirit of dialogue obscures the extent to which American Catholics shared the shortcomings of their European brethren of three decades ago. The confusion of national and religious values, the emphasis on prudence at the expense of justice and charity, and the view of Communism as the embodiment of anti-Christian forces, all these tendencies existed among American Catholics as they did within the German Catholic community. Catholics in America, like many elsewhere, were sure that Communism constituted a far greater menace to God and country than did Fascism, and they too saw the struggle in Spain as a confrontation of Christ and anti-Christ. Their responses to events had some unique characteristics, as Allen Guttmann—in *The Wound in the Heart* (Free Press, 1962)— has demonstrated in regard to the Spanish Civil War; but the basic problem of defining the Christian position in the face of the brutality of modern war and mass society remained the same, whether set in Germany, Spain, or the United States.

Although the record of the American Church on anti-Semitism in the thirties was perhaps somewhat brighter than on other issues of the day, the question may be of immediate interest. Recent commentators have been willing to admit the responsibility of all Christians for the destruction of Europe's Jewish population; but they have sometimes overlooked the more direct responsibility of American Catholics for the treatment of their Jewish neighbors at home and for their failure to present an adequate response to the rise of the Nazi evil. While proportionately few Catholics took part in the anti-Semitic activities of the decade in this country, the presence of such activity and the Catholic response to it were for many a source of scandal and despair.

Dislike of Jews has always been present in the United States and anti-Semitism has been a characteristic of nativists from the Know Nothings to the Ku Klux Klan. Populist orators often drew upon the symbol of the Jewish banker in their warfare against Wall Street and the money power. In the 1930's more serious assaults took place, and they were not confined to Fascists like Gerald Winrod or to the western plains. Gangs attacked Jews on the streets of Brooklyn and other eastern cities with little interference from the police, while organizations calling themselves the Christian Front or the Christian Mobilizers conducted "Buy Christian" campaigns, cheered the Fuehrer and denounced prominent American Jews. The American hero of these groups was a Catholic priest, the radio voice of Royal Oak, Michigan, Father Charles E. Coughlin.

Early in the Depression Father Coughlin had emerged as one of the nation's most powerful men, the champion of the common man and the "shepherd of discontent." His Sunday radio sermons on socio-economic topics had a huge audience; at his call letters and telegrams flooded Congress, and his was generally acknowledged to be the "most persuasive voice in America." He lashed out at the greed and hypocrisy of the old order, its low wages, its unstable farm prices, its financial speculation. Franklin Roosevelt welcomed his support in 1932 and in the early days of his administration. Calling for active government assistance to relieve the distress caused by the Depression, he assisted his listeners in making the transition from the traditional American fear of federal action to the positive government initiated by the New Deal. As a Catholic priest, he did more to popularize knowledge of the social encyclicals than all previous American spokesmen combined. His indictment of the plutocracy and support for inflationary schemes, together with his role as a priest, enabled him to draw support both from western farms and industrial cities, areas sharply divided in the days of Prohibition and the Klan.

Gradually, however, he drifted away from the New Deal and from the sources of his support. Adopting the debtor-oriented schemes of the earlier populists, he became increasingly dogmatic, insisting that drastic fiscal reorganization was a prerequisite for any just and lasting social reform. He identified the monetization of silver and the destruction of the Federal Reserve System with the dictates of Christianity and became increasingly critical of New Deal hesitations and half measures. The Administration's refusal to carry through drastic monetary reforms he took as evidence of its continuing alliance with the plutocracy, while its labor policies and the increased centralization of government he began to denounce as Communistic. Intensified by personal slights, these disagreements culminated in the radio

orator's break with Roosevelt and his organization of a new political party to contest the presidential election of 1936. Father Coughlin challenged his Catholic followers traditional loyalty to the Democratic party and their gratitude to Roosevelt for the substantial gains they received at the hands of the New Deal. On the other hand he challenged as well the traditional suspicion of the Church and its clergy among his agrarian Protestant followers. It was a desperate gamble and Coughlin lost; with the overwhelming defeat of his candidates he retired from the air, disillusioned with the American people of whom he had thought himself the spokesman. But several months later he was back, determined to save the nation from the consequences of its action in choosing the politicians, the plutocrats and the Communists over Christian and American principles.

In the late thirties Father Coughlin became even more desperate, predicting the early advent of a Communist society in the United States and finding indications in the penetration by the "reds" into all sectors of American life. But there was a new element in his thought, one that had been implicit earlier and which admirably served to tie together the twin evils of Communism and plutocracy: anti-Semitism. Most, though not all, of the financial oligarchy were Jewish, he discovered. They controlled the press and propagandized against Christians, most notably during the Spanish Civil War. They were also the key figures in the Communist movement, having dominated the Russian Revolution and subsequent party activity. Nazism, like Fascism before it, was a "defense mechanism" against Communism; to prevent a "red" takeover Hitler, Mussolini and Franco had acted "as patriots rising to a challenge," he said in *Social Justice,* November 20, 1936. Fascism, Coughlin contended through his weekly paper, *Social Justice,* "was and is Europe's answer to Russian Communism's threat of world revolution, and it is the bulwark against long active agencies of destruction."

The Jews were persecuted abroad, according to Father Coughlin, because of their association with Communism and their lack of patriotism. For the same reasons they would eventually suffer in the United States, he believed, particularly if they continued to demand action against Nazism while ignoring the plight of Christians under persecution in Russia, Mexico and Spain. He reminded them that to destroy Nazism it was first necessary to eliminate its cause, Russian Communism. He denied that he was anti-Semitic; for him it was "not a question of anti-Semitism; it is a question of anti-Communism."

Father Coughlin professed to desire to save the Jews from themselves. "Anti-Semitism is spreading in America," he wrote in *Social Justice,* December 5, 1938, "because the people sense a closely interwoven relationship between Communism and Jewry. . . . It is the *duty* of American Christians to aid their Jewish fellow citizens in shaking off Communism before it is too late." He claimed that he was not opposed to "religious Jews," only to those who supported Communism. As early as 1936, he called upon the Jews to abandon the law of "an eye for an eye" and to adopt the law of Christ. Later he admitted that the real need was for Jews to "openly profess the divinity of Christ" and that there would always be a "Jewish problem" so long as they would not accept the "spiritual brotherhood of Christ." In his organ, *Social Justice,* Coughlin reprinted the discredited *Protocols of Zion;* invited the contributions of Nazi sympathizer, George Sylvester Viereck; attributed the

disasters of modern history to Jewish influence; and in sum, conformed to the public image of an anti-Semite. Repeating the arguments again and again, the radio priest became the rallying point for pro-Nazi and anti-Jewish organizations, all the while denying any particular dislike of the Jews or admiration for the Nazis.

As in his earlier economic talks, Coughlin avoided too great an emphasis on specifically Catholic support for his position, instead relying on the general Christian symbols which had proven so effective earlier. His favorite reference was to the work of an Irish priest, Father Denis Fahey, who in turn relied on continental and British Catholic anti-Semitic sources. Coughlin, however, shied away from Fahey's view of the world as a battleground between the mystical body of Christ and a corresponding spiritual union of Satanic forces, for such a framework would have allied him with the visible Church rather than with the broad Christian consensus whose fundamentalist wing supplied recruits both for monetary panaceas and anti-Jewish crusades. But the vision of the world as the scene of struggle between good and evil was basic to all Coughlin's rhetoric. Again and again when distinguishing his policies from those of his enemies, he challenged his listeners to choose between "God's side" or that of "His Enemy who goeth about like a roaring lion . . . roaring in the press, roaring on the radio, roaring on the silver screen." Thus, whether the issue was re-evaluation of gold, the New Deal, the CIO, or the Spanish War, the choice was always "civilization or Communism; Christ or chaos."

In addition to Father Coughlin, there was another source of Catholic anti-Semitic propaganda in the United States in the 1930's, less influential but more explicitly Catholic. Edward Koch of Germantown, Illinois, edited a monthly magazine, *The Guildsman,* through which he attempted to spread knowledge of the corporate social thought of the German Catholic social movement. Koch was vigorously anti-capitalist and regularly attacked Catholics who supported labor unions or social legislation, both of which, he believed, only perpetuated the existence of immoral capitalism and delayed the introduction of a social system based on a hierarchy of functional groups. A strong supporter of Franco and an apologist for Fascism, Koch upheld dictatorship as a method of overcoming private interests and introducing the new order. He admired the economic and diplomatic accomplishments of the Third Reich and praised Hitler's *Mein Kampf* for its devotion to German greatness and its concern for the common people. He thought he detected in Hitler's writings the influence of Pius XI's *Quadragesimo Anno* and of the Austrian social Catholics, Lueger and Vogelsang. He drew on German and Austrian sources to excuse the persecution of the Jews, who rejected "everything distinctly Christian," controlled the socialist movement, and represented the "money power." He argued that all supporters of the unjust social order were opposed to Hitler and used the defense of democracy as a shield for their exploitation. He denied that the Church had everything to gain from democracy and attacked Catholics who combatted Nazism or anti-Semitism. After the war had begun in Europe he predicted that, if successful, Hitler and Mussolini would "initiate a new Christian civilization."

Koch's writings were scarcely noticed, but Coughlin's work was a source of division and difficulty for the Catholic community. *Commonweal,* whose editors were regarded as traitors by Coughlin and his supporters because of the magazine's opposition to Franco, from the be-

ginning consistently denounced anti-Semitism, Coughlin, and the Christian Front. The *Catholic Worker* likewise was openly opposed to the priest and took the lead in combatting anti-Semitism, distributing a press service of news of Catholic opposition to persecution of the Jews. John Ryan and George Shuster both publicly refuted Coughlin's charges against the Jews while Father Joseph N. Moody rebutted the old canards of Jewish financial power and Jewish radicalism. A group of liberal Catholics formed an organization to fight anti-Semitism and published a new journal for this purpose, *The Voice.* Cardinal Mundelein of Chicago stated that Coughlin was not authorized to speak for, and his views did not represent, "the doctrines and sentiments of the Church." Several other prelates, including Milwaukee's Archbishop Stritch and Coughlin's own superior, Archbishop Mooney, spoke out forcefully against anti-Semitism.

For others, repudiation of Father Coughlin was less easy. Coughlin had skillfully tied his anti-Semitism to the issue of Communism and to the fears of the Catholic minority of the supposed bigotry of non-Catholic America. Opposition to Communism provided him with a convenient point of reconciliation with those Catholics who disliked his earlier activities. Cardinal O'Connell of Boston had deplored Coughlin's appeals to class hatred and his involvement in politics in the first half of the decade. Later Coughlin was denouncing the New Deal and the unions as Communistic because they set class against class and declaring that politicians and parties could never come to grips with America's problems. His about-face and his focus on the Communist issue provided a firm basis for alliance with other Catholics who, though they might deplore his anti-Semitism, found little occasion to condemn him by name and undoubtedly welcomed his powerful support in their battle to avoid involvement in a war against Germany, a war which most agreed could only help the Communists.

With very few exceptions, American Catholic spokesmen agreed with Coughlin's major premise that, in the present as well as in the future, Communism was a greater menace to the Church and to America than was Nazism or Fascism. As Father Parsons of *America* put it, the Church opposed the Nazis on political and economic grounds in the name of democracy while it opposed Communism on religious grounds in the name of God. Bishop Noll of Fort Wayne, who had denied support of Coughlin in 1936, later praised his work and endorsed his call for a "Christian Front" against Communist penetration in the United States. The bishop's fear, like that of many of his fellow Catholics, was that the nation was being led into war against Fascism while neglecting the Communist menace. "There has been such a vigorous campaign against Fascism in the American press and furthered by numerous groups of men and women," Bishop Noll wrote in 1939, "that the attention of the people has been at least temporarily withdrawn from the even greater evil of Communism."

American Catholics were hurt and puzzled by the failure of their countrymen to share their view of events in Mexico, Spain and, later, their view of the war. Widespread indifference to the persecution of the Church in Mexico was seen by Catholics as evidence of the continued existence of the bigotry they had witnessed in 1928. The Mexican situation was a sore-point in relations between Catholics and other groups throughout the decade and provided a foundation of bitterness on which the intense feelings about Spain could be built. The Civil War

was seen by Catholics as a clearcut choice between Christianity and Communism; opposition to Franco was not only pro-Communist and un-American, it was anti-Catholic as well. When George Shuster abandoned Franco for neutrality, he came under the most bitter and personal attacks. *America's* Father Talbot accused him of incompetence and even the gentle Father John LaFarge was led to compare the *Commonweal* editor to Nero, standing by neutral while the Church was destroyed.

The same individuals and groups who had ignored the fate of the Church in Mexico and were actively supporting the anti-Catholic forces in Spain appeared to Catholics to be the leading sympathizers with the persecuted German Jews. Even Father James M. Gillis of *The Catholic World*, among the most outspoken opponents of anti-Semitism, deplored the fact that Catholics under persecution did not receive the same understanding and support as their Jewish counterparts. At the other end of the Catholic spectrum, the Brooklyn *Tablet* had long decried the sympathy for the Jews among those who showed little concern for Catholics. The *Tablet* became Coughlin's leading supporter in the east, resisting efforts to suppress anti-Semitism and supporting the Christian Front which had been organized under Coughlin's inspiration, though he evaded responsibility for its actions.

In Brooklyn, anti-Semitism found a solid social foundation. The Irish population, which had arrived in the city in the mid-nineteenth century, had risen to the lower middle class, but as Daniel Moynihan has pointed out, they were slow in ascending beyond this level of the social scale while their Jewish neighbors, arriving far later, rapidly attained comparable and even higher status. The resulting tensions were felt for years and came to the fore in the thirties. Patrick Scanlan of the

Tablet gave expression of those feelings when he asked of the editors of *The Voice,* the Catholic journal which combatted anti-Semitism: "Why do they not assail the discrimination against the Germans, Italians, Irish and other races of New York who are fast being reduced to the most inconspicuous places?" It was in this context that the incendiary writings of Father Coughlin were received and acted upon; though he might deny being anti-Semitic, he was sure to be taken seriously in an area predisposed to view the Jews with dislike and suspicion. The priest himself was not reluctant to play upon Catholic frustrations, urging "the spineless Christians of America to wake up and demand that their coreligionists in other parts of the world be offered the same protection, the same sympathy and the same comfort which four million American Jews demand for their co-nationals."

Convinced that Communism was a greater danger than Fascism, Catholics were naturally suspicious of opposition to Germany on the part of those who appeared to ignore the totalitarianism and aggression of Soviet Russia. Resentful of the indifference of their countrymen to the murder of priests and nuns at the hands of the "Reds," a picture forcefully drawn by their hierarchy and press, Catholics were not likely to be attracted to action against the Fascists states based upon their persecution of the Jews or their infringement of civil liberties. At the same time that Catholics were becoming increasingly anti-Communist, however, their fellow Americans were awakening to the dangers of Nazism, a development which intensified the ever-present self-consciousness and sense of isolation of American Catholics. In this situation Father Coughlin's activity was particularly deplorable. His skillful argument fixing responsibility on the Jews for Catholic isolation and the drift toward war were

sure to seem plausible to some Catholics. Those who resisted the anti-Semitic conclusions, on the other hand, were fearful of dividing the Catholic body in the face of war pressures on the part of individuals and groups who were thought to be anti-Catholic and pro-Communist.

Yet the failure to condemn Father Coughlin exacerbated the very conditions which were thought to make unity essential. The honest fears of many Americans that the Church was moving toward an accord with Fascism were given added weight by the refusal of his superiors to discipline Father Coughlin and the failure of much of the Catholic press unequivocally to disassociate itself from him. Archbishop Mooney may have feared another McGlynn scandal, a possibility which *Social Justice* had raised in 1937. Others, with far less grounds for inaction, were too preoccupied with their own fears of Communism and bigotry to recognize and repudiate the priest's propaganda. Whatever the motives involved, Coughlin's presence and his popularity in some heavily Catholic areas constituted a standing rebuke to the Church in America.

For Catholics of another generation, the memory of Father Coughlin's work and the Catholic response to it offers a warning against self-righteousness and a reminder that American Catholics of thirty years ago were no more courageous in facing their problems than were their German brethren. Too many American Catholics were—and remain—susceptible to demagogic appeals to the fears and frustrations arising from a largely self-imposed minority consciousness. Realization of this, like awareness of the German experience, is only of value if it assists the development of a real and vital sense of Christian commitment rising above the limitations of exclusive national, racial or sectarian loyalties.

In his investigations of Negro-Jewish relations KENNETH B. CLARK (b. 1914), professor of psychology at the City College of the City University of New York, president of the Metropolitan Applied Research Center, Inc., and author of *Prejudice and Your Child* (1963), *The Negro Protest* (1963), and *Dark Ghetto* (1965), finds evidence of mutual antipathy. Although he details numerous incidents of Jewish discrimination and Negro concern, how much attention does he give to Jewish anxiety about Negro activities? Is Clark's analysis still relevant today? Have any other black concerns emerged since 1946 which are not discussed in this essay?*

Kenneth B. Clark

Candor About Negro-Jewish Relations

Three Negro women appeared before a mediating panel of clergymen with complaints that a Jewish butcher was "refusing to sell meat to many Negro residents of the neighborhood, but selling to white Irish Catholics who live outside of the area but formerly lived within it." Furthermore: "The complainants report that this sort of discriminatory practice occurs elsewhere in the neighborhood— that in two instances angry Negro customers threatened the storekeeper—and in one instance also injured the storekeeper so that he was obliged to close up for a few days."

The following quotation appeared last January in a national Negro newspaper. Leading Negro women of the community —commenting on the Baltimore department. store situation—stated:

It is a poor excuse for Jewish merchants who own and control the major downtown department stores which set the policy in Baltimore to say their patrons force them to employ discriminatory practices against Negroes. . . .

Boycott and picket is the real solution to the problem. In this way we can call attention to the Jewish merchants who are guilty of Hitlerism here in Baltimore.

Some Negro domestics assert that Jewish housewives who employ them are unreasonable and brazenly exploitative. A Negro actor states in bitter terms that he is being flagrantly underpaid by a

Jewish producer. A Negro entertainer is antagonistic to his Jewish agent who (he is convinced) is exploiting him. He vents his feelings to his friends, but admits that "If the Jews didn't get us bookings or parts we wouldn't work—but they make a gold mine out of us."

Antagonism toward the "Jewish landlord" is so common as to have become almost an integral aspect of the folk culture of the northern urban Negro. To him, almost all landlords are automatically Jewish and all his obvious housing ills are attributed to the greed and avarice of the "Jewish landlord."

In short, in practically every area of contact between the Negro and Jewish peoples some real or imagined grounds for mutual antagonism exist. Undoubtedly, many personal relationships between Jews and Negroes are exceptions to the general pattern, and among highly politically or intellectually developed Negroes and Jews there is little overt indication of antagonism. Yet on the whole the picture cannot be considered a favorable one.

One Jewish Approach

Efforts are being made to remedy the situation. Whether these efforts are well advised is, however, another question. And it is most certainly open to question whether, well-meaning as they may be, they have any vital effect. Let us cite a single case in point.

In the latter part of November 1945, an Institute on Judaism and Race Relations was called by the Commission on Justice and Peace of the Central Conference of American Rabbis. Its stated purpose was "to aid in the preparation of a statement relating the teachings of the prophets of Israel to the problems of race in the modern world." One of the six round tables of which the Institute was composed concerned itself with the problems of "the Negro in the United States."

It was felt by the writer that on-the-spot observation and analysis of this particular round table might provide some valuable insights into the problem of Jewish-Negro relations. So far, the social psychologist has not made enough use of direct observation of real-life social interaction as a way of developing and checking his interpretations.

The round table on "The Negro in the United States" began by analyzing and modifying a statement prepared by its chairman. This statement, as originally presented, contained the following: (1) an introductory paragraph pointing out the relation between Nazi excesses against Jews and the Jews' understanding of the suffering of others—"... because our religion is based upon the belief in the *oneness* of humanity; because our trials and suffering have given us both understanding and unusual sympathy, we are perhaps in a position to appreciate fully the plight of the Africans and Asiatics under white imperialism and especially the plight of our Negro brothers"; (2) a section listing social status gains made by Negroes during the war; (3) a list of the more obvious injustices the Negro still suffers in spite of the listed "gains"; (4) a general statement about the need for a just society free from racial jingoism and exploitation.

Most of the ensuing discussion dwelt on small points of terminology, coherence and language. And the conclusions finally agreed upon by the round table did not differ significantly from the chairman's statement. However, the final statement by the editorial committee of the Institute varied from that of the round table discussion by eliminating the introductory paragraph and reducing the final paragraph to the following: "These considerations are valid for all Americans. Because they are so deeply consonant with Jewish teaching and reinforced by Jewish experience, we shall lend our strongest efforts to secure justice for the Negro."

It is significant that in neither the original statement nor the one finally released was any mention made of the specific problems of Jewish-Negro relations as such. There appeared to be a general reluctance to deal with those aspects of Negro life in America that directly and concretely involved Negro-Jewish relations.

Avoiding the Issue

Rabbi Ferdinand M. Isserman of Temple Israel, St. Louis, Missouri, chairman of the Commission on Justice and Peace, joined the round table for a few hours during its discussions and made strenuous attempts to get the group to include in that portion of the statement dealing with the injustices toward Negroes a specific statement about anti-Negro practices in Jewish hospitals and certain department stores. He stated: "We must point the fingers at ourselves too. Jewish hospitals have followed the prevailing discrimination against Negroes in the selection of students, nurses, internes, and staff members. . . . We could direct an appeal to Jewish hospitals to admit Negroes as patients and members of their staffs."

Another member of the panel said that the problem of "department stores owned by members of our congregation" who discriminate against Negroes (particularly in border cities such as Baltimore) had him "baffled." He was even more disturbed because he found that "Negroes

were more bitter toward Jewish owners than toward non-Jewish owners who discriminated against them."

Another member declared that he was "not too sure" whether these specific recommendations were "pertinent" to the statement under consideration. It was agreed, however, at the insistence of Rabbi Isserman, that some specific statement about discriminatory practices in "Jewish hospitals" should be included in the statement.

After Rabbi Isserman left, the question of specific mention of discrimination in Jewish hospitals was reopened. It was felt that the group was not justified in singling out Jewish institutions; they were not the only ones guilty of discrimination against Negroes. Instead of a specific statement on this point, the final, very general, summary statement quoted above was suggested to "take care of this."

It was at this point, too, that one of the participants, who had not taken too active a part before, said: "We have been discussing the problems of the Negro as if his condition was to be blamed on others. . . . Shouldn't we point out somewhere in the statement that the Negro should assume some responsibility to help himself? We can help them by showing them that they can help themselves—we can help them by pointing out their deficiencies." This suggestion was met by what appeared to be embarrassed silence. Then another participant, who had demurred against the singling-out of Jewish hospitals and proposed the substitution of the summary statement, said: "If I were a Negro and saw such a statement coming from a Jewish group I would be morally indignant. It would be the extreme of poor taste for a group such as this to make such a statement publicly. . . . There are things which we can say to our Negro friends in private that we cannot say for public consumption." And there the matter ended and the round table closed.

The round table well reflected the dilemma of Jewish-Negro relations in contemporary American society. Here were a number of Jewish persons, all armed with the best intentions, and yet unable to free themselves from prevailing American attitudes toward the Negro. Most typically perhaps this attitude reveals itself in condescension. On the face of it, it appears commendable that one minority group should be concerned with the status of another oppressed group. But the question arises as to what Jews and others would think if a conference of Negro leaders were to devote a round table to the problem of "The Jew in the United States."

Some parts of the originally prepared statement also revealed either a basic lack of understanding of the nuances of the American Negro's position or an unconscious acceptance of an attitude toward him not significantly different from the prevailing attitude. The following part of the original statements seems particularly pertinent here:

"The war against fascism has been marked by some gains for our Negro citizens. Among these . . . the opportunity given Negroes in our fighting forces to display their fine heroism and their patriotism. . . ."

Now the status of Negroes in the armed forces happens to be a humiliating one and not compatible at all with such terms as "opportunity," "heroism" or "patriotism" It fits the pattern of institutionalized fascist racism far more closely.

At no time during these discussions did an almost elemental point seem to be clearly understood: that mere generalities highly charged with moralizing senti-ment mentality cannot bring about desired social changes. It is obviously true that the problems of the Jew and the Negro in America have moral implications, but they cannot be dealt with by mere words. In fact, moral verbalization has often been used precisely to cloak the perpetuation of injustice.

No, what we need here are facts, first of all, and then concrete action. But what are the facts?

Some of the Facts

An investigation of inter-group attitudes in one of the larger, more isolated communities that make up metropolitan New York, found that nearly 60 per cent of Jews held some unfavorable stereotyped reaction toward Negroes and 70 per cent of Negroes had some unfavorable stereotyped reaction toward Jews. Those Jews who looked unfavorably upon Negroes felt that they "have no ambition—they are lazy—they drink a lot—they have low intelligence—they are low class, rowdy, dirty, and noisy." Negroes antagonistic toward Jews tended to feel that "Jews own everything—they are more aggressive—they engage in sharp business practices."

The findings of many studies of racial attitudes, particularly among college students, show in general that Jewish students are relatively less negative in their attitudes toward Negroes than are average Gentile whites. On the other hand, the average Negro student tends to have the same general stereotype of the Jew that the Gentile white has.

This pattern of relationship between Jews and Negroes as a whole has been used to prove "the fact" that prejudice is normal and inescapable. "You see, even

members of a minority group are antagonistic to other minorities—Jews don't
let Negroes enter their hotels; why should
they expect Gentiles to permit Jews into
theirs?" The only aim of such reasoning,
however, is to justify majority prejudice
against minorities in general. It is another
version of "divide and conquer."

Against this, the most prevalent "positive" attitude in the speeches and articles
of "right-thinking" Jews and Negroes
consists in *bemoaning and deploring the
facts*. "This should not be—we must work
together—Negroes and Jews should stand
together and fight." This attitude, however, contributes little either to an understanding of the facts or to the solution of
the basic problem.

A second attitude is that of *denying
the facts*. It attempts to emphasize the
common bonds between Jews and Negroes: "Jews are fighting with Negroes
for full civic, political and economic
rights—Jews and Negroes are friends—
there is no real problem between our
two peoples."

Still a third attitude is one of *ignoring
the facts*. This makes it possible for each
group to concern itself with its own peculiar problems, independent of those
of the other group. It is an attitude that
seems to be basic in the work-a-day activities of established Jewish and Negro
organizations. An elaborate research institute formed by a national Jewish organization admitted that it had under-
taken a project to improve Jewish-Gentile
relations in a border city under the expressed condition, laid down by some of
the white Gentile participants, that the
problem of Negro-white relations was *not*
to be raised. This was a city in which at
the time there was intense feeling among
Negroes against "Jewish" department
store owners. The Institute implicitly
justified its decision on the ground that

the problems of Negro-white and Negro-
Jewish relations were secondary to the
problem of Jewish-Gentile relations.

A final attitude is the fatalistic one of
accepting the facts. This admits the sad
facts but assumes that not much can be
done about them. This state of mind can
arise from intellectual cynicism, or from
a deep-going political-economic view of
the causes of social psychopathologies,
or from resigned acceptance of all social
realities that do not constitute an immediate threat.

The Cost of Insecurity

There still appears to be need for an objective analysis of the active factors involved in the pattern of Jewish-Negro
relations. Through such an analysis, one
ought to arrive at an understanding upon
which a real program for improvement on
both sides could be founded.

Here one crucial fact must always be
kept in mind. To be sure, each group has
a relatively insecure status in the dominant American culture; each suffers from
the psychological threats of humiliation;
each has been the victim of organized
bigotry. But it is naive to assume that,
because Negroes and Jews are each in
their own way oppressed and insecure,
this will necessarily lead to a feeling of
kinship and understanding. Actually, the
psychological reactions of individuals
to insecurity are not so simple and direct.
The common ground of insecurity itself
may lead to antagonism toward individuals sharing that insecurity. It may
also lead to an intensification of fear,
suspicion and active hostility as each
group competes in efforts to escape rele-
gation to the lowest status.

For in each group there may be a feeling—usually unexpressed—that the pres-

ence of another rejected group will deflect the full brunt of the antagonism of the majority from itself. The other group may be looked upon as a buffer—but with protective value only as long as its marginal, insecure status persists.

Further, it appears that insecurity arising from racial and religious persecution tends to develop and intensify a protective ethnocentricism that makes for antagonism toward all other groups, including other minority groups.

Another thread in this whole complex pattern is the tendency of each rejected minority to seek some basis for identification and contact with the attitudes of the dominant majority, especially if by so doing it is able to escape subjectively and temporarily the full impact of its own minority status. Anti-Semitic whites not infrequently involve some Negroes in their bigoted conversations. When a Gentile white condescendingly says to a Negro, "Why John, you are closer to us whites than those dirty Jews are," the Negro is strongly tempted to take advantage of this admittedly shaky and temporary bridge to the self-validation otherwise denied him by caste prejudice. By the same token, a Jew may establish an equally fragile bond with the Gentile white by discussing the "shiftlessness and unreliability of Negro servants and porters," or "the catastrophe it would be to let Negro families move into 'white' neighborhoods."

Nor should one ignore the amount of ego satisfaction an insecure Jew or Negro gains from his antagonism to members of the other group. It serves to compensate him for his own feeling of inferiority. The part played by personal instability and neuroticism in feeding racial prejudice has not been adequately explored. It does seem, however, that the need for personal status and for a good opinion of oneself—based on the inferiority of others—is often more intense in a person belonging to a group that is generally rejected.

Another, even less tangible factor, is that of projected self-hatred. If the attitude of the dominant society is predominantly negative to one's own group the members of that group may be influenced even to the point of hating themselves as a group. This self-hatred, being in direct conflict with one's need for self-respect, may be repressed and may disguise itself in the form of hostility toward another minority group.

In any specific situation, any one or more of the factors in this theoretical analysis may emerge in one proportion or another.

The Negro's Handicap

For additional clarity let us examine some of the specific problems involved in Jewish-Negro relations in the light of the economic, political, and social realities of the contemporary power-pressure culture of America.

L. D. Reddick, writing on "Anti-Semitism Among Negroes" in the *Negro Quarterly,* summer of 1942, states: ". . . essentially the 'Jewish struggle' and the 'Negro struggle' are one."

Such a statement ignores the very wide difference between Jewish and Negro social, political, and economic status. Many Jews have won economic and political eminence. Jews have become Supreme Court Justices, Presidential advisers, etc.; Jews have been able to establish some sort of economic stability in spite of severe discrimination. These facts are known to the Jewish people at large and afford them some basis for positive group self-respect. Negroes too are aware of these facts and are not likely to see the Jewish plight as "identical" with their own. Accordingly, many Negroes view with suspicion any Jewish appeal to them that argues "we are both in the same boat." This they consider unrealistic, and probably insincere.

Many Negroes, rightly or wrongly, see the struggle of Jews in American society as primarily a conservative one, to consolidate gains already made; and secondarily to expand these gains to a higher level of economic, political, educational and social integration with the dominant group. Though not oblivious to the difficulties of Jews, many Negroes are nevertheless disinclined to view their struggles as fundamental or as critical as their own—the struggle of the Jew is after all not one of life and death, to wring from society the bare necessities of life. The Negro sees his own struggle as an essentially aggressive fight to break down strong traditional barriers that have kept him from obtaining minimally decent housing and food, and the right to other than the most menial jobs; and it is also a struggle to break down barriers that keep him from even minor positions of political and economic power.

Accordingly, Jewish statements about equality, however well intended, may seem to Negroes to minimize real differences and imply acceptance of the status quo.

A part of the complexity of the feelings of the Negro about the Jew is his awareness that Jews have seemed, in general, less negative toward him than have other whites. More Jews have shown active concern about racial problems and more Jews have been willing to hire Negroes for various types of jobs. The Negro's interpretation of this has not, however, been altogether favorable. There is sometimes the lurking suspicion that all this is motivated by a desire on the part of the Jew to use him as a shield and reflects a not too well disguised concern about his own status.

It is an oversimplification, therefore, to assume that the pattern of anti-Semitism among Negroes is always identical with the anti-Semitic attitudes of Gentile whites. When found in a Negro, anti-Semitism tends to be confused, ambiguous, and not directly traceable to organized bigotry. And while there may be some degree of economic jealousy, anti-Semitism in a Negro does not appear to be rooted directly in economic competition.

Patterns of Hostility

The following appear to be the basic psychological functions that are supported by and support anti-Semitism in a Negro:

1. Anti-Semitism may offer a pretext for the release of aggressions that come from the insecurity and humiliation of his status.

2. It may canalize and put into words his feeling against whites in general. Often the term "dirty Jew" in a Negro's mouth means essentially "dirty white."

3. It may offer a way of solidarizing and identifying himself with the dominant white group.

4. It may help him gain inner group security and may re-inflate deflated racial self-respect. An extreme form of this is the brazen anti-Semitism which in a few cases became an integral part of the appeal of intensely chauvinistic Negro organizations.

Similarly the Jewish attitude toward the Negro is somewhat different from the general attitude of Gentile whites.

Here the background of motivation

seems saturated with guilt feelings, anxiety and conflict. There is a conflict between the desire to detach oneself from a group that in this country appears to be even more despised than one's own, and the tendency of a member of one insecure group to identify himself and cooperate with persons of another insecure group.

This pattern of conflict and guilt feelings may lead to a confusion that expresses itself either in exaggerated, awkward sentimentality toward the other group, or in defensively negative and hostile behavior.

Anti-Negro attitudes among Jews appear to serve the following functions:

1. They offer a basis for subjective identification with the dominant white Gentile, serving as one of the bridges toward assimilation of status with the dominant group.

2. They offer a protective covering behind which a Jew can hope to escape the full impact of anti-Semitism. It is relevant here to note that the status of Southern Jews is more secure than the status of Jews in regions where Negroes form a smaller proportion of the population and where there is less active anti-Negro feeling.

A Problem of Human Relations

The barbaric excesses of Nazism have made it impossible to escape the full implications of racial and religious prejudice, no matter what its form. These prejudices have been revealed as a crucial symptom of a basic psychopathology in the given society, and attention has been focused on the fact that they seriously threaten the life and the essential dignity of every human being, whether oppressor or oppressed.

An America that heretofore was prone to accept its prejudices as a normal, if somewhat deplorable, aspect of its tradition is now concerned enough to examine them. Indeed, many individuals and groups are not content with verbal catharsis and casual expiation of the sins of our society, but demand practical action that will ameliorate or do away with prejudice.

That such action is necessary and desirable is undebatably true. But the success or failure of such action may well depend upon the soundness of the analysis, the validity of the data, and the social value and stability of the ideological base upon which such action is taken.

It appears clear from what has been said that a sentimental, primarily moralistic, blaming, or ostrich approach to the problem of Negro-Jewish relations is inadequate from a theoretical and practical point of view. This sector of race relations, like all other problems of relations between racial, religious and cultural groups, must be approached within a framework of objectivity and realism. There must be a tough-minded search for facts that are meaningful; they must be placed within a strong ideological framework constructed of human values; and a clear concept must be formed of the goals of an efficiently functioning democratic society. Fear of facts, wishful thinking, an attitude of opportunistic expediency, a willingness to make concessions to some symptoms of the sickness afflicting the dominant society while decrying others will inevitably render hollow whatever apparent improvement may be made in race relations.

We should also understand that the problem of Jewish-Negro relations probably has no important significance in itself, but serves rather to indicate the extent to which the pathologies of the dominant society infect all groups and individuals within that society. They reflect, with modifications in terms of the status of each group, the general social fact that prejudice has a certain political, economic and psychological function in the over-all pattern of American society. If this is correct, it would seem to follow that it is a futile task to attempt to attack the problem of the mutual antagonism of Negroes and Jews as if it were a special, isolated phenomenon.

The chances of success would appear to be greater if enlightened Jews and Negroes and their progressive organizations, instead of approaching each other specifically, pooled their efforts with all other enlightened human beings working to rid society of the virus-like affliction which is one man's hatred of other men. The obvious obstacle here would be a tendency on the part of any group of human beings—Jewish, Negro, or other—to be limited by narrow group loyalties and ethnocentric considerations. The seriousness of the threat that these, our still unsolved problems present, may well demand a much more resolute effort to discard traditional group loyalties, or at least to submerge them in larger group loyalties, as a prerequisite to their solutions. Loyalty to mankind may have to be given priority over all other loyalties.

If this cannot be, Jews and Negroes may be merely two among the many human casualties of history.

JAMES BALDWIN (b. 1924), a brilliant contemporary novelist and author of *Giovanni's Room* (1956) and *The Fire Next Time* (1963), herein attempts to explain why the black man is antisemitic. Baldwin sees the Jew as a displacement substitute but is bitter about him nonetheless. If the Negro is antisemitic because he's antiwhite, why has the Jew been selected as the target for the black man's wrath? Why doesn't the Negro confront the real culprit? Why is a substitute necessary?*

James Baldwin

Negroes Are Antisemitic Because They're Antiwhite

When we were growing up in Harlem our demoralizing series of landlords were Jewish, and we hated them. We hated them because they were terrible landlords and did not take care of the building. A coat of paint, a broken window, a stopped sink, a stopped toilet, a sagging floor, a broken ceiling, a dangerous stairwell, the question of garbage disposal, the question of heat and cold, of roaches and rats—all questions of life and death for the poor, and especially for those with children—we had to cope with all of these as best we could. Our parents were lashed down to futureless jobs, in order to pay the outrageous rent. We knew that the landlord treated us this way only because we were colored, and he knew that we could not move out.

The grocer was a Jew, and being in debt to him was very much like being in debt to the company store. The butcher was a Jew and, yes, we certainly paid more for bad cuts of meat than other New York citizens, and we very often carried insults home, along with the meat. We bought our clothes from a Jew and, sometimes, our secondhand shoes, and the pawnbroker was a Jew—perhaps we hated him most of all. The merchants along 125th Street were Jewish—at least many of them were; I don't know if Grant's or Woolworth's are Jewish names—and I well remember that it was only after the

Harlem riot of 1935 that Negroes were allowed to earn a little money in some of the stores where they spent so much.

Not all of these white people were cruel —on the contrary, I remember some who were certainly as thoughtful as the bleak circumstances allowed—but all of them were exploiting us, and that was why we hated them.

But we also hated the welfare workers, of whom some were white, some colored, some Jewish, and some not. We hated the policemen, not all of whom were Jewish, and some of whom were black. The poor, of whatever color, do not trust the law and certainly have no reason to, and God knows we didn't. "If you *must* call a cop," we said in those days, "for God's sake, make sure it's a white one." We did not feel that the cops were protecting us, for we knew too much about the reasons for the kinds of crimes committed in the ghetto; but we feared black cops even more than white cops, because the black cop had to work so much harder—on *your* head—to prove to himself and his colleagues that he was not like all the other niggers.

We hated many of our teachers at school because they so clearly despised us and treated us like dirty, ignorant savages. Not all of these teachers were Jewish. Some of them, alas, were black. I used to carry my father's union dues downtown for him sometimes. I hated everybody in that den of thieves, especially the man who took the envelope from me, the envelope which contained my father's hard-earned money, that envelope which contained bread for his children. "Thieves," I thought, "every one of you!" And I know I was right about that, and I have not changed my mind. But whether or not all these people were Jewish, I really do not know.

The Army may or may not be con-trolled by Jews; I don't know and I don't care. I know that when I worked for the Army I hated all my bosses because of the way they treated me. I don't know if the post office is Jewish but I would certainly dread working for it again. I don't know if Wanamaker's was Jewish, but I didn't like running their elevator, and I didn't like any of their customers. I don't know if Nabisco is Jewish, but I didn't like cleaning their basement. I don't know if Riker's is Jewish, but I didn't like scrubbing their floors. I don't know if the big, white bruiser who thought it was fun to call me "Shine" was Jewish, but I know I tried to kill him—and he stopped calling me "Shine." I don't know if the last taxi driver who refused to stop for me was Jewish, but I know I hoped he'd break his neck before he got home. And I don't think that General Electric or General Motors or R.C.A. or Con Edison or Mobil-oil or Coca-Cola or Pepsi-Cola or Fire-stone or the Board of Education or the textbook industry or Hollywood or Broadway or television—or Wall Street, Sacramento, Dallas, Atlanta, Albany, or Washington—are controlled by Jews. I think they are controlled by Americans, and the American Negro situation is a direct result of this control. And anti-Semitism among Negroes, inevitable as it may be, and understandable, alas, as it is, does not operate to menace this control, but only to confirm it. It is not the Jew who controls the American drama. It is the Christian.

The root of anti-Semitism among Negroes is, ironically, the relationship of colored peoples—all over the globe—to the Christian world. This is a fact which may be difficult to grasp, not only for the ghetto's most blasted and embittered inhabitants, but also for many Jews, to say nothing of many Christians. But it is a fact, and it will not be ameliorated—

in fact, it can only be aggravated—by the adoption, on the part of colored people now, of the most devastating of the Christian vices.

Of course, it is true, and I am not so naive as not to know it, that many Jews despise Negroes, even as their Aryan brothers do. (There are also Jews who despise Jews, even as their Aryan brothers do.) It is true that many Jews use, shamelessly, the slaughter of the six million by the Third Reich as proof that they cannot be bigots—or in the hope of not being held responsible for their bigotry. It is galling to be told by a Jew whom you know to be exploiting you that he cannot possibly be doing what you know he is doing because he is a Jew. It is bitter to watch the Jewish storekeeper locking up his store for the night, and going home. Going, with *your* money in his pocket, to a clean neighborhood, miles from you, which you will not be allowed to enter. Nor can it help the relationship between most Negroes and most Jews when part of this money is donated to civil rights. In the light of what is now known as the white backlash, this money can be looked on as conscience money merely, as money given to keep the Negro happy in his place, and out of white neighborhoods.

One does not wish, in short, to be told by an American Jew that his suffering is as great as the American Negro's suffering. It isn't, and one knows that it isn't from the very tone in which he assures you that it is.

For one thing, the American Jew's endeavor, whatever it is, has managed to purchase a relative safety for his children, and a relative future for them. This is more than your father's endeavor was able to do for you, and more than your endeavor has been able to do for your children. There are days when it can be

exceedingly trying to deal with certain white musical or theatrical celebrities who may or may not be Jewish—what, in show business, is a name?—but whose preposterous incomes cause one to think bitterly of the fates of such people as Bessie Smith or King Oliver or Ethel Waters. Furthermore, the Jew can be proud of his suffering, or at least not ashamed of it. His history and his suffering do not begin in America, where black men have been taught to be ashamed of everything, especially their suffering.

The Jew's suffering is recognized as part of the moral history of the world and the Jew is recognized as a contributor to the world's history: This is not true for the blacks. Jewish history, whether or not one can say it is honored, is certainly known: The black history has been blasted, maligned and despised. The Jew is a white man, and when white men rise up against oppression, they are heroes: When black men rise, they have reverted to their native savagery. The uprising in the Warsaw Ghetto was not described as a riot, nor were the participants maligned as hoodlums: The boys and girls in Watts and Harlem are thoroughly aware of this, and it certainly contributes to their attitude toward the Jews.

But, of course, my comparison of Watts and Harlem with the Warsaw Ghetto will be immediately dismissed as outrageous. There are many reasons for this, and one of them is that while America loves white heroes, armed to the teeth, it cannot abide bad niggers. But the bottom reason is that it contradicts the American dream to suggest that any gratuitous, unregenerate horror can happen here. We make our mistakes, we like to think, but we are getting better all the time.

Well, to state it mildly, this is a point of view which any sane or honest Negro will have some difficulty holding. Very few Americans, and this includes very few Jews, have the courage to recognize that the America of which they dream and boast is not the America in which the Negro lives. It is a country which the Negro has never seen. And this is not merely a matter of bad faith on the part of Americans. Bad faith, God knows, abounds, but there is something in the American dream sadder and more wistful than that.

No one, I suppose, would dream of accusing the late Moss Hart of bad faith. Near the end of his autobiography, "Act One," just after he has become a successful playwright, and is riding home to Brooklyn for the first time in a cab, he reflects:

"I stared through the taxi window at a pinch-faced 10-year-old hurrying down the steps on some morning errand before school, and I thought of myself hurrying down the streets on so many gray mornings out of a doorway and a house much the same as this one. My mind jumped backward in time and then whirled forward, like a many-faceted prism—flashing our old neighborhood in front of me, the house, the steps, the candy store— and then shifted to the skyline I had just passed by, the opening last night, and the notices I still hugged tightly under my arm. It was possible in this wonderful city for that nameless little boy—for any of its millions—to have a decent chance to scale the walls and achieve what they wished. Wealth, rank, or an imposing name counted for nothing. The only credential the city asked was the boldness to dream."

But this is not true for the Negro, and not even the most successful or fatuous Negro can really feel this way. His journey will have cost him too much, and the price will be revealed in his estrangement —unless he is very rare and lucky—from other colored people, and in his continuing isolation from whites. Furthermore, for every Negro boy who achieves such a taxi ride, hundreds, at least, will have perished around him, and not because they lacked the boldness to dream, but because the Republic despises their dreams.

Perhaps one must be in such a situation in order really to understand what it is. But if one is a Negro in Watts or Harlem, and knows why one is there, and knows that one has been sentenced to remain there for life, one can't but look on the American state and the American people as one's oppressors. For that, after all, is exactly what they are. They have corralled you where you are for their ease and their profit, and are doing all in their power to prevent you from finding out enough about yourself to be able to rejoice in the only life you have.

One does not wish to believe that the American Negro can feel this way, but that is because the Christian world has been misled by its own rhetoric and narcotized by its own power.

For many generations, the natives of the Belgian Congo, for example, endured the most unspeakable atrocities at the hands of the Belgians, at the hands of Europe. Their suffering occurred in silence. This suffering was not indignantly reported in the Western press, as the suffering of white men would have been. The suffering of this native was considered necessary, alas, for European Christian dominance. And, since the world at large knew virtually nothing concerning the suffering of this native, when he rose he was not hailed as a hero fighting for his land, but condemned as a savage, hungry for white flesh. The Christian world considered Belgium to be a civilized country; but there was not only no reason for the Congolese to feel that way about Belgium; there was no possibility that they could.

What will the Christian world, which is so uneasily silent now, say on that day which is coming when the black native of South Africa begins to massacre the masters who have massacred him so long? It is true that two wrongs don't make a right, as we love to point out to the people we have wronged. But *one* wrong doesn't make a right, either. People who have been wronged will attempt to right the wrong; they would not be people if they didn't. They can rarely afford to be scrupulous about the means they will use. They will use such means as come to hand. Neither, in the main, will they distinguish one oppressor from another, nor see through to the root principle of their oppression.

In the American context, the most ironical thing about Negro anti-Semitism is that the Negro is really condemning the Jew for having become an American white man—for having become, in effect, a Christian. The Jew profits from his status in America, and he must expect Negroes to distrust him for it. The Jew does not realize that the credential he offers, the fact that he has been despised and slaughtered, does not increase the Negro's understanding. It increases the Negro's rage.

For it is not here, and not now, that the Jew is being slaughtered, and he is never despised, here, as the Negro is, *because* he is an American. The Jewish travail occurred across the sea and America rescued him from the house of bondage. But America *is* the house of bondage for the Negro, and no country can rescue him. What happens to the Negro here happens to him *because* he is an American.

When an African is mistreated here, for example, he has recourse to his embassy. The American Negro who is, let us say, falsely arrested, will find it nearly impossible to bring his case to court. And this means that *because* he is a native of this country—"one of our niggers"—he has, effectively, no recourse and no place to go, either within the country or without. He is a pariah in his own country and a stranger in the world. This is what it means to have one's history and one's ties to one's ancestral homeland totally destroyed.

This is not what happened to the Jew and, therefore, he has allies in the world. That is one of the reasons no one has ever seriously suggested that the Jew be nonviolent. There was no need for him to be nonviolent. On the contrary, the Jewish battle for Israel was saluted as the most tremendous heroism. How can the Negro fail to suspect that the Jew is really saying that the Negro deserves his situation because he has not been heroic enough? It is doubtful that the Jews could have won their battle had the Western powers been opposed to them. But such allies as the Negro may have are themselves struggling for their freedom against tenacious and tremendous Western opposition.

This leaves the American Negro, who technically represents the Western nations, in a cruelly ambiguous position. In this situation, it is not the American Jew who can either instruct him or console him. On the contrary, the American Jew knows just enough about this situation to be unwilling to imagine it again.

Finally, what the American Negro interprets the Jew as saying is that one must take the historical, the impersonal point of view concerning one's life and concerning the lives of one's kinsmen and children. "We suffered, too," one is told, "but we came through, and so will you. In time."

In whose time? One has only one life.

One may become reconciled to the ruin of one's own life, but to become reconciled to the ruin of one's children's lives is not reconciliation. It is the sickness unto death. And one knows that such counselors are not present on these shores by following this advice. They arrived here out of the same effort the American Negro is making: They wanted to live, and not tomorrow, but today. Now, since the Jew is living here, like all the other white men living here, he wants the Negro to wait. And the Jew sometimes—often—does this in the name of his Jewishness, which is a terrible mistake. He has absolutely no relevance in this context as a Jew. His only relevance is that he is white and values his color and uses it.

He is singled out by Negroes not because he acts differently from other white men, but because he doesn't. His major distinction is given him by that history of Christendom, which has so successfully victimized both Negroes and Jews. And he is playing in Harlem the role assigned him by Christians long ago: he is doing their dirty work.

No more than the good white people of the South, who are really responsible for the bombings and lynchings, are ever present at these events do the people who really own Harlem ever appear at the door to collect the rent. One risks libel by trying to spell this out too precisely, but Harlem is really owned by a curious coalition which includes some churches, some universities, some Christians, some Jews, and some Negroes. The capital of New York is Albany, which is not a Jewish state, and the Moses they sent us, whatever his ancestry, certainly failed to set the captive children free.

A genuinely candid confrontation between Negroes and American Jews would certainly prove of inestimable value. But the aspirations of the country are wretchedly middle-class and the middle class can never afford candor.

What is really at question is the American way of life. What is really at question is whether Americans already have an identity or are still sufficiently flexible to achieve one. This is a painfully complicated question, for what now appears to be the American identity is really a bewildering and sometimes demoralizing blend of nostalgia and opportunism. For example, the Irish who march on St. Patrick's Day do not, after all, have any desire to go back to Ireland. They do not intend to go back to live there, though they dream of going back there to die. Their lives, in the meanwhile, are here, but they cling, at the same time, to those credentials forged in the Old World, credentials which cannot be duplicated here, credentials which the American Negro does not have. These credentials are the abandoned history of Europe —the abandoned and romanticized history of Europe. The Russian Jews here have no desire to return to Russia either, and they have not departed in great clouds for Israel. But they have the authority of knowing it is there. The Americans are no longer Europeans, but they are still living, at least as they imagine, on that capital.

That capital also belongs, however, to the slaves who created it here; and in that sense, the Jew must see that he is part of the history of Europe, and will always be so considered by the descendant of the slave. Always, that is, unless he himself is willing to prove that this judgment is inadequate and unjust. This is precisely what is demanded of all the other white men in this country, and the Jew will not find it easier than anybody else.

The ultimate hope for a genuine black-white dialogue in this country lies in the recognition that the driven European serf merely created another serf here, and created him on the basis of color. No one can deny that the Jew was a party to this, but it is senseless to assert that this was because of his Jewishness. One can be disappointed in the Jew—if one is romantic enough—for not having learned from his history; but if people did learn from history, history would be very different.

All racist positions baffle and appall me. None of us is that different from one another, neither that much better nor that much worse. Furthermore, when one takes a position one must attempt to see where that position inexorably leads. One must ask oneself, if one decides that black or white or Jewish people are, by definition, to be despised, is one willing to murder a black or white or Jewish baby: for *that* is where the position leads. And if one blames the Jew for having become a white American, one may perfectly well, if one is black, be speaking out of nothing more than envy.

If one blames the Jew for not having been ennobled by oppression, one is not indicting the single figure of the Jew but the entire human race, and one is also making a quiet breathtaking claim for oneself. I know that my own oppression did not ennoble me, not even when I thought of myself as a practicing Christian. I also know that if today I refuse to hate Jews, or anybody else, it is because I know how it feels to be hated. I learned this from Christians, and I ceased to practice what the Christians practiced.

The crisis taking place in the world, and in the minds and hearts of black men everywhere, is not produced by the Star of David, but by the old, rugged Roman cross on which Christendom's most celebrated Jew was murdered. And not by Jews.

ROBERT GORDIS (b. 1908), professor of religion at
Temple University and professor of Bible at Jewish
Theological Seminary, is the author of numerous works,
including *A Faith for Moderns* (1960) and *The Book of
God and Man: A Study of Job* (1965). Rabbi Gordis
does not deny that blacks in the United States have
good reason to be bitter and hostile to the white
community, but he vigorously protests singling out
the Jews as being primarily responsible for the Negro's
condition. On the contrary, Gordis argues, Jews have
done more than other whites to help the black man.
He accuses Baldwin, moreover, of being an apologist
for Negro antisemitism. Do you think Rabbi Gordis'
charge is justified?*

Robert Gordis

Negroes Are Antisemitic
Because They Want a Scapegoat

The brilliant Negro writer, James
Baldwin, wrote a characteristically articu-
late and frank article on Negro anti-
Semitism in *The New York Times Magazine* two weeks ago. His thesis was clearly
expressed in the headline: "Negroes
Are Anti-Semitic Because They're Anti-
White." In a prefatory note we are informed that Mr. Baldwin resigned from
the black nationalist magazine *Liberator,*
which had published a series of anti-
Semitic articles, saying, "I think it is
distinctly unhelpful, and I think it is
immoral, to blame Harlem on the Jew.
. . ." He concludes his piece with these
words: "The crisis taking place in the
world, and in the minds and hearts of
black men everywhere, is not produced

by the star of David, but by the old,
rugged Roman cross on which Christendom's most celebrated Jew was murdered. And not by Jews."

Thus, he graciously absolves the Jews
from the crime of deicide which for centuries, in Israel Zangwill's words, "has
made the people of Christ the Christ of
peoples." Baldwin also declares, "I know
that if today I refuse to hate Jews, or anybody else, it is because I know how it
feels to be hated." Here is impressive
evidence indeed of James Baldwin's anti-
anti-Semitism.

These credentials notwithstanding,
he devotes the bulk of his lengthy article
to a passionate justification of Negro
anti-Semitism today. In the process he

utilizes all the time-honored devices of propaganda perfected in our century. For decades Negroes have been battling energetically to destroy the white man's various stereotypes of the Negro as shiftless, irresponsible, happy-go-lucky and contented with his inferior lot. Nevertheless, Baldwin does not hesitate to set up a series of stereotypes of the Jew in Harlem in order to explain the anti-Jewish prejudice of Negroes.

The landlord who exploits the Negro tenant, the grocer and the butcher who overcharge and shortweight their customers, the pawnbroker who battens on the misery of the Negro—all these, we are told, are Jews, and the Negro therefore hates the Jews. Baldwin "does not know" whether Grant and Woolworth are Jewish names, but the Negro hates the Jews. He hates the welfare worker and the policeman; "we hated black cops even more than white cops." Though Jews on the police force are not particularly numerous, the Negro hates the Jews. Not all public school teachers in the Negro ghetto are Jews, but he hates the Jews. He feels the same way toward the union to which his father belongs, which is "a den of thieves." So, too, with the Army which *may or may not be controlled by Jews; I don't know and I don't care* [italics mine]. I know that when I worked for the Army I hated all my bosses because of the way they treated me." The same reaction applies to the great business corporations, to Hollywood and Broadway, to the post office, to the television industry and to Wall Street. To be sure, Baldwin doesn't *think* that they are all controlled by Jews, but the consequence is anti-Semitism, which is both "inevitable and understandable."

Baldwin would dismiss as irrelevant such factual questions as the degree to which Jewish businessmen and landlords

dominate Harlem and other Negro ghettos stretching from Boston to Miami, from New York to Seattle, from Washington to Los Angeles.

It does not occur to him to compare the exploitation of Negroes allegedly practiced by Jews with the treatment they receive at the hands of non-Jewish merchants and landlords, both white and black. He ignores the fact that preliminary studies by social scientists at the University of California suggest that the attitude of Negroes toward Jews is less negative than toward white non-Jews, and that Negroes tend to recognize that Jews have often treated them with a greater degree of fairness and decency than have white Christians.

Since the substantial funds contributed by Jews to the civil-rights movement are denounced as "conscience money," it is fatuous to expect any recognition—let alone any appreciation—of the disproportionate role that Jews have played in the civil-rights struggle. The deaths of Jewish civil-rights workers are passed over in total silence. To recall the earlier work of Julius Rosenwald in Negro education and of Joel E. Spingarn in the founding of the N.A.A.C.P., or the current efforts of Morris Milgram in interracial housing, would obviously be out of place.

It is a truism of military strategy that the best defense is an offense. We are warned against examining critically the exaggerations which Baldwin seriously advances as legitimizing Negro anti-Semitism. Thus, he writes: "The uprising in the Warsaw ghetto was not described as a riot, nor were the participants maligned as hoodlums: the boys and girls in Watts and Harlem are thoroughly aware of this, and it certainly contributes to their attitude toward the Jews."

Baldwin recognizes that his comparison

of Watts and Harlem with the Warsaw ghetto "will be immediately dismissed as outrageous" and declares that there are many reasons for this. He overlooks the only important reason: the comparison is totally false. In the Warsaw ghetto, defenseless men, women and children were systematically attacked and butchered by the world's most powerful military machine. In the Watts and Harlem riots, Negro youths, abetted by their elders, were the attackers, beating and killing white men and women upon whom they chanced to come, and looting and destroying millions of dollars of property. Whatever reasons the rioters had for resentment and bitterness, there was no physical attack upon their lives to justify the resort to mass violence.

In the best tradition of the purveyors of prejudice, the Jew is blamed for his virtues as well as for his vices. Thus the complaint is advanced that "the Jew is recognized as a contributor to the world's history: this is not true for the blacks." Here again the distortion underlying the comparison is patent.

It is no criticism of Bulgarians or Algerians—or, for that matter, of Belgians or Swiss—to say that their group contributions to Western civilization are less than that of the Jewish people, and that their respective literature and history are correspondingly less familiar to the rest of the world than the traditions enshrined in the pages of the Hebrew Bible. There can be no doubt that the time is long overdue for a greater knowledge and appreciation, by whites as well as by blacks, of Negro culture created both in Africa and in America. But to offer this condition as an apology for anti-Semitism (since no note of objection is interposed) is indeed going far afield. Nor is it true to say that the American Jew tells the Negro "his suffering is as great as the

American Negro's suffering. We suffered, too, but we came through, and so will you. In time."

Baldwin's reticence in opposing anti-Jewish prejudice is all the more striking when contrasted with the vigor of style he employs in criticizing Jews. He declares, "It is true that many Jews use, *shamelessly,* the slaughter of the 6,000,000 by the Third Reich as proof that they cannot be bigots—or in the hope of not being held responsible for their bigotry." (Italics mine).

The italicized adverb is deeply revealing and disturbing. The statement, of course, is false. I challenge Baldwin to offer evidence that the slaughter of 6,000,000 Jews by Hitler is used by Jews, shamelessly or otherwise, to prove that they cannot be bigots. Jews have demonstrated their capacity for bigotry—and, by that token their link with all humanity—time and again. And not only vis-à-vis non-Jews, but also in their relations with one another! It may be true that, in general, Jews are like other people, only more so. In their relations with Negroes, they, like all other white Americans, have been guilty of major sins both of commission and of omission. But their record, though far from admirable, is nonetheless at least as good as and in most respects better than that of others.

If Baldwin is right and the Jew is "singled out by Negroes not because he acts differently from other white men, but because he doesn't," Negro leadership is confronted by a crucial moral issue and not merely a problem of strategy and finances.

What is most disturbing in the approach of Baldwin and other apologists for Negro anti-Semitism is not so much what is said, but what is left unsaid.

One searches in vain in the article for any forthright recognition that hatred is as disastrous to its perpetrator as to its victim. No effort is made to grapple with the problem of a possible cure or amelioration of the disease. Nowhere is there one word of admonition or warning addressed to the Negro community, urging them to fight the incubus of Jew-hatred which he finds both ubiquitous and justified. Instead, all the ills of contemporary society in general and the plight of the Negro in particular are placed at the doorstep of the Jew, the scapegoat of the ages.

Jews and all white men of decency and good will do wish to speak with their Negro brothers in fruitful confrontation. But the undertaking does not become easier in the face of the exaggerations and distortions which are being advanced.

One of the gravest intellectual errors of which men are capable—and its consequences in the practical sphere are devastating—is simplism. The phenomenon of Negro anti-Semitism is tragically oversimplified and by that token dangerously distorted when it is explained—and justified—in terms of one cause only. Undoubtedly the social and economic factor is a basic element in the anti-Semitic complex. But other strands are woven into the age-old chain of Jew-hatred.

Anti-Semitism in the Christian world derives its original impetus, and much of its present hold on men's spirit, from religion. This remains true even in an age marked by both unbelief and ecumenicalism, and the two phenomena are not unrelated. Yeoman efforts are being made today to extricate Western society from the burdens of prejudice and ill will inherited from the earliest period of traditional Christianity. When the Christian church first came into being, its leaders confidently expected that Jews would flock to its fold since it claimed to be the new Israel, the heir and suc-cessor of the old. The hoped-for mass conversion, however, did not take place and Jews, by and large, refused to accept the new dispensation. The church expressed its resentment by charging the Jewish people not merely with the rejection of the Savior but with His death: Thus the Jew became the cosmic villain in the Christian drama of salvation.

In every age there were a few greatsouled exemplars of religion who spoke out for brotherhood and love, but they were usually voices crying in the wilderness. For 19 centuries Jew-hatred was not merely condoned but glorified as a religious virtue. Even today, anti-Semitic prejudice is difficult to dislodge because it is so often sustained by a conviction of self-righteousness, and piety.

When the American Negro was kidnaped from his native Africa and brought to the United States and east into slavery, he was converted to Christianity in its most literalistic form. Lacking the education and sophistication which even his white masters rarely possessed he could hardly be expected to counter the outspoken anti-Jewish bias of the Gospels. He therefore tended to identify the Jew, whom he knew from the New Testament, with the enemy of God.

The seeds of prejudice, having been sown in the soil of faith, continued to produce their bitter fruit in the arena of life. When the Negro met Jews, rarely in the rural South, but more commonly in the urban North, and often in situations of economic hostility, the religious basis for anti-Semitism was strengthened. This prejudice has remained even with the Negro who has surrendered or attenuated his commitment to Christianity. As Zangwill pointed out with bitter irony years ago, many a Christian who is sure that Jesus never existed is certain that the Jews killed him.

Both the religious and economic motives for Negro anti-Semitism have provided the basis for a deep psychological need in the lives of many Negroes. Oppressed, exploited and despised by the white majority, often suffering from the malaise of a sense of inferiority, he needs an avenue of relief. He often finds it in anti-Semitism because here, at least, he can identify with the dominant white majority, give vent to his pent-up hostilities and indulge a sense of imaginary superiority.

The same psychological mechanism explains why "poor whites" in the South have historically been among the most rabid supporters of "white supremacy" and the most active practitioners of violence against their Negro neighbors. Similarly, the Negro anti-Semite who echoes the prejudice of white Americans compensates for his sense of inferiority by believing that he is "better than the Jew."

It is only when this deeply intertwined complex of factors in Negro anti-Semitism —religious, psychological and socio-economic—is understood and clearly recognized that we can hope to attack the disease by its roots. Without abating an iota of their zeal in the battle for equality on every front, Negro leaders have an obligation to fight black anti-Semitism, not merely because it is a dangerous diversion from the long and arduous struggle for Negro freedom and equality, but for the sake of their own moral and intellectual integrity.

Nearly 70 years ago, the Socialist leader August Bebel, speaking of the Jew-hatred endemic in his native Germany, declared: "Anti-Semitism is the socialism of fools." We may add that black anti-Semitism is the democracy of charlatans.

In the difficult struggle for racial justice that confronts Negroes and all Americans, Jews have not been altogether idle. Without minimizing in the slightest the obligation of white Americans, individually and collectively, toward the Negro community, and in deepest friendship and sympathy for their problems, American Jews are perhaps more conscious than others of another moral challenge confronting Negro leadership: the obligation to mobilize its resources for self-help and mutual responsibility. Here, the past experience of the American-Jewish community is by no means irrelevant.

During the four decades from 1880 to the outbreak of World War I most Jewish immigrants to America arrived penniless and from backward countries. They were unfamiliar with the language and the customs of the new land, faced by countless temptations and exposed to poverty, overcrowding and disease. It is true that some agencies for the new arrivals were established by their coreligionists who had settled here earlier. But the East European Jews who crowded the ghettos of our great cities were not long content to be recipients of help, even from their fellow Jews. Almost immediately they created a vast network of institutions of philanthropy, education, recreation and culture of their own.

I do not suggest that the pattern of the American-Jewish experience can be taken over ready-made by the American Negro, but there is a lesson to be derived nevertheless. To the outside observer, however sympathetic, there seems to be too little evidence of self-help and mutual responsibility within the Negro community.

Growing numbers of Negroes are today well-to-do, if not wealthy. Many thousands of Negroes employed in government, industry and commerce live considerably above the subsistence level. Yet in Harlem, in Bedford-Stuyvesant, and in other areas of Negro settlement throughout this city and nation, Negro-sponsored and Negro-maintained settlement houses and schools, cultural, vocational and welfare institutions are few and far between.

It is true that Jewish immigrants to America possessed one great and incalculable advantage. In Judaism there has existed for centuries love of learning and a tradition of mutual responsibility. The Negro, on the other hand, is a comparative newcomer to the Western world. In the face of intolerable brutality and oppression he has had to close the gap of centuries in one or two generations. His position has been heartrendingly difficult since his period of physical slavery lasted until only a century ago and his social and economic burdens have remained heavy.

Particularly in view of the grave responsibility the American people must bear for the condition of the Negro, both before and since the Emancipation Proclamation, the Negro cannot be expected to "go it alone" in raising his present status and his future prospects. But he still has the obligation to put forth his best efforts to do as much as he can for himself. Help from others, however necessary, inevitably breeds ill will, ingratitude and a sense of inferiority.

La Rochefoucauld observed that we are never able to pardon those we have injured. As a corollary one might say that the existence of Negro anti-Semitism testifies that we can rarely forgive those who have helped us.

As the battle for the removal of all external restraints on the Negro enters its next, difficult phase—and it must be crowned with success if America is to survive—we need to recall a truth, painfully discovered by Moses when he liberated the Israelites from Egyptian bondage. The Negro, like Everyman, can attain real freedom not through emancipation but through self-emancipation.

Twenty centuries ago, a Hebrew sage set forth what might well become the slogan of the American Negro: "If I am not for myself, who will be for me? But if I am only for myself, what good am I? And if not now, when?" Mature and intelligent men and women in the Negro community should recognize—and act upon the recognition—that hatred of whites in general, and of Jews in particular, points not to liberation but to perdition. There is a better way.

Suggestions for Further Reading

There is no book which deals with the history of antisemitism in the United States. There is not even a good history of the Jews in the United States which deals with the problem, although Oscar Handlin, *Adventure in Freedom* (New York, 1954) and Rufus Learsi, *The Jews in America* (New York, 1954) cover Jewish experiences in a readable fashion.

For insight into what antisemitism is and why it occurs one should turn to two other extraordinarily good books of essays: Isaque Graeber and Stewart Henderson Britt (eds.), *Jews in a Gentile World* (New York, 1942) and Ernest Simmel (ed.), *Anti-Semitism: A Social Disease* (New York, 1946). Another book worth consulting is Melvin M. Tumin, *An Inventory and Appraisal of Research on American Anti-Semitism* (New York, 1961). Tumin not only lists the projects but writes a brief analytical paragraph about each one.

On the roots of antisemitism, there is a considerable amount of material. The Survey Research Center of the University of California has just completed a five-year study of antisemitism in the United States which was directed by sociologist Charles Y. Glock. Two of the books are particularly revealing. *The Tenacity of Prejudice: Anti-Semitism in Contemporary America* (New York, 1969) by Gertrude J. Selznick and Stephen Steinberg, concludes that antisemitism is still quite prevalent in the United States and that "lack of education is the primary factor in its acceptance." An earlier work in the project, *Christian Beliefs and Anti-Semitism* (New York, 1966) by Charles Y. Glock and Rodney Stark, emphasizes Christian teaching, which still blames the Jews for killing Christ, as the single most important factor contributing to antisemitism. This view, of course, substantiates Horace Kallen's opinions which were elaborated upon in *Judaism at Bay* (New York, 1932). Lucy S. Dawidowicz, "Can Anti-Semitism Be Measured?" *Commentary*, 50 (July 1970), pp. 36–43, is a telling critique of the Survey Research Center studies.

Psychologists, psychiatrists, and sociologists have acknowledged many aspects in the development of antisemitism, including xenophobia, economic and social insecurity, and displaced aggression. Some of the best of these studies are T. W. Adorno, *et al.*, *The Authoritarian Personality* (New York, 1950); Nathan Ward Ackerman and Marie Jahoda, *Anti-Semitism and Emotional Disorder* (New York,

1950); Else Frenkel-Brunswick and R. Nevitt Sanford, "Some Personality Factors in Anti-Semitism," *The Journal of Psychology*, XX (1945), 271–291; Bruno Bettelheim and Morris Janowitz, *Social Change and Prejudice* (New York, 1964); Selma G. Hirsch, *The Fears Men Live By* (New York, 1955); Rudolph M. Loewenstein, "The Historical and Cultural Roots of Anti-Semitism," *Psychoanalysis and The Social Sciences,* I (1947), 313–356; James Travis, "The Secret of Antisemitism," *Catholic World*, CLVI (January 1943), 420–429; Israel S. Wechsler, "The Psychology of Anti-Semitism," *The Menorah Journal*, XLI (April, 1925), 159–166; Bruno Bettelheim, "The Dynamism of Anti-Semitism in Gentile and Jew," *The Journal of Abnormal Psychology*, XLII (1947), 153–168; and Joseph D. Herzog, "The Emergence of the Anti-Jewish Stereotype in the United States," unpublished thesis, Hebrew Union College, 1953.

Daniel Bell in "The Face of Tomorrow," *Jewish Frontier*, XI (June, 1944), 15–20, labeled modern antisemitism "a product of the insecurities and fears generated by capitalism," while David Reisman wrote, in "The Politics of Persecution," *Public Opinion Quarterly*, VI (Spring, 1942), 41–56, that the adjustment of social and economic difficulties in society would go "a long way towards arresting the tide of anti-Semitism and its complete eradication. . . ." A socialist's view can be found in Daniel De Leon, *Anti-Semitism, Its Cause and Cure* (New York, 1921). An article by psychologists Nancy C. Morse and Floyd H. Allport, "The Causation of Anti-Semitism: An Investigation of Seven Hypotheses," *The Journal of Psychology*, XXXIV (1952), 197–233, stresses national involvement as the single most potent contributor to antisemitism but the authors also concede that "no one factor is the cause of *all* the forms of anti-Semitism." I think that Dennis Wrong is much too optimistic in "The Rise and Decline of Anti-Semitism in America," in *The Ghetto and Beyond*, edited by Peter I. Rose (New York, 1969), pp. 313–334.

Historical treatments of antisemitism in the United States are few in number and uneven in quality. John Higham's essays: "Anti-Semitism in the Gilded Age: A Reinterpretation," *Mississippi Valley Historical Review*, XLIII (March, 1957), 559–578, and "Social Discrimination Against Jews in America, 1830–1930," *Publications of the American Jewish Historical Society*, XLVII (1957–1958), 1–33, are the first pieces that interested readers should consult. Also worth looking at, but with caution for while they are informative in detail they are spotty in analysis, are Oscar and Mary Handlin, *Danger in Discord: Origins of Anti-Semitism in the United States* (New York, Anti-Defamation League of B'nai B'rith, 1948) and Carey McWilliams, *A Mask for Privilege: Anti-Semitism in America* (Boston, 1948); Donald S. Strong, *Organized Anti-Semitism in America* (Washington, D.C., 1941); and two books by Lee Joseph Levinger: *The Causes of Anti-Semitism in the United States* (New York, 1925), and *Anti-Semitism Yesterday and Tomorrow* (New York, 1936).

Jewish organizations have been particularly concerned with the causes and fluctuations of antisemitism in the United States. They have continually sponsored research studies and some of these are excellent scholarly endeavors. The American Jewish Committee is responsible for Charles Herbert Stember, *Jews in the Mind of America* (New York, 1964); *The Many Faces of Anti-Semitism* (New York, 1967); and *A Community Survey of Prejudice: Baltimore, Md.* (New York, 1949). The Anti-Defamation League of B'nai B'rith sponsored *Anti-Semitism in the United States* (New York, 1947); Ruth Weintraub, *How Secure These Rights?* (Garden City, N.Y., 1949); and Arnold Forster, *A Measure of Freedom* (New York, 1950).

Specific incidents of antisemitism in the United States are dealt with in Morris U. Schappes, "Anti-Semitism and Reaction, 1795–1800," in *The Jewish Experience in America* edited by Abraham J. Karp (New York, 1969), I, 362–390, and Nina Morais, "Jewish Ostracism in America," *The North American Review*, CXXXIII (1881), 265–275. Mark Twain complains of Jewish aggressiveness in business in "Concerning the Jews," *Harper's Magazine*, XCIX (1899), 527–535, while Burton J. Hendrick, in two outrageous articles, asks whether Jews have in themselves "the stuff of which Americans are made": "The Great Jewish Invasion," *McClure's Magazine*, XXVIII (January, 1907), 307–321, and "The Jewish Invasion of America," *McClure's Magazine*, XL (March, 1913), 125–165.

For discussions of antisemitism among agrarians in the late nineteenth century, interested students might consult Irwin Unger, *The Greenback Era* (Princeton, N.J., 1964). Unger supports Hofstadter's contention and clearly indicates that "at its most unbalanced,

rural anti-bankism of the 1860's and 1870's was tinged with anti-Semitism." For a defense of the Populists, though, see Norman Pollack, "The Myth of Populist Anti-Semitism," *American Historical Review*, LXVIII (October, 1962), 76–80; C. Vann Woodward, "The Populist Heritage and the Intellectual," *The American Scholar*, LIX (Winter, 1959–1960), 55–72; and Walter T. K. Nugent, *The Tolerant Populists* (Chicago, 1963).

There are a few books which discuss aspects of American antisemitism even though this is not the authors' main focus. Among the best of these are Bertram Wallace Korn, *American Jewry and the Civil War* (Philadelphia, 1951); Morton Rosenstock, *Louis Marshall, Defender of Jewish Rights* (Detroit, 1966); and John P. Roche, *The Quest for the Dream* (New York, 1963), which is a history of the Anti-Defamation League's efforts to eradicate prejudice in the United States.

Leonard Dinnerstein, *The Leo Frank Case* (New York, 1968) analyzes the forces at work which produced the worst episode of southern antisemitism, 1913–1915. Harry Golden, who claims that the South is, and has a heritage of, philo-Semitism, develops a case for the opposite conclusion in "Jew and Gentile in the New South: Segregation at Sundown," *Commentary*, XX (November, 1955), 403–412, as does Stanley Meisler, "The Southern Segregationist and His Anti-Semitism," *The Chicago Jewish Forum*, XVI (Spring, 1958), 171–173.

For the 1920s, 1930s, and 1940s some of the best source material comes from contemporary periodicals. H. L. Mencken reasons that Jews and Gentiles should stick with their own in "The Curse of Prejudice," *American Mercury*, XXIII (May, 1931), 123–126; Ralph Philip Boas insists that there is little evidence of antisemitism in the United States, but does offer the opinion that Jews have no manners and should be more aware of their own "shortcomings" in "Jew-Baiting in America," *Atlantic*, CXXVII (May, 1921), 658–665.

Two articles critical of Father Coughlin are William C. Kernan, "Coughlin, the Jews, and Communism," *The Nation*, CXLVII (December 17, 1938), 655–658; and George Seldes, "Father Coughlin: Anti-Semite," *New Republic*, XCVI (November 2, 1938), 353–354.

Other essays which pinpoint antisemitism in either time or place are: Johan J. Smertenko, "Hitlerism Comes to America," *Harper's*, CLXVII (November, 1933), 660–670; Horace Sutton, "Bigotry in B-Flat: How the Berkshires Face the Music," *The Nation,* CLXIV (July 28, 1947), 768–769; and William Schack, "The Conquest of Sea Gate," *Menorah Journal,* XVIII (January, 1930), 52–58, for discrimination in resort areas; Dan W. Dodson, "College Quotas and American Democracy," *American Scholar,* XV (July, 1946), 267–276, discusses restrictive admission policies in colleges; Walter R. Harte does the same thing in "Anti-Semitism in New York Medical Schools," *American Mercury,* LXV (July, 1947), 53–63; F. L. Marcuse discusses job discrimination in "'Gentleman's Agreement' in Science," *School and Society,* XCIV (September 8, 1951), 152–153; and Lois Waldman summarizes the findings on "Employment Discrimination Against Jews in the United States—1955," in *Jewish Social Studies,* XVIII (July, 1956), 208–216. In the mid-1940s *Chicago Jewish Forum* published a series of articles which also exposed American bigotry: Edward Wahl, "Anti-Semitism and Labor," IV (Spring, 1946), 163–166; Ashley Montagu, "Anti-Semitism in the Academic World," IV (Summer, 1946), 219–225; and Charles I. Glicksberg, "Anti-Semitism in American Literature," V (Spring, 1947), 159–163.

For the 1950s and 1960s, three informative books are David Caplovitz and Candace Rogers, *Swastika 1960,* the epidemic of anti-Semitic vandalism in America (New York, Anti-Defamation League of B'nai B'rith, 1961), and two by Benjamin R. Epstein and Arnold Forster: *"Some of My Best Friends . . ."* (New York, 1962) and *Cross-Currents* (Garden City, N.Y., 1956). An essay worth looking at is Shad Polier, "The Jew and the Racial Crisis," *Congress Bi-Weekly,* XXXI (September 14, 1964), 5–8. For an analysis of the explosive outburst in Wayne, New Jersey, in 1967 see Rodney Stark and Stephen Steinberg, "Jews and Christians in Suburbia," *Harper's Magazine,* August, 1967.

For black antisemitism most of the literature is of recent vintage. A good survey of black attitudes before the 1880s is Eugene I. Bender, "Reflections on Negro-Jewish Relationships: The Historical Dimension," *Phylon,* XXX (Spring, 1969), 59–65. Louis Harris and Bert E. Swanson, *Black-Jewish Relations in New York City* (New York, 1970), is a sophisticated analysis of the topic while Robert G. Weisbord and Arthur Stein, *Bittersweet Encounter* (Westport, Conn., 1970) gives a detailed history of the relationships between blacks and Jews in the United States. Weisbord and Stein also have an extraordinarily good bibliography.

Aside from Kenneth Clark's article there are three other essays specifically acknowledging Negro antisemitism in the 1940s and 1950s: L. D. Reddick, "Anti-Semitism Among Negroes," *Negro Quarterly,* I (Summer, 1942), 112–122; James Baldwin, "The Harlem Ghetto: Winter 1948," *Commentary,* V (February, 1948), 165–170; and Marguerite Cartwright, "Do I Like Jews?" *Negro History Bulletin,* XXI (November, 1957), 38–39.

Rabbi Richard C. Hertz wrote about the "Rising Tide of Negro-Jewish Tensions" in *Ebony,* XX (December, 1964), 117–118 ff., but no one paid much attention. "Some Facts About Rising Anti-Semitism Among Negroes," *Jewish Digest,* XII (December, 1966), 63–66 continued the discussion started by Hertz. Horace Mann Bond elaborates on "Negro Attitudes Toward Jews" in *Jewish Social Studies,* XXVII (January, 1965), 3–9, while the intensity of black frustrations and the consequent resentment of Jews is most striking in Eddie Ellis' three articles, ". . . Semitism in the Black Ghetto," *Liberator,* VI (1966), January, 6–7; February, 14–15; and April, 14–16. Contemporary commentators—some twenty-odd—also attempt to explain black attitudes towards Jews and *vice versa* in Shlomo Katz, editor, *Negro and Jew: An Encounter in America* (New York, 1967), and James Baldwin, *et al., Black Anti-Semitism and Jewish Racism* (New York, 1969).

The 1968 New York City school teachers' strike generated too many hysterical reactions and a wave of defensive articles from more Jews than could possibly be listed here. Perhaps the most sophisticated and intelligent of these are three essays which appeared in *Commentary,* XLVII (1969): Earl Raab, "The Black Revolution and the Jewish Question," January, 23–33; Milton Himmelfarb, "Is American Jewry in Crisis?" March, 33–42; and Nathan Glazer, "Blacks, Jews & Intellectuals," April, 33–39. Himmelfarb's essay met with a series of strenuous objections, and they are published in "American Jewry in Crisis?" June, 6–25. A good journalistic piece which analyzes the treatment given by the New York City newspapers to the strike is Fred Ferretti, "New York's Black Anti-Semitism Scare," *Columbia Journalism Review,* VIII (Fall, 1969), 18–29.